FISHING
KENAI
RIVER

GUNNAR PEDERSEN

FISHING ALASKA'S KENAI RIVER

ISBN 1-57833-296-6

Library of Congress Control Number: 2005921695

Printed in the USA on acid-free paper.

Fishing Alaska Publications
P. O. Box 90557
Anchorage, AK 99509

Fish species illustrations and map line drawings by *Gunnar Pedersen*. Fish mounts courtesy of Ken and Carol Guffey of *Ken's Taxidermy* and Tom Elias of *Hunter Fisher Taxidermy*.

Front Cover Photo (Main): Drift fishing on Upper Kenai River. *G. Pedersen*, (Inset #1): Client and guide with trophy rainbow trout. *Mystic Waters*, (Inset #2): Large sea-run Dolly Varden on flyrod. *R. Limeres*, (Inset #3): Anglers boating another Kenai king. *King of the River Charters*.

Back Cover Photo (Inset #1): Red salmon spawning in Quartz Creek. *G. Pedersen*, (Inset #2): Guide and client posing with Kenai king. *King of the River Charters*, (Inset #3): Anglers fishing for red salmon on Upper Kenai. *G. Pedersen*.

Inside Photos
Section I, Header: Guide and client with trophy king salmon. *Alaska Clearwater Sportfishing*, Section II, Header: Guide netting large rainbow trout for client. *Alaska Clearwater Sportfishing*, Section III, Header: Rafting Upper Kenai River in autumn. *G. Pedersen*.

Photo Credits
Introduction - *G. Pedersen*, Chapter(1) *S. Pedersen*, (2) *R. Limeres*, (3) *T. Cappiello* (4) *Mystic Waters*, (5-10) *G. Pedersen*, (11) *E. Pedersen*, (12) *S. Pedersen*, (13) *E. Pedersen*.

Table of Contents

ALASKA'S KENAI RIVER DRAINAGE

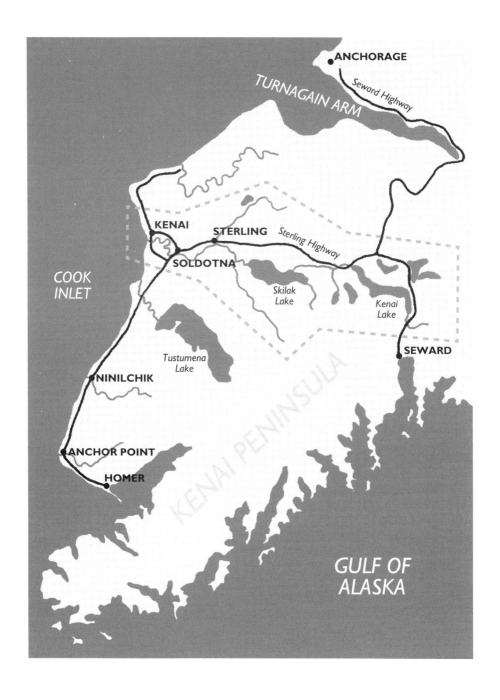

INTRODUCTION

Words From The Author

Welcome to *Fishing Alaska's Kenai River*, the first book in a series of publications highlighting the magnificent fisheries of the state. Described within these pages are details regarding the main game fish species in the drainage and summary chapters of the more productive locations in which to catch them.

I believe that what makes the Kenai River so special is its prosperity in terms of the general well-being of the fishing population as well as the scenic and logistic values it portrays. It is my hopes that through this book people gain a better understanding of the uniqueness the Kenai River drainage displays in its diversity of fish species through not just their numbers but also distribution and habits. *Fishing Alaska's Kenai River* is as much an educational tool of awareness as it is a guidebook for anglers.

Enjoy the book and good luck on the water.

Gunnar Pedersen

Alaska's Kenai River Drainage

The Kenai is an incredible river. Its glacial-green waters and adjoining tributary streams and lakes support fourteen species of game fish in varying abundance, from a million or more fish to as few as several hundred specimens. The Kenai River is the most popular sport fishery in the state of Alaska and attracts anglers from all around the world to its turquoise waters. Its reputation is owed at least in part to the fact that it is easily accessible, offers a reasonable opportunity to land trophy-sized king salmon, has phenomenal runs of red and silver salmon, fantastic fly fishing for rainbow trout and Dolly Varden, and an extended active angling season that runs continuously from May to October with the possibility of year-round fishing. In addition, wildlife along the river is thriving and the scenery magnificent.

Viewing the Kenai drainage in sections, it becomes very clear how different they all are. Even the mainstem Kenai differs greatly between the upper and lower portions, not to speak of the smaller streams and lakes that pour out of mountain valleys and lowland marshes to join this 2,200-square mile system.

The bluish-green or turquoise color of the Kenai derives from very fine silt. Visibility changes according to the seasons and output of sediment from area glaciers but lighting conditions interact as well. Most of the waters in the drainage, however, consists of clear-flowing rivers and streams.

It has been stated that the silty Snow River is the true starting point of the Kenai River drainage, pouring into the 20-mile long and fairly narrow Kenai Lake with a spectacular backdrop of the Chugach Mountains. From here, the "upper" Kenai River exits the lake and runs to Skilak Lake, another major glacial lake in the system. The next river section, popularly known as the "middle" Kenai, flows out of Skilak and continues its journey to the town of Soldotna and the Sterling Highway Bridge. From here on to its terminus at Cook Inlet, the meandering river is known as the "lower" Kenai. The elevation drop from Kenai Lake to sea level is 430 feet, the total river length being 82 miles.

The Sterling Highway parallels the Kenai as it travels through the Chugach National Forest and the Kenai National Wildlife Refuge, with several side roads and pull offs that aid in the accessibility to the river. The Seward Highway provides additional access to the eastern half of Kenai Lake and adjoining lakes and streams. Being only 100 miles from Anchorage, Alaska's largest city, it is no wonder the Kenai River system is a major playground for substantial numbers of anglers in the region.

The Kenai River's flow is sustained year-round through glacial melting and runoff from precipitation, water levels varying to a great extent between the mid-summer and winter months – commonly by three to four feet. Periodic flooding adds to the volume, the river rising up to three feet or more in a short span of time as a result of rainstorms, ice-jams, and the collapse of glacial dams, the latter occurring every three years or so. At the gauging station in Soldotna, the Kenai has an average annual discharge of some 5,000 cubic feet per second.

Along its course, the mainstem Kenai is joined by three other sizable drainages; namely the Russian, Killey, and Moose rivers. The clear-flowing Russian in particular is famous for its incredible onslaught of red salmon, arguably some of the best angling in the world for the species. The Moose is better known for its productive silver salmon action while tributary lakes contain excellent rainbow trout opportunities for more adventurous anglers using canoes.

The Kenai River flows deep and swift throughout much of its length but does display an abundance of braided channels, gravel bars, and some islands that are easily waded and fished from shore. There is essentially prime spawning habitat for salmon along the entire river with superb sporting opportunities for trout and char.

Next to fishing off the banks, the Kenai has a sizable fleet of both powerboats and drift boats. Most of the powerboats are driven by 35-horsepower engines (the maximum allowed on the Kenai) and measure some 18 to 20 feet in length. They are almost exclusively used on the lower Kenai with some usage on the middle river section as well. More than a hundred boats can be seen at one time when the kings are running at a peak in July. The drift boats and rafts, however, are mainly stationed on the upper Kenai, which is a "drift"-only area (no powerboats permitted) and adds immeasurably to the quality of the experience. Drift boats are also common on the middle river and some are even to be found on the lower Kenai. There are many boat launches present from Kenai Lake to the rivers' mouth at Cook Inlet.

The Alaska Department of Fish & Game, considering the popularity of game fish available and the myriad of user groups chasing them, is doing an excellent job of managing the resources to make certain the various species and stocks remain healthy. Recognizing this enormous responsibility, rules and regulations are conservatively placed to obtain the goal of sustainable yield. New restrictions are added or changed frequently to an already regulation-saturated river. It is a very complex process of comprehension and organizing these nuances of nature and applying rules that stand to reason in the eye of conservation, at the same time meeting demands of the sport and commercial fishing industries, is a daunting task.

One of the ways the department manages the Kenai's salmon runs is through enumeration by the use of sonar and weir. The sonar, located 8.6 miles from the river mouth on the Kenai, monitors the day-to-day entrance of early- and late-run king and late-run red salmon. The Russian River weir is located at the outlet of Lower Russian Lake, approximately 78 miles from Cook Inlet, and counts red salmon passing into the middle and upper reaches of the Russian. It takes the fish about a week to ten days to reach the weir from the mouth of the Kenai.

The Kenai River is a special place. Sound management by the state, conservative harvest guidelines by the fishing community, and an overall view of custodianship to make certain the river stays healthy through habitat protection is the key to the long-term survival of the river system.

SECTION 1:
KENAI'S SPORTFISH

PACIFIC SALMON
in the Kenai River

An Introduction

There are five species of Pacific salmon in the state of Alaska, all of which are present in the Kenai River in varying degrees of abundance. Although the cyclic pink (hump-back) salmon is the most abundant species in even-numbered years, the Kenai is much more famed for its mammoth strain of king (chinook) and massive runs of red (sockeye) salmon, and the late-arriving silver (coho) is increasingly gaining notoriety. Chum (dog) salmon is not a common species in the Kenai drainage. Anglers flock from around the country – even from every corner of the world – to partake in the annual salmon migrations that boom into the turquoise river and its tributaries from spring through fall.

Salmon in the Kenai River, like elsewhere in its range, are almost exclusively anad-romous. That is, the fish are hatched in freshwater, the juvenile salmon migrating to the sea after a period of a few weeks up to some years, spend a year to five years eating and growing in the nutrient-rich marine environment, and then returning to the Kenai and the exact place of birth to reproduce. It is an amazing life cycle and can be witnessed at least in part by anyone, especially during the latter half of the season when in-migrating, spawning, and dying salmon are present within the watershed.

The king salmon is the first to come back to the river starting in May, followed by the red in June, and pink and silver salmon in July. Each is present for a certain time frame, usually lasting two to four months, depending on the species. And as all local anglers know and visiting anglers soon come to learn, these yearly migrations are referred to as "runs." Not only that but some types of salmon, like king, red, and silver, display two separate runs each. For example, king salmon come into the Kenai in two distinct pulses or runs, the first in May and June (coined "early" run) and a second showing in July and August ("late" run).

Runs are a result of each population of salmon reflecting unique conditions within the Kenai River drainage. The Kenai represents a very large system comprising a multitude of tributary rivers, creeks, and lakes, each with its own character based on various geological and biological factors. It is these factors that help shape the habits as well as physical attributes of the fish that are present. Water temperature is believed to be one of the major contributing reasons behind distinct run developments and in the Kenai drainage there are a many temperature regimes that influence run timing behavior.

Another way to analyze it is by understanding that salmon eggs develop slower in colder water, which means stocks in predominantly cold streams and lakes appear earlier than those in warmer streams where egg development is faster. Of course, this explanation is oversimplified, as there are also several additional factors that play a role as well.

Anglers are able to find excellent fishing for several of the salmon species in season, with red, pink, and silver salmon offering particularly fast-paced action. King salmon in the Kenai are not based on quantity as much as quality: Trophy and potential record fish. Most activity takes place along the mainstem Kenai River from the headwater at Kenai Lake downstream to its terminus at Cook Inlet; however, the total distribution of salmon is much more extensive and includes almost every tributary lake and stream.

Not all waters are open to salmon fishing throughout the year. Some drainages, especially the smaller ones, have seasonal or total closures for salmon, or perhaps tackle and gear restrictions. The Alaska Department of Fish & Game through the Board of Fisheries establishes rules and regulations in order to protect salmon at a time when they are vulnerable to harvest or angling activity. It is particularly the spawning period which is of concern for most species, like king, red, and silver salmon, yet other species such as pink salmon are of lesser importance regulatory speaking due to the huge volume of fish and relatively little angling interest.

The following chapter sections describe all five species of salmon in the Kenai River drainage and details the what, when, where, why, and how's of sport fishing for them, including biological information that can prove very valuable in understanding the nature and behavior of the salmon and the application it has on angling for them.

Chapter Content:

KING SALMON
Scientific Name: *Oncorhynchus tshawytscha.*
Common Name(s): Chinook.

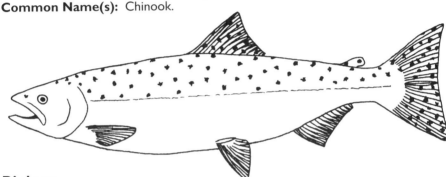

Biology
Description: Black markings/spots on back, upper sides, tail fin, and top of head. Back is dark, sides silvery, and belly white. Spawning fish are dark red on back and sides with black belly.
Size: Average 20 to 40 pounds (early run), 30 to 50 pounds (late run), up to 70 or 80 pounds or more. State/World Record is 97 pounds, 4 ounces (Kenai River, 1985).
Distribution: Clearwater tributaries (early run) and mainstem Kenai River (late run).
Abundance: Total drainage population size ranging from 50,000 to 75,000; 10-25,000 (early run) and 30-60,000 (late run).

Sport Fishing
Regulatory Season: January 1 through July 31; may be extended into August by emergency order.
Timing: May to August, peaking in June (early run) and July (late run).
Gear: Seven- to eight-foot rod spin/bait caster; nine- to 10-foot, 10-weight fly rod; 25- to 30-pound test line/tippet.
Tackle: Spinners, attractors, plugs, roe clusters, and flies. An attractor/roe combination is deadly. Plug with sardine wrap also good.
Methods: Drifting, back-bouncing, back-trolling.
Hot Spots: Lower and middle stretches of Kenai River, best around river mile 10 to 18.

KING SALMON in the Kenai River

Life Cycle

All stocks of king salmon in the Kenai River drainage are anadromous. In other words, the fish are born in fresh water, migrate to the sea to feed for a period of time ranging from a year to five years, and return to the place of birth as is common with all species of Pacific salmon.

Mature adults enter the Kenai on a rising or high tide from spring until fall in two temporal runs to reproduce in the mainstem river or one of its numerous tributaries. Upstream migration is typically slow although some fish are known to travel up to 18 miles per day with peak movement occurring in late afternoon and evening.

All kings display black irregular cross-markings on the back and upper sides. Both lobes of the tail fin and top of the head are covered with black spots. The tongue and gum line on lower jaw is black. When arriving fresh from the ocean, kings have a greenish-blue back, the lower sides and belly being silvery to white. The flesh color is orange-red.

After a week in fresh water a slight coloration begins to set in, and after three weeks the silvery shine is barely visible on the scales. Flesh tone is usually pink. As a month to six weeks passes, fish have taken on the spawning phase. At this time, kings are generally dark red on the back and sides with belly being black. Some specimens may take on a copper, brown, or even almost black hue. Males develop a kype, large teeth protrude from their jaw, and the spine converts to a ridgeback condition. Flesh color is white.

Spawning area selected may be as diverse as the tidal section of the swift main river channel to small clearwater mountain streams only a couple of feet deep. Loose, clean gravel or smaller rock bottom structure is preferred. In the mainstem Kenai, locations consisting of vegetated islands and considerable meandering of the river attract spawning fish. Females deposit anywhere between 2,000 and 14,000 eggs in one or more redds, a process that may take several days. Eight weeks after entering the river the kings have completed spawning and will decease within ten days.

The eggs hatch in late winter or early spring with the newborn salmon emerging from the gravel soon after. The juveniles usually remain in the Kenai River about one year, subsisting on zooplankton, young insect, and other small organisms before migrating downstream to the ocean. Diet of immature kings in salt water consists mainly of fishes and crustaceans.

Early & Late Runs

The Kenai River supports two distinct pulses, or "runs," of king salmon during the spring and summer season, unlike most watersheds in Alaska that only has one. Early run fish are primarily destined for clearwater tributaries such as Funny and Killey rivers while late run kings spawn for the most part in mainstem Kenai River. Biologically speaking, the distinction of early runs and late runs is not as easy as splitting the two groups into exact calendar periods but it does makes absolute sense in regulatory terms to make for easier management of the commercial and sport fisheries.

For many years the state has regulated the populations under "early" and "late" categories, this being May and June and July and August, respectively. Yet the fact remains that at least some tributary fish enter the Kenai in July and mainstem Kenai kings in June or even earlier, creating a natural blending of the two main populations. In other words, Kenai's salmon stocks do not always fit neatly into two distinct categories. To make things more interesting, there are indications that a few stocks may fall between the two groups.

Early Run Kings

The first, or early, run of kings on the Kenai is very similar to other stocks on the peninsula and around northern Cook Inlet in that the run timing is basically the same. Returns happen between mid-May and early July, with the peak in-migration occurring during the first ten days of June. A few scouts, however, are typically present in the tidal area of the river starting in late April. The number of bright in-river fish peaks in mid-June. By the third week of June, there is a noticeable drop in fresh kings coming into the Kenai and the run will gradually subside through the month and on into July. Very few tributary fish are believed to enter the drainage beyond the third week in July but an occasional straggler may even show up as late as August. The physical condition of late-arriving fish is usually, yet not always, quite poor as the fish are already ripe and ready to spawn.

The appearance of dark kings in May is fairly common as some fish return to the river very early in the season or even come in from the ocean already blushed. The latter is more typical of late-run kings but is quite normal in the later stages of the early run as well.

Killey River by far supports the largest population of tributary fish with numbers in the thousands, followed by Funny River. Kings enter these drainages starting in late May and continue through mid-July. Concerning tributary stocks of the upper Kenai, it appears that a few kings do move through the lower river sections and Skilak Lake rather quickly, yet the majority of the fish spend two or three weeks or more getting to their destination. Available data suggests that early run kings may take anywhere from four days to more than six weeks to migrate from the river mouth to the Sterling Highway Bridge in Soldotna. Additionally, the bulk of these fish have passed the bridge by the third week of July.

As is common with all tributary stocks, many fish display the habit of milling around the mouth of spawning streams until nearly ripe before proceeding upstream to spawn. This behavior may be connected to water levels in the spawning stream. Although water flow may not be much of an issue in some tributaries early in the season as runoff from snowmelt is still ongoing, later in the summer may see very low water levels in some of the smaller streams. It is in these that fish may delay migration upstream for weeks. In larger tributaries, such as Killey and Funny, this period of milling is relatively short with virtually all kings ascended the rivers by the third week in July. In smaller streams, like Slikok Creek, a few fish may still be found at the mouth until the first of August.

There are not many tributaries of the Kenai that support sizable runs. Most stocks contain fish only numbering in the dozens to a few hundred. Killey, as mentioned above, is the main producer but Funny River is also important. Smaller to very small and sporadic populations exist in Beaver, Slikok, Benjamin, and Soldotna creeks and Moose River of the lower and middle Kenai, while on the upper river and Kenai Lake there is Russian and Trail rivers, and Quartz, Grant, and Ptarmigan creeks. Very minor populations are present in Juneau, Daves, and Falls creeks.

Spawning commences in mid-summer, usually from mid-July to early August, but has been reported to occur as early as mid-June and as late as early September. Early run kings spend an average of some two weeks on the spawning beds.

"Middle" Run Kings

There often appears to be a spike in numbers of fresh kings coming into the Kenai the last week of June (according to sonar counts), a sort of "middle" run, which some guides and ADF&G biologists speculate to perhaps be a specific population of fish with a unique run timing. One source states the possibility that at least some of these "middle" returns are attributed to the Quartz Creek king stock. These fish also spawn slightly later, primarily in August, than what is the norm in other tributaries. Another stock that may contribute to the middle run factor is Russian River, which has a run timing similar to Quartz. Additionally, semi-bright kings may occasionally be present as late as mid-August in the clear waters of the Russian.

Late Run Kings

It has long been established that the beginning of the late run commences in late June, numbers of fish entering the mouth of Kenai building into July with peak in-migration during the second and third weeks of the month. The number of bright in-river kings peak in mid- to late July. In some years, strong returns may continue through the month and the end of the regulatory sport fishing season (July 31). Mostly, however, the run starts subsiding in late July in terms of fresh kings entering the system. Fair numbers of fish keep coming in until mid-August and from then on only a small trickle of kings will be arriving through the remainder of the month and into early September. In very rare circumstances, dime bright king salmon are reported as late as the end of September and early October in the lower and middle Kenai River.

It is very common for kings in the July-August time period to enter the Kenai quite blushed already, this being particularly true of fish heading into the river during the month of August and later. Since a good portion of the kings spawn in the lower river it is very common for anglers toward the end of the season to catch quite dark fish, even in tidal areas. Guides and other anglers fishing the Kenai and marine waters of Cook Inlet south of the river mouth sometimes refer to these late summer stragglers as "copper kings" due to the fishes' copper or bronze skin tone.

The majority of salmon entering the Kenai River in July and August are mainstem spawners. That is, these kings spawn in the swift main channel of the river. The distribution of fish within the drainage is quite extensive but there are a couple of river sections that are more commonly used for reproductive purposes than others. Good numbers of late run kings utilize the upper Kenai between river miles 64 and 80, or from the inlet of Skilak Lake upstream to Fisherman's Bend. Yet the bulk of the kings concentrate in the lower and middle portions between river mile 16 and 34, or from a point about two miles upstream of Big Eddy Hole to approximately a couple of miles downstream of the Moose River. Salmon can also be found spawning in other areas of the river, from tidewater at river mile 10 (Beaver Creek) to the outlet of Kenai Lake (river mile 82), just not in great numbers.

With such an abundance of available spawning habitat, it really is no wonder that the

Kenai River produces a large quantity of late-run kings. Procreation throughout the drainage begins in late July, peaks during the second half of August, and ends in mid-September. It is not unusual, however, to observe a few fish spawning into October in some years. The kings average approximately three weeks on mainstem spawning beds.

Recently, through exhaustive scientific studies of king salmon in the Kenai River drainage, it has come to light that not all mainstem spawners fit in the late run category, or, conversely, not all early run kings spawn in tributaries. A certain segment of the May-June population actually selects specific areas of the main Kenai for reproductive purposes. Studies regarding these fish are ongoing but the results thus far has sparked some speculation within the angling community that it is possible a few of the very large kings (75 to 85 pounds or more) that are caught in May and June are actually early run mainstem fish and not of tributary stock as earlier assumed. In addition, the state/world record king salmon of 97 pounds that was caught on May 17 may just have been a mainstem Kenai fish. More research is definitely warranted.

Size & Age

King salmon in the Kenai River may measure anywhere between 16 inches or less to a weight of nearly 100 pounds or more. Still, the average fish invariably falls in the 20- to 50-pound category with a decent number of 60-pounders present during the season. It is quite rare to find kings that weigh in excess of 85 pounds but a few are caught every couple of years or so. There is also a size difference when it comes to comparing early-run with late-run kings.

The common or broader average weight for early kings is 20 to 40 pounds and fish of 50 to 60 pounds are not unusual. Salmon exceeding 70 pounds are the exception. It is broadly recognized that fish in the May-June time period are not as heavy as kings in the July-August population, yet there are several examples of specimens weighing 80 pounds or more being produced. The world record sport-caught king salmon of more than 97 pounds, for instance, was taken in mid-May.

Kings of the late run are generally larger, however, and in addition display a greater proportion of very big, trophy fish. Here the average size range is approximately 30 to 50 pounds with 60 pounds being common. A small percentage of salmon stretching from 70 to 90 pounds are present in the Kenai River in any given year but the actual number of these mammoth kings varies from season to season. The size of late run kings could have developed to cope with the deep water and strong currents of the Kenai but more than likely there are other factors involved as well. Whatever the actual reason(s), it is a perfect blend to create a genetically distinct stock of king salmon.

A small portion of Kenai kings are "jacks," a male salmon that has spent one year of growth in the ocean and measure only 14 to 20 inches in length. "Two ocean" fish weigh between 10 and 20 pounds and are also predominantly males. The majority of kings return after having spent three to four years at sea and weigh anywhere from 25 to 60 pounds. The 97-pound world record specimen spent one year in fresh water, five years at sea, and returned to the river in its seventh year of life. About 60% of both early and late runs are made up of 6-year-old fish, but there are usually twice as many 7-year-old kings in the late run as the early run.

Kings of the same age will vary in size from stream to stream, perhaps due to genetics. A "four ocean" fish in most Alaska streams rarely weigh 40 pounds, in the Kenai the same age fish will typically weigh 50 pounds.

Abundance Estimates

The Kenai River supports many stocks of king salmon. Some are quite small, perhaps only a few dozen to a hundred or more specimens, while others may consist of fish numbering in the thousands into tens of thousands. Including kings harvested in the sport fishery, the early run comprises approximately 16,500 salmon, while the late run averages some 41,000 specimens. In years when both runs see healthy returns the total population base may exceed 75,000 kings.

FISHING FOR KENAI KINGS

Many standard techniques employed in fishing for kings in clearwater river and streams do not necessarily work in the Kenai. Some methods are similar but require some modification. Additionally, if an angler has never fished Kenai kings before, chances are good that he or she will leave the river skunked. Consider that over 60% of all kings caught on the Kenai are taken by guided anglers, while the other 40% are caught by anglers that have at least some experience fishing the river and the techniques and methods required.

The Kenai River is by far the most popular king salmon fishery in Alaska with most activity occurring on the stretch of water downstream of Soldotna. Up to 115,000 or more angler days per season is spent on kings, resulting in between 7,000 and 30,000 or more kings being harvested with an average annual take of 17,000. While the lower and middle Kenai is open to king fishing, all tributaries and waters above Skilak Lake are protected by regulation.

Fishing for Kenai kings is largely a boat fishery and for good reason. The river is wide and deep, the current strong, the fish big, and the spots to actually hook and land a huge king from land few and far between. Also, the advantage of fishing from a boat is that an angler can follow that fish a little easier than if one had to run along the riverbank. Of all the kings that are harvested in the Kenai, over 99.99% of them are taken from a boat. Most of the information contained in this chapter as it relates to king fishing assumes a boat is employed; however, there is also a small section toward the end of this section that deals with shore fishing for kings.

Hire a Guide

On average it requires approximately 29 hours of fishing effort before an angler boats a king. One can improve chances significantly by hiring a professional guide, especially if one is either a novice angler or an experienced angler with little time to spend and/or lack suitable equipment. On the Kenai, guided anglers are about twice as efficient as non-guided anglers. Guides know the rules and will apply the technique to match the river currents of the day since they can change in hours.

Rules & Regulations

The first run of king salmon has suffered from weak returns in the past decade and special restrictions are in place to cull anglers' success rate. Currently there is a bait ban in effect through June 30 that is lifted only if there are sufficient enough numbers of salmon making it into the river and the minimum escapement goal is assured. Furthermore, the confluences of spawning tributaries and Kenai River are closed to king fishing most of the season to protect early run fish that stage there. Consult the ADF&G Sport Fishing Regulations for more information.

The late run of kings is doing well and appears very healthy. Emergency orders to extend regulatory fishing time from July 31 into the first week in August are implemented from time to time.

Kenai's Giants

Kenai River king salmon are amongst the largest strain of the species in the world. Although there have been kings taken in several other locations in Alaska, British Columbia, and the Lower 48, as well as in Russia, comparable in size to some of the biggest fish in the Kenai, few – if any – drainages can match the consistency of yielding trophy salmon that this river has become famous for. And it is not just the belief that intense angling pressure has a way of dredging the largest fish out of the river and if any other king river was subject to such bombardment we would see huge fish come out of those locations as well. No, these fish truly are in a class of their own, even by Alaska standards. There is a real reason why the Alaska Department of Fish & Game (ADF&G) lists the minimum weight for a trophy king salmon in the Kenai River as 75 pounds while each and every other watershed in the state it is only 50 pounds. Kenai kings are just bigger.

In any given year, the largest king to come out of the river invariably weighs somewhere between 75 and 85 pounds with tales and rumors of even bigger fish that got away always circulating the angling community. But the numbers speak for themselves considering that seven out of the top ten record king salmon from the Kenai River weighed in excess of 90 pounds (see chart below) with the next three fish all being in the 89-pound plus range. In addition, the majority of the top ten are late-run salmon. Anglers in the know concede that the Kenai stands a very good chance of one day breaking the Holy Grail of records, the almost magical 100-pound mark. And there is ample evidence to support this notion.

Test-netting for research purposes by the ADF&G a few years ago turned up one fish that by length and girth calculations would have weighed somewhere between 103 and 106 pounds. On occasion spawned-out kings are found washed up on the riverbank in fall that by all reasonable estimates are believed to have weighed more than 100 pounds when the fish first came into the river from the ocean. Commercial fishers in Cook Inlet report from time to time catches of kings that they think may have exceeded the mark. One fish was estimated to have weighed 135 pounds.

Time is of the essence concerning that almost mythical giant 100-pound plus king salmon. Sport fishing for kings on the Kenai is still a relatively new issue. The fishery never got started to any degree until the early 70s and there is yet much to learn about this mammoth race of salmon. One day the Holy Grail will be found.

Top 10 Kenai River Kings

#	Pounds - Oz.	Inches	Date	Year	Angler
1.	97 - 0	58.75	May 17	1985	Lester Anderson
2.	95 - 10	59.5	July 17	1990	Patrick Plautz
3.	92 - 4	57.25	July 9	1985	James Cato
4.	91 - 10	58.25	July 5	1988	Clint Moeglein
5.	91 - 4	53.0	n/a	1987	James Luton
6.	91 - 0	57.5	June 27	1995	Butch Kaping
7.	90 - 4	59.5	July 19	1995	Clyde Odin
8.	89 - 4	57.5	July 31	2002	Frederick Houtman
9.	89 - 3	57.5	July 5	1989	Richard Sargent
10.	89 - 1	57.0	July 15	1995	Garold Waldrip

Success Rate

What is considered good or excellent fishing for king salmon on the Kenai River may not necessarily be true of other drainages around Alaska. The Kenai is not a quantity fishery but rather a quality fishery. That is, what the river lacks in consistent fast-paced action so typical of some king salmon hot spots it makes up for by yielding the absolutely biggest fish. As a matter of fact, according to trophy fish statistics compiled by the ADF&G, the Kenai has produced the top catches of king salmon year after year for decades.

As mentioned earlier in this section, it takes on average an angler about a day-and-a-half to catch one king on the Kenai whereas in some of the better king locations in the state one or two fish per hour is the norm. But in all fairness, during the peak of the runs and if a guide and right tackle is used, that average may drop significantly. It is not unheard of for anglers to pull in two or three or more kings per day with a quite decent chance of at least one of those fish weighing 50 pounds or so. Many king streams in Alaska hardly ever see a fish over 60 pounds while on the Kenai fish of that size are caught practically every day during the July run. Besides, what more of a thrill can an angler ask for knowing that that one particular strike could prove to be a monster of 70 or 80 pounds – perhaps even the next world record.

Anglers should know that although equally productive action can be had for king salmon in both the early and late runs, the July-August component of the population is much larger in terms of numbers of fish present as well as size of fish. Additionally, the late run has more than double the number of older kings that are prone to reach trophy proportions.

When & Where

King salmon are available in the Kenai from May through July with emergency openings sometimes extending the season into early August. The best time to be on the water to hit the absolute peak of the early and late runs is in mid-June and mid-July, respectively. This is when the in-migration of salmon has reached its zenith and good numbers of kings are found distributed throughout most of the area open to fishing. However, good fishing can also be had before and after the peak. The early morning hours are generally thought of as being optimal for success but anytime coinciding with tidal movements is recommended as well.

Mainstem River

The lower Kenai River produces the most kings for anglers during the first half of June and most of July. Guides and anglers in the know target fish in the lower river extensively as each tide brings in a solid influx of fresh, aggressive salmon. The area between river mile 10 and 18 is very productive for incoming kings.

The early run of kings are concentrated in the middle portion of river during the second half of June while the late run dominates the second half of July. Some guides and private anglers will target fish here but not nearly as many as on the lower river.

Although a good number of fish are in the upper Kenai, it is currently closed to all king salmon fishing.

As for targeting kings in tributaries, only the mouth of Moose River is currently open; all other waters are closed to king salmon fishing.

Structure

King salmon can be found most anywhere in the Kenai, from near-shore shallows to the deepest holes at 10 to 15 feet. However, both early and late run fish do prefer the deeper sections of the river and pattern their migrations upstream accordingly. Some spots are better early or late in the season as variations in current and depth create different situations in terms of suitable structure. Wherever there are deep pockets, holes, and runs – even in areas with a fair clip of current – expect to find concentrations of kings. Big fish are especially fond of structure and prefer to hold in very deep and heavy water.

Seek out structure in terms of mid-stream islands, submerged islands and shallow reefs, jetties, boulders, and big rocks as these are ideal concentration points. Migrating kings will often not just hold in the slack water downstream of a structure but will actually surround it, front to back and along the sides, this being particularly true with islands and reefs. Many salmon will hold in front of boulders, not behind. Migratory pathways or holding areas are often established by the contour of a riverbank, with fish situated within approximately 10 to 50 feet or more of shoreline structure.

What to Use

If presented properly, there are few things that will not catch a king salmon. However, after decades of trial and error, guides and local anglers have arrived at a few lures and methods that consistently work better than others. Plugs and attractor/bait combination are by far the top producers of kings in the Kenai River and the current and lighting conditions often determine what set-up and technique must be employed. A back-trolled plug is best in strong current while back-bouncing attractors and bait and deeper-diving plugs are best in deeper water. In some years, spoons and spinners may be the thing. Even flies can be used with some success.

Gear

The Kenai River has big kings and heavy and deep currents so equipment selected must absolutely be of good quality. A 7.5-8.5 medium-heavy action graphite rod with a limber tip and stiff spine is the rule, while a reel in the Ambassadeur/Garcia 7000 category filled with 25- to 40-pound test line. High visibility lines are preferred.

Plugs

During times when bait is restricted, anglers like to back-troll plugs, particularly in areas with moderate to strong current flow. Plugs reach maximum depth at moderate speed and can be used with or without a planer. Due to low water and only moderate current flow in May and most of June, a planer is not necessary but becomes required later in the season (late June on) as melt-water increases river flow significantly.

Wiggle Wart (best in May/June), Kwikfish (best in late June/July), Tadpolly, Hot Shot (Nos. 20-30), and Flatfish (size U-20 or the X-4/X-5) are all used on the Kenai and proven effective. The larger varieties are the most popular yet some of the smaller sizes may work very well early in the season if the water is low and clear.

If using a planer with a size K-16 Kwikfish, for example, the planer should be monitored to its deepest-running setting, and string the tuned plug back four feet from the swivel. A plug running at four or five feet will not produce desired results if kings are suspended at 10 or 15 feet. Anglers must always be familiar with the depth of the location fished, as some are considerably shallower or deeper than others, as well as diving characteristics of the plug. In more shallow to moderate depths, a planer may not be necessary. Shy away from deep-diving plugs when working water only a few feet deep because of gravel.

Grass or other floating debris may be a problem in summer in the upper layers of water and a plug that dives deeper the fastest will not collect as much debris. Foreign material suspended on the hook(s) of a plug is likely to inhibit the wobbling effects necessary to catch fish.

Some anglers do use plugs along with bait. Wrapping a fillet of sardine or herring onto the underside of the plug using thread or a rubber band is a deadly setup for kings.

When fishing plugs timing is crucial, hesitate and the fish is gone. If rod dips two or three times, set the hook, but not before.

Attractors & Bait

There are probably few things that are as effective on catching Kenai kings as an attractor and bait combination. Scent is a big issue and it is a fact that bait catches more fish, hence the regulatory restrictions of prohibiting bait if salmon runs are in danger of not reaching minimum escapement goals. Artificial scents work also but not quite to the same degree as natural bait. Some anglers use both scent and bait at the same time.

Popular attractors include the all-time favorite Spin-N-Glo, but Cheaters are used to some degree as well. A hootchie skirt or strings of colored yarn may be attached to hook(s) in place of bait if restrictions mandate a no-bait policy.

Typical rigs include a large Spin-N-Glo, 18 to 24 inches of leader (black plastic-coated wire leaders rated at 40 lbs. are commonly applied), a teardrop sinker, and a chunk of salmon roe the size of a golf ball. Sliding sinkers sleeves and a selection of one-half to three-ounce Teardrop sinkers and wire twist-ons for attaching weight to sleeves are a necessity. Use one or a series of red, green, or chartreuse plastic beads, such as Corkies, for bearings and additional attractors. Rig lure with a size 4/0 to 6/0 single hook. Using planers, anglers also back-troll this setup with a longer leader. Roe attached to an attractor will increase mass and scent, creating a wobbling action that is deadly for kings.

Spoons & Spinners

Anglers can do quite well at times using standard hardware. The techniques used may have some degree of resemblance to fishing with plugs or attractors yet a slight variation must be employed for the specific conditions. Although boaters do use hardware now and then, it is usually anglers fishing from shore that use it as the weight of the lure is more ideal and streamlined for long casts.

Spoons are usually on the larger side, at least half an ounce to ideally around one ounce to properly penetrate layers of water several feet deep in moderate current. The 7/8th-ounce variety of Pixie or similar weight Krocodile is popular. Let the lure tumble downstream or apply a slow retrieve through a likely hole or run.

Spinners in sizes five and up do take some fish. Because of the lighter weight compared to spoons, a one-half to one ounce sinker may be attached. A slow retrieve through deep water of moderate current flow or less is best. The size 6 chrome Vibrax and T-Spoon have been used with good results when buzzed downstream along the bottom with the current.

Lure Color

Water turbidity and time of year will dictate the best color. In May and through the first half of June, when the lower Kenai is plugged with literally millions of silvery smelt (hooligan), solid colors are most productive since salmon appear to become immune to glitter. Try fluorescent red, orange, chartreuse, and hi-glo pearl and peach hues. Later in the season, about late June and on, kings will strike more readily on lures with silver and gold flash as these assist in visibility and thus enhances the aggravation response.

Fluorescent colors are best in low-light or murky water conditions. Red, green, yellow, and chartreuse are all productive and can be used throughout the king season. Overall, lures with a chartreuse hue are the most versatile, working in a wide range of water and lighting conditions, as are nickel-plated ones. The silver K-16 Kwikfish with a chartreuse head or tail is on every boat fishing for kings on the Kenai.

In bright sunshine or if the kings are finicky, darker hues such as metallic blue, green, and purple are good choices of color anytime during the season since they do not exhibit a great deal of flash which may spook the fish. White and black combination can be effective. These darker shades also work great if the water is low as it often is early in the season.

Tips
- High visibility lines are popular and help to know where fish is and help others keep out of the way of a running fish.
- Many anglers replace manufacturer hooks with stronger, sharper hooks.
- Strikes are sometimes very soft, as the fish will gently mouth the lure.
- The longer a king can see a lure coming towards it, the better it is.
- Be aware of the Strike Zone of fish. It is defined as an area within a physical distance where a fish is most likely to hit a lure, and this area expands and contracts depending on water temperature and clarity. If conditions are right, the king will strike.
- Universal sign on the river for a "fish on" is a raised landing net. Give boat the widest berth possible.

How to Fish

There are four methods that are proven to catch Kenai king salmon. Back-trolling, drifting, and back-bouncing are all effective and utilized by both guides and private anglers. Guides prefer back-trolling because it is easier to keep their lines under control. The fourth method, anchoraging, used to be a popular way of catching kings but is no longer considered appropriate as an anchored boat and line is viewed more as an hindrance for other boats to fish the same hole or run. Additionally, the other three methods cover more water and thus are more efficient and effective. For more detailed description of each method, see chapter 4 on techniques, page 91.

Back-trolling

The boat is motored upstream slightly slower than the speed of the current, thus boat slips slowly downstream, enabling angler to cover a lot of area and place lure in front of fish for extended periods of time. Large lures are most effective. Attractors such as big Spin-N-Glo's, preferably with eggs, and plugs are best.

Drifting

Anglers drift with current, allowing lure to bounce along the bottom at the speed of the current. An effective method but not as much as back-trolling or back-bouncing. Attractor with or without bait is the typical lure application.

Back-bouncing

Boat is constantly under power and slowly backed down the river. As the boat backs through a hole or drift, the angler bounces the lure along the bottom of the river. Attractor and attractor/bait combinations are best applied to this method.

Anchoring

A boat is kept stationary in a hole or run by employing an anchor. This method is done in areas with slow to moderate current. Plugs and attractors are used. Bait fished alone is also an option. This method is not recommended in congested high-traffic areas of the Kenai such as that found on the lower river.

Fishing from the Bank

Although a good number of kings have been caught from shore, many anglers still doubt that it can be done, or at least consistently. The size of the river and the fish could easily support the notion of impracticality and an exercise in futility. However, there are a handful of anglers that accomplishes this seemingly impossible feat every season and have the logistics and technique required handling big fish down to a science. As a matter of fact, fish in the 50- to 60-pound range are landed every summer and catches up to 70 and even 80 pounds have been made. The first thing to look for is a suitable location, the second proper gear, and the third is tackle.

Locations

There are several places anglers have caught kings from shore but the more known locations include Centennial Campground and the boardwalk near the Sterling Highway Bridge in Soldotna. This portion of the river (from the bridge down to about river mile 20.4) is closed to fishing from boats so anglers here have no competition so to speak. The calm water just downstream of the small island at the campground is a relative hot spot and one of the best places for kings on the river.

Two other locations where kings are being caught from shore include Swiftwater and Morgan's Landing on the middle river. The former spot may be difficult to fish early in the season but both produce fish during the late run.

The confluence of Moose River and Kenai River is another location where anglers tangle with big kings. The slow waters of Moose is a fly-fishing only area and not really suitable for effectively catching fish but a few are caught every season. Anglers here should concentrate on the waters just upstream and down of the confluence for better opportunity.

Tackle & Gear
Hardware is usually what takes fish from the riverbank. Heavy spoons weighing about one ounce are recommended, as long casts are required to reach holding areas. The 7/8th-ounce Pixie and similarly-sized Krocodile are proven spoons. Some anglers even modify their offerings by connecting two spoons together for added mass. These lures are then cast into likely structure and allowed to drift with the current, the angler making a slow retrieve. Large spinners (size 5 or 6) can also be used if a sinker is attached to the line. Apply color code as described in "What to Use" section above.

Attractors with a cluster of roe accompanied with a one-ounce sinker also work well. Again, the lure is allowed to drift with the current. Some anglers use enough weight as to keep the attractor/bait combination stationary on the bottom, a difficult task considering the heavy current.

Quite a few anglers have shown success using side planers (plastic diving plane), a tool of sorts that works with the current to keep the lure away from shore and positioned in the hole or run desired. Plugs and attractors both can be used with this innovative technique.

Heavy action rod and level-wind reel is recommended with at least 40-pound test line. With the advent of ultra-thin braided lines, anglers have the liberty to make longer casts with exceptionally heavy line.

Fly Fishing
There is a very modest increase of fly fishers attempting to hook and land Kenai kings every year. A boat is almost certainly required as space – crowds of other anglers and thick shoreline vegetation – may be a problem if casting from shore. The long casts necessary to reach holding spots of kings can interfere with surrounding fishers making much shorter flips for reds or other near-shore species.

Successful fly fishers are using fast sinking-tip lines and shooting heads. Sinking-tips are the variety with longer than average tip sections, 15 to 25 feet in length, and are made with lines of the fastest sink rate. However, even these lines may not be enough to slice through the Kenai's heavy current so attaching lead sinkers may be the only other option.

A 10-weight rod or larger and big game fly reel with a good drag and at least 150 yards of backing is standard equipment. Reel must be rigged with shooting heads with a sinking rate of three inches per second. As these are big kings in heavy current, a fighting butt on rod helps.

Bright fluorescent flies work best, orange alone or in combination with green and chartreuse are best. Flies are preferably large and gaudy, the King Killer and Fat Freddie being of choice. Bulk orange yarn, white marabou, and silver Krystal Flash tied on a 1/0 hook is proven effective.

World Record King Salmon

On May 17, 1985, the late Lester "Les" Anderson of Soldotna caught one of the huge kings that Kenai is known around the world for, a fish of 97 pounds, 4 ounces.

Les and his brother-in-law, Bud Lofstedt, were fishing in a spot between the Pillars and Honeymoon Cove at approximately 6:30 in the morning when Les, using a red and green Spin-N-Glo in combination with a chunk of salmon roe, hooked into the great king. The giant fish led the men on a chase upstream and it was not until an hour later that Les and his companion finally had the king tired. However, three failed attempts at netting the king prompted the men to reach a decision to beach it instead, which they did. The anglers at first did not realize the actual size of the king and kept on fishing for another three hours after that before returning to shore.

After leaving the river, Les and Bud stopped by Peninsula Ford (in which Les was a co-owner) in Soldotna to show the catch to the employees there. Upon encouragement of the workers to have the fish weighed, Les and his companion took the fish to the Tackle Box in Soldotna where the giant king tipped the scale at over 96 pounds. But since this scale was not certified to official standards, the two surprised anglers headed to Echo Lake Lockers where a certified scale could be found.

Hanging on the peg, the massive fish buried the scale to 97 pounds, 4 ounces and thus officially a new state and world record. By the time the king was finally weighed, six hours had gone by since it was landed and dehydration and blood loss had set in. Considering this, it is plausible that the true weight of the monster was closer to 99 pounds.

Les Anderson's trophy still stands as both the Alaska state record and IGFA world record king salmon caught on rod and reel.

Concerns

There appears to be indications that the very large kings that are present during the early run in May and June are declining in numbers. The exact reason or reasons is not completely understood at this time but suspicions is that the sheer number of anglers present on the river are negatively impacting the population by selecting and retaining big fish, thus weakening the genetic stock. Although not given much merit in years past, it is now realized that trophy-sized specimens are vital in producing progeny with the same genetic programming: to grow big. Size slot limits are currently in place on these fish in hopes of ensuring that the Kenai will continue to yield trophy kings into the future.

RED SALMON
Scientific Name: *Oncorhynchus nerka*.
Common Name(s): Sockeye and Blueback.

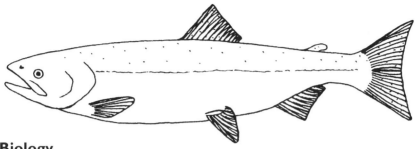

Biology

Description: Dark blue on back, sides silvery, silvery white on belly. No spots. Spawning fish are crimson red on back and sides with dark belly. Distinctive olive green head.

Size: Average 6 to 8 pounds (early run), 5 to 10 pounds (late run), up to 12-14 pounds or more. State record is 16 pounds (Kenai River, 1974).

Distribution: From river mouth to headwater tributaries, mostly in lake-associated drainages.

Abundance: Total drainage population size ranging from 650,000 to over one million.

Sport Fishing

Regulatory Season: No species-specific regulations in place, except for Russian River; general restrictions apply.

Timing: May to September, peaking in June (early run) and July-August (late run).

Gear: Seven- to eight-foot rod spin/bait caster; seven- to nine-foot, 7-weight fly rod; 10- to 20-pound test line/tippet.

Tackle: Flies.

Methods: Casting and flipping.

Hot Spots: Lower, middle, and upper Kenai River; Russian River.

RED SALMON in the Kenai River

Life Cycle

With few exceptions, all stocks of red salmon in the Kenai River drainage are anadromous. The fish are born in fresh water, migrate to the sea to feed for a period of time ranging from a year to four years, and return to the place of birth as is common with all species of Pacific salmon.

Mature adults enter the Kenai on a rising or high tide in summer in two distinct runs to reproduce in the mainstem river or one of its tributaries. When fresh from the sea, reds are dark steel blue to greenish blue on the back, the sides silvery, fading to silvery white on the belly. Very minute black freckles may be observed on the back but usually none at all. Flesh color is ruby red.

A slight coloration begins to show after the salmon has been ten days or so in the river environment. At three weeks the silvery shine has disappeared, a slight pink to a grayish hue dominates, and the head is starting to turn olive green. Flesh tone is orange at this point. After four to five weeks, the salmon is usually in full nuptial coloration. The body is brilliant red but can also be dirty brown, pale red, dark purplish to almost black. The head is a distinct olive green. Males develop a slight humped back and a tooth-filled kype. Flesh is now white in color.

Red salmon do show a particular fondness of selecting spawning streams that are tied into lake or pond environments. Some stocks commonly spawn along lake shorelines or on reefs with gravel or pebble bottom structure. Breeding grounds are from the middle Kenai upstream to headwaters. Females deposit 2,000 to 4,500 eggs that hatch in late winter or early spring. Six to seven weeks after entering the river the reds have completed reproduction and will decease within approximately ten days.

Young salmon remain in the Kenai drainage from one to three years, eating insects and zooplankton. Fish migrate to sea in spring and early summer, immature adults feeding on crustaceans.

The landlocked version of red salmon, called kokanee, lives year-round in larger lakes that have an abundant supply of various organisms including insect life and zooplankton. These fish take on the same appearance as sea-run fish, being silvery in color most of the year, bodies turning red with green heads in fall as they prepare to spawn in suitable structure on the lake bottom. Kokanee also die after the reproductive process is done.

Early & Late Runs

As with kings and silvers, red salmon are represented in the Kenai drainage by two distinct runs or populations. There is a very slight overlap between the runs in the first part of July but they are generally even more separated than that of other salmon species. The early reds are bound for various tributaries within the drainage while the late run is a combination of both tributary and mainstem fish.

Early Run Reds

A few scouts begin entering the mouth of the Kenai in the second week of May but reds do not show in any numbers until the last ten days of the month. By the first week of June, the run should be coming in at an increasing rate on every tide, the migration peaking during the second week. If the run is heavy sustained numbers of fish will last through the third week. Late June marks the period when the early run begins to dwindle but a trickle of reds continue to arrive until mid-July. The lower and middle Kenai experiences the peak of bright in-river fish during mid-June, while the upper river sees the most reds during the second half of June.

The upstream migration of the first run of reds is the fastest of any salmon species on the Kenai. It is quite common for these fish to cover a distance of almost 75 miles in a matter of just three or four days. The pace at which these salmon swim also contributes to the very brief seasonal appearance in the mainstem Kenai River.

The single largest producer of early salmon is the Russian River with smaller runs also occurring in Quartz Creek and Moose River. As water conditions can be quite high still in June from mountain snowmelt, the fish generally do not hold at the Kenai confluence more than a few days at the most before ascending spawning streams. In low water years, the upstream movement may be delayed for two weeks or longer.

Spawning takes place in late summer, starting in mid-July and peaking during the first half of August. The majority of the run has finished the process by the first of September.

Late Run Reds

The second wave of red salmon is by far the largest, the first few late run scouts into the Kenai coinciding with the last of the early run around the first of July. Numbers build slowly through the second week and, as is typical of Kenai reds, the run bursts into the river in mid-month. The arrival of these fish can usually be described as an assault as tens of thousands of salmon arrive on each tide. In fact, some days during the peak of the run will see 100,000 or more fish coming into the river all at once. This onslaught continues through the third week of July, the run then beginning to wane the rest of the month and into early August. By the first of September, the run is down to a trickle. A few fresh reds are known to continue entering the Kenai until late September, with semi-bright specimens present in the upper river through early October.

In most years, there is one last big push of reds that comes into the river mouth sometime in the first half of August, believed by some guides and biologists to be a distinct "third" run of fish representing a discreet stock. However, some argue that many of these fish are actually pink or silver salmon and not reds as the sonar unit indicates.

The number of bright in-river salmon peaks during the second half of July on the lower and middle river, and late July and early August on the upper Kenai.

The majority of reds are mainstem fish that will spawn along the middle and upper river and in areas of Kenai and Skilak lakes. Russian River also sees a significant return, with approximately 16% of the total Kenai late run heading there. Additionally, important stocks are destined for tributaries of Kenai Lake, including Ptarmigan Creek and the Trail River drainage.

Beginning in early August and peaking from late August to mid-September late run reds can be observed in the various stages of the breeding cycle. Most salmon have completed the process by October.

A very small segment of the run is comprised of fish that select spawning sites along the middle and upper mainstem Kenai consisting of sloughs or side channels with upwelling springs. These fish are physically smaller and spawn later than their late run counterparts. Breeding may continue through fall and into mid-November or later in these locations.

Size & Age

Red salmon in the Kenai River drainage are present in a wide range of sizes, from "jacks" measuring only 16 inches or less to trophy mainstem spawners that can weigh as much as 15 pounds or more.

Early run reds average six to eight pounds with some specimens reaching 10 to 11 pounds. In this run it is actually quite rare to find salmon smaller than the average because of the age of the fish. It has been found that the early fish in Russian River spend two years in freshwater and three years at sea before returning in their sixth year of life to spawn and die. This compared to late run fish in Russian that spend two years in freshwater and only two years at sea, hence they have one year less of ocean growth and are physically smaller (averaging four to seven pounds).

Late run fish in the mainstem Kenai, however, are very broad and heavy and considered to be one of the largest strains of reds in Alaska. Fish average six to 10 pounds with some males exceeding 12 pounds. A few specimens can weigh up to 14 or 15 pounds. The Alaska state record was taken in the Kenai River and weighed 16 pounds. Bigger reds may exist as one fish estimated at 18 pounds was caught on the upper Kenai many years ago.

Kokanee, as they miss the nutrient-rich ocean environment, only average 12 to 14 inches with very few fish bigger than 16 inches.

Abundance Estimates

The exact number of early run reds in the Kenai River is uncertain given the lack of sonar surveillance, but as the Russian River is the main producer of this stock and weir counts are being conducted there, a good estimate can be made. The average return is approximately 55,000 salmon, which in some years may be double that. The Moose River return is very small, around 1,000 or less, but the Quartz Creek population is quite large and estimated at about 10,000.

Yet it is the late run that truly has the numbers. From 650,000 to 1.5 million fish are counted by the sonar unit on the lower river. In actuality, barring commercial fishery interception, the possible production of the Kenai could be three or four million red salmon.

FISHING FOR KENAI REDS

The red salmon on the Kenai River and its tributaries is almost exclusively a bank fishery. The only advantage to employing a boat or other watercraft is to access more secluded or remote locations in which to fish from shore.

The average annual harvest of red salmon is approximately 100,000 fish, not counting the ones that are caught and then released which would raise the tally substantially.

Many anglers in the know search various locations along the river for signs of reds moving through, only stopping to make an effort if salmon are rolling or people are catching fish. It is particularly important on the lower river to be aware of the numbers of fish coming through. When the ADF&G-operated sonar unit observes a big push of reds entering the mouth, these fish will be available to anglers for only a few days at the most before moving further upstream into the middle river and disappearing into Skilak Lake. Locals that fish the lower river on a regular basis have come to recognize that for good and consistent action to take place, a push of some 20,000 fish per day is necessary. Anything less and anglers will have to work for their fish.

Kenai reds enter the river in pulses and there are typically several days between each pulse. The exact reason for such entrance pattern is unknown but thought to be a combination of tidal influence, wind direction, water temperature, water clarity, commercial fishing pressure, and several other factors. Yet this is not unusual of salmon and most coastal waters do experience if not the exact same at least similar patterns of entry.

The middle and upper river does not generally see this drastic change in fish density from day to day as the reds are more spread out and action quite steady and consistent.

Rules & Regulations

The restrictions for red salmon in the Kenai River are for the most part very liberal, especially on bag limits in years of big returns (up to six fish per day). Only the Russian River has a seasonal restriction that runs June 11 through August 20. The regulatory season may be extended through August 31 by emergency order if the late run is strong.

Top 10 Kenai River Reds

#	Pounds - Oz.	Inches	Date	Year	Angler
1.	16 – 0	31.0	n/a	1974	Chuck Leach
2.	15 – 11	31.5	August 17	1989	Jerry Lemon
3.	15 – 3	30.6	n/a	1987	Stan Roach
4.	14 – 12	29.0	n/a	1979	Vince Fernelus
5.	14 – 8	31.0	August 2	1994	Archer Richardson
6.	14 – 8	30.75	n/a	1973	Alwin Krause
7.	14 – 8	30.5	July 22	1995	Raymond Mong
8.	14 – 8	30.0	July 27	1996	Raymond Mong
9.	14 – 8	29.4	n/a	1982	Elmer Dewitt
10.	14 – 8	29.2	July 28	2000	Gary Adams

When & Where

Red salmon are basically available in the Kenai River system from June into September. The peak of the early and late runs occur in mid- to late June and mid-July through early August, respectively. Most angling pressure is on the lower river during the late run and at the Russian River. In terms of both angler participation and harvest, the Kenai River is the largest salmon fishery in the state.

Mainstem River

The early run of reds are generally not targeted to any extent on the lower or middle Kenai due to the comparatively small number of salmon necessary to sustain a viable and productive fishery. Some effort does take place but not even close to what one would find later in the season. Additionally, the fish travel with great speed through the entire lower section of the Kenai River and Skilak Lake before slowing down near the Russian River confluence. The upper Kenai, however, does promote some activity as the run becomes much more concentrated and the river narrower and holes and runs more defined. Good fishing is the norm here.

The late run with its exceptional heavy numbers of fish is the main red fishery on the Kenai. The lower Kenai sees the peak in-migration during the second half of July with excellent action typical at the height of each pulse. As one big push of reds enters the mouth of Kenai, anglers can expect these fish to pass through the Soldotna area the very next day, a distance of approximately 20 to 22 miles. It is common to be able to pursue the salmon on a day-to-day basis as the pulse progresses upstream.

As the late run hits the middle river, foremost the upper end above Naptowne Rapids, many of the salmon begin to slow down their quick upstream movement, as this is a major spawning ground for a good portion of the run. Anglers experience excellent fishing in late July and early August along nearly the entire length of the Kenai with the exception of the area at the outlet of Skilak Lake, which has an abundance of very slow, quiet water.

By the time the late run hits in force on the upper Kenai, a fair number of fish will be starting to turn, requiring anglers to sort through the older reds to get to the fresh ones. But in the early part of the season, in late July, there should be a large contingent of dime bright salmon available.

Tributaries

The only tributary of the Kenai River that has any decent red salmon fishing to offer is the Russian River. The majority of the early run and many late run salmon are found in its clear waters, the action typically being excellent in most years. Moose River has some fairly productive fishing at its mouth where it enters the mainstem but these are almost all Kenai or Russian reds. Relatively very few reds spawn in the Moose River drainage.

The only other tributaries that see significant returns of red salmon are the streams draining into Kenai Lake; however, they are all closed to salmon fishing year-round.

Structure

Red salmon are not much different from silvers in their preference for holding water or paths of upstream migration. Generally, the fish choose to swim close to shore, approximately three to 15 feet from the bank, where currents are not as strong, thus expediting the speed of migration and saving much needed energy at the same time. Schools or long bands of salmon are commonly spotted moving up the Kenai, making it easy for anglers to target the fish. In slack water, such as the lower few miles of river near its terminus or the first couple of miles of water just downstream of Skilak and Kenai lakes, the reds often tend to spread out more and can be located across the width of the river.

As with all salmon species, the fish move rapidly through high-velocity currents, resting in sloughs and back channels for a few hours up to several days. Although most salmon are ideally targeted in the resting areas, the best action for reds is actually in locations with at least moderate current flow. Seek out spots with a good clip of moving water, preferably about two feet deep, upstream of large holes and pools as schools of salmon will be moving through in pulses after having rested. On the lower Kenai, most anywhere with favorable current and depth is likely to see a number of salmon as the fish in this stretch of river are related to tidal movements and the perceived urgency in which they travel upstream.

In the only tributary with viable red action – Russian River – anglers can cast to schools or individual salmon easily as the clear water permits superb opportunities for sight fishing. Here the fish are spread throughout the river and do not necessarily travel close to shore. As the water is only two to three feet deep at most, anywhere on the river is a good spot to hook reds. The fish move through the shallows with speed and can be readily intercepted. When the salmon rest in holes and runs they become even easier targets as the current is almost never too slow to properly present an offering.

What to Use

It has been stated that red salmon do not bite artificial offerings at all and any fish caught in the mouth are actually legally snagged so to speak. There is some truth

FISH SPECIES FOUND IN ALASKA'S KENAI RIVER DRAINAGE

King Salmon

King Salmon, spawning color phase

Red Salmon

Red Salmon, spawning color phase

Pink Salmon

Pink Salmon, spawning color phase

Chum Salmon

Chum Salmon, spawning color phase

Silver Salmon

Silver Salmon, spawning color phase

Rainbow Trout

Rainbow Trout, spawning color phase

FISH SPECIES FOUND IN ALASKA'S KENAI RIVER DRAINAGE

Steelhead Trout

Lake Trout

Arctic Char / Dolly Varden

Arctic Char / Dolly Varden, spawning phase

Arctic Grayling

Round Whitefish

Northern Pike

Burbot

to that statement but it is not the whole story. Most offerings anglers toss at red salmon are not ideal in that they do not mimic something these fish can relate to in respect to food sources. Remember, the main source of sustenance of red salmon in the ocean is mainly small crustaceans. Spoons, spinners, plugs, and most flies do not look at all similar to what reds used to eat and therefore do not trigger a response to bite. What they do, however, is sometimes activate an anger or stress response, especially in larger males.

What should also be considered is that red salmon are not hunters by nature. They do not have a very acute sense of giving chase, which certainly is not the case with the other salmon species. Therefore, reds do not generally have any tendency to follow and attack lures or flies.

Most anglers having fished for red salmon on the Kenai River and its tributary, Russian, know that flies is the offering of choice. Most streamer flies are good for only one thing and that is as a visual reference point for the angler to know where the hook is, a very valuable function in sight fishing especially. And it works exceptionally well. Yet there are certain colors that will draw actual strikes under the right water and lighting conditions though usually reds are being "lined" (see description below or in chapter 4, page 94). But they will bite given the right fly and right water conditions. The decision then becomes to choose an offering that will, with persistence, draw a true strike, or a creation that will effectively hook a fish in the mouth. The bottom line, of course, is that the hook is legally set.

Gear

Spin/bait Casting: Seven- to eight-and-a-half-foot rod, matching reel, 8- to 15-pound test line.

Fly Fishing: Eight- to 10-foot, 7- or 8-weight rod and matching reel, 8- to 15-pound test tippet.

Note: In areas with strong current and/or large crowds of other anglers, use 17- to 20-pound test for better control of fish.

Flies

By far the most favorite fly used on the Kenai and Russian rivers is the Coho. A huge variety of colors exist with most anglers picking red/white, red/yellow, and green/white combinations; these may not necessarily be the most productive but anglers like them and they do catch a lot of fish. The vast majority of reds caught on the Coho are "lined" and therefore color is not an important factor. However, experienced anglers generally recognize that some of the brighter hues (orange, red, yellow, pink) work best in the glacial Kenai while the darker colors (blue, purple, green, black) are most productive in the clear Russian, which lends some credibility to the salmon actually mouthing these flies instead of being just "lined."

Pieces of colored yarn tied on a single hook is a very easy and inexpensive fly to tie and it works just as well as anything else and at times even better. These creations are most often used on the mainstem Kenai reds. Chartreuse and red are effective hues, while flaming orange can draw some surprisingly savage strikes on dark days or in very early morning and late evening. The yarn should be about one- to one-and-a-half-inch long. The larger, fuller yarn flies work best in murky conditions, especially on the far lower end of the river in the slow-flowing tidal zone. One gaudy commercially made pattern that is deadly is the Fat Freddie.

To entice reds to strike flies in a "feeding" response in the relatively clearer water of the middle and upper river, flies in orange, red, green, chartreuse, and pink colors are good. Original or modified patterns include Flash Fly, Battle Creek, Polar Shrimp, Boss, Sockeye Orange, Simple Stealth, Comet, Silver Brown Buck, Fall Favorite, Sportsman Special, Mary Ann, San Juan Worm, Green Butt Skunk, Egg-Sucking Leech, and Soft Hackle Stealth in sizes 6 to 10, depending on water and weather conditions.

In very clear water, such as that of the Russian River, darker pattern hues often rule with purple, brown, metallic or dark blue and green, and black being excellent color choices. White sometimes does well too. However, there are times reds will hit a small red or orange Glo Bug with enthusiasm. The most important thing to keep in mind is that flies need to be simply tied with sparse hackle, be it in the Kenai or Russian.

Lures

It is rare that red salmon will pursue spoons, spinners, plugs, or any other full-action hardware. Some fish are taken on plugs intended for kings and silvers on the lower Kenai but this is rather an exception than a rule. Small spinners (size 1 or 2) may also entice a fish to hit when retrieved slowly through a holding school of salmon.

Very small attractors such as Spin-N-Glo's, Cheaters, and Corkies may catch fish as well, particularly if fished stationary in a channel with moderate flow and lots of salmon moving through. Small red or orange beads stripped in at a snails pace through a hole or pool stacked with reds can actually be quite effective. But for all practical purposes, stick to flies.

Bait

Small clusters of salmon roe fished on the bottom fairly close to shore in the lower tidal reaches of the Kenai does promote some reds to bite. The take is usually very soft and subtle. Single salmon eggs work as well when drifted through promising holes and runs further upstream.

How to Fish

Unlike when fishing for other game fish, reds will not move any distance to intercept a fly or any other lure. Flies are good, but only when properly presented. Allow fly to work the water column in the fish's line of vision, not a foot above or below as it will more than likely be ignored. Select an area with moderate to fairly swift current flow for best results.

Use a split shot, rubber core, pencil lead or any other sinker attached about 18 inches to three feet above the fly. Enough weight must be used to feel a tap along the bottom every couple of feet or so. Adjust as necessary according to current velocity and depth.

In flat or very slow current, use very long leader (preferably with a floating line), 5 to 7 feet or more between sinker and fly, working the offering with short and smooth strips of line. When sinker hits bottom, pull in two to three feet of line and let it slowly sink again.

Flipping

This is the most effective and efficient method of presenting a fly to migrating red salmon. Casts (or flips) are short – perhaps 12 to 15 feet – with the angler working water that lies in the arc 45 degrees above to 45 degrees below his or her position. Line is pulled in with one hand through rod guides, rod swinging around in a circular whip, and let line go again. Feel the sinker bounce along the bottom and repeat procedure.

"Lining"

This is a method that has proved extremely productive on tight-lipped reds. The basic procedure is the same as the "flipping" technique described above. The length of line between fly and sinker is about three to five feet. The fly and sinker create a trap in which the fishing line between the two slides into the mouth of the fish and with the help of the current pulls the fly right into the fish. Through the drift, the angler keeps the rod tip low, sweeping it downstream ahead of the current, pulling the line with one hand to keep it tight but slow enough to keep sinker along bottom.

Hot Spots

All sections of the mainstem Kenai River provide excellent opportunities for red salmon, with the possible exception of the first couple of miles of river downstream of Kenai and Skilak lakes. The area around Soldotna and Sterling, and between the inlet of Skilak Lake and the mouth of Russian River, is superb and affords some of the best action anywhere for the species.

The Russian River has world-class, clearwater sight fishing for reds. Expect good to excellent action during the height of the runs with 40 to 50 or more hookups per day possible.

Fishing For Kokanee

The use of a boat or other watercraft is highly recommended in pursuing kokanee as the fish have a tendency to move around quite a bit, often in offshore areas as structure allows. They are often quite timid and may require some persistence to get to strike; however, there are times when fish appear very aggressive as well.

A variety of small flies, spoons, spinners, and jigs work in sizes 0 and 1 or 1/32-ounce weight. Fly fishers do best using size 12 to 16 nymph, midge, shrimp, or scud patterns. Popular colors include orange and pink but darker hues in brown, black, and deep purple are also well received.

Cloudy days or in early morning or late evening is best time to be out on the water, as fish are usually found quite shallow. If casting, lure or fly should be retrieved erratically just under the surface for best effect.

Troll the lure or fly at varying speeds through a range of water column from the bottom to near the surface, hitting areas of structure such as reefs, around vegetation mats, and small islands. Remember, kokanee thrive in schools so when one fish is hooked, stay in the immediate location and depth as more salmon are likely to be found. Many anglers to cut down on search time use a fish locator.

Try tiny pieces of bait if kokanee appears finicky. Scuds, shrimp, grubs, and maggots all take fish, either fished alone on a small single hook with a small flasher attached two feet above on the line or with a lure.

Given the typical small size of kokanee, use ultra-light gear with 2- to 4-pound test line or tippet.

Hidden Lake supports the largest population of kokanee on the peninsula and action can be good at times early in the season (May-June).

SILVER SALMON
Scientific Name: *Oncorhynchus kisutch.*
Common Name(s): Coho.

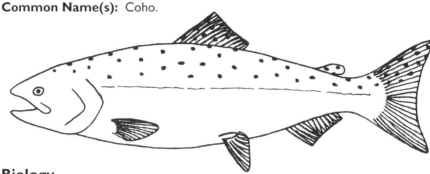

Biology
Description: Black spots on back, upper sides, tail fin, and top of head. Back is dark, sides silvery, and belly white. Spawning fish are dark red on back and sides with black belly.
Size: Average 6 to 10 pounds (early run), 8 to 15 pounds (late run), up to 20 pounds or more.
Distribution: Found from mouth of river to headwater tributaries.
Abundance: Total drainage population size unknown but believed to number approximately 100-150,000.

Sport Fishing
Regulatory Season: July 1 through October 31 in mainstem Kenai River; July 1 through September 30 in tributaries. General restrictions apply.
Timing: July to November, peaking in August-September (early run) and September-October (late run).
Gear: Seven- to eight-foot rod spin/bait caster; eight- to nine-foot, 8-weight fly rod; 10- to 20-pound test line/tippet.
Tackle: Spoons, spinners, attractors, plugs, flies, and bait.
Methods: Casting, drifting, back-bouncing, back-trolling, and stationary.
Hot Spots: Lower, middle, and upper Kenai River; Moose and Russian rivers.

SILVER SALMON in the Kenai River

Life Cycle
Most all stocks of silver salmon in the Kenai River drainage are anadromous. In other words, the fish are born in fresh water, migrate to the sea to feed for a period of time ranging from a year to three years, and return to the place of birth as is common with all species of Pacific salmon.

Mature adults enter the Kenai on a rising or high tide in summer and fall in two separate runs to reproduce in the main channel of the river or one of its tributaries. Moderately small black spots cover the top of the head, back, and upper lobe of the tail fin. Silvers have a white gum line (compared to black in kings) and the base of the tail is thick. When straight out of the ocean, fish are metallic blue on the back, silvery on the side, and white on the belly. Flesh color is orange red.

After spending about a week in the river, a slight coloration starts to show and after three weeks the silvery hue is gone, replaced by a pink or light orange coloration. In the fourth or fifth week of freshwater residence, the salmon display full spawning phase. The fish is now brilliant red (may also appear bronze, greenish brown, or black) with a dark olive green to faded red or copper back. Males develop a very distinct hooked snout, prolonged teeth, and a slightly humped back. Flesh color is white.

Breeding grounds are very diverse and may be located from the tidal section of the lower river to small clearwater streams. Preferred spots include anywhere with suitable gravel or pebble bottom structure and sufficient current flow in about two to three feet of water. Females deposit 1,400 to 5,700 eggs that hatch in winter or spring. Six to seven weeks after entering the river the silvers have completed reproduction and will decease within about ten days or so. It must be noted, however, that some stocks have a considerably longer freshwater lifespan.

Juvenile silvers remain in Kenai River for about one or two years, subsisting on a diet of insects and salmon fry. Fish migrate to the ocean in spring and early summer, where they will eventually consume fish and crustaceans.

At least one documented report of self-sustaining resident silvers is known, from Engineer Lake (tributary of Hidden and Skilak lakes). These fish became landlocked by natural means and are apparently able to survive on the lake's zooplankton in order to grow and may reach 20 inches and several pounds.

Early & Late Runs

Like king and red salmon, silvers also appear in two distinct runs in the Kenai. The early run is primarily tributary fish that display a timing scheme similar to other streams on the Kenai Peninsula, while the late run consists of mainstem Kenai salmon with a timing pattern reminiscent of Kodiak Island and Southeast Alaska stocks. There is some overlap of the two populations during the month of September and a few discreet stocks may not fit exactly into either run category.

Early Run Silvers

Some fish begin arriving in mid-July yet a very few scouts may be in the river mouth as early as the first week of the month. The run builds slowly until about the first of August when fair numbers of silvers start coming in on every tide. As time progresses, fish are increasingly stacking into the lower Kenai until the in-migration peaks in mid-August. Good numbers continue to enter the river through the month. After Labor Day, the run subsides rapidly with fresh tributary silvers still coming in on the tides down to a trickle by mid-September with a few stragglers present into early October.

The number of bright in-river fish is at a peak in the second half of August on the lower and middle river but not until late August and early September in the upper section.

Tributaries that support important or large runs of early-run salmon include Funny,

Killey, Moose, and Russian rivers as well as streams draining into Kenai Lake such as Quartz and Ptarmigan creeks and others. It is common for silvers bound for smaller drainages to stage at the confluence with mainstem Kenai for a period of one or two weeks or more waiting for a rise in water levels associated with autumn rainfall before proceeding to the breeding grounds. These fish are often ripe upon ascending the streams.

Spawning commences in late fall, usually from early October to early November, but has been reported to occur as early as mid-September and as late as mid-December. Early run silvers spend approximately two weeks on the spawning beds.

Late Run Silvers

The first few mainstem spawners show up the last week of August, building in numbers until the in-migration peaks during the second and third weeks of September. The run begins to deteriorate with the approach of October but a fair number of silvers will sporadically continue to arrive on the tides into November. Given a lack of complete data, it is assumed that the majority of the late run is in the river by mid-November with a trickle of fish still coming in through December or even later. It has been suggested by some sources that fresh silvers may enter the frozen river considerably later as evidence seems to support.

The number of bright in-river salmon is at a peak in the second half of September on the lower river, late September to mid-October on the middle, but not until mid- and late October on the upper Kenai. Unlike early-run silvers, fish of the late run keep their silvery ocean coloration for a longer duration of time, apparently up to four weeks or more is commonplace.

These fall salmon are primarily mainstem Kenai River fish, selecting areas for reproduction that may be anywhere from the upper reaches of the tidal zone near the mouth to the outlet of Kenai Lake. Most fish utilize portions of the middle river and the whole length of the upper river. Spawning begins in mid-November, peaks during the month of December, and ends in mid-January. However, silvers that spawn at the outlet of Kenai and Skilak lakes display a much later timing cycle (see section below).

"Winter" Run Silvers

It is recognized that a certain component of the late run of silvers do not fit exactly into the category of the typical mainstem Kenai fish in that the maturity process, in-river behavior, and selection of spawning areas are quite unique.

Whereas most species of salmon do not spend more time than perhaps a couple of months in freshwater before breeding and dying off, this particular stock of silvers are capable of surviving up to four or five months or longer. Although scientific research in the Lower 48 has verified a correlation between water temperature and the speed of maturation (cold water delays nuptial coloration), it is not known if this factor alone or other variables are at play.

It appears that large schools of fish sometimes stage in areas of Skilak and Kenai Lake until reaching full or partial maturity before moving onto the spawning grounds. Only the lake outlets and the first few miles of river are used for reproduction, unlike mainstem silvers that may utilize the entire length of the Kenai River. The process starts in mid-January, activity peaking from mid-February to mid-March, with most salmon spent by mid-April. A few spawned-out silvers can be observed into May.

When exactly this stock of salmon ascends the Kenai from sea is up to speculation. It is known, however, that dime bright silvers are present in decent numbers in the upper reaches of middle and upper Kenai through December, and fairly common even into February. A few seemingly fresh specimens are known to occur as late as March.

Size & Age

Silver salmon in the Kenai River drainage may be present in a wide range of sizes, from "one ocean" jacks measuring 16 inches or less to trophy status specimens of 20 pounds or more. The majority of salmon invariably weigh in the order of six to 15 pounds, depending on the time of year as late run silvers are generally larger than those of the early run.

Fish of the first run average six to 10 pounds with a fair number of silvers reaching 15 pounds. Exceptional specimens up to 18 pounds or more are not unheard of. The second – or late – run have bigger fish on average as most are in the order of eight to 15 pounds. Trophy class salmon in the 20- to 22-pound category are present every season with silvers up to 24 pounds reported.

Abundance Estimates

There is little documented information exactly on how large the silver salmon populations are in the Kenai River drainage. Moose and Russian rivers are most likely responsible for the majority of early run fish production because of the ideal habitat conditions. Some of the smaller streams may see no more than a few hundred specimens while bigger drainages have silvers numbering at least into the thousands, even tens of thousands in good years. The late mainstem run is believed to be the heavier of the two runs. Scientific studies began only just recently and are still ongoing. It is assumed that the total number of silvers may be as high as 100-150,000 fish or more.

FISHING FOR KENAI SILVERS

The Kenai River is one of the largest silver salmon fisheries in Southcentral Alaska with the average annual catch being 41,000 fish. It is not just the numbers of salmon available but also the length of time fish are present, achieved by the system providing two distinct populations of silvers covering several months of activity.

Rules & Regulations

Restrictions regarding silver salmon fishing on the Kenai River are quite liberal. The official season runs from July 1 through October 31. Streams draining into Kenai Lake, however, are closed to salmon fishing year-round. Consult the ADF&G Sport Fishing Regulations for more information.

When & Where

Silver salmon are available in the Kenai River system from July through October. The peak of the two runs that occur on the river is mid-August through early September and late September through mid-October. Successful anglers target the early morning hours and, if fishing on the lower river, time their excursion to coincide with a high tide.

Mainstem River

Silver salmon tend to move fairly rapidly through the lower reaches of the Kenai with fish generally spending no more than a few days at the most before moving into upper areas. Although a few silvers will spawn in a couple of the smaller tributaries (Beaver and Slikok creeks) and the mainstem Kenai, the vast majority is bound for waters upstream of Soldotna. Large schools of fish arrive on the tides during mid-August and again in mid-September but action can be worthwhile from a week before to a week after the peak in-migration. Many guides operate on the lower river for silvers and there are a multitude of great holes and runs to choose from.

The middle stretch of the Kenai River sees far less guide traffic than lower in the drainage but has some terrific fishing just as well. Salmon move through the Sterling area and up into the Kenai Keys at their thickest in late August-early September and late September-early October. The speed at which the fish travel has slowed somewhat since there are a few spawning grounds located here. Oftentimes during the early run, silvers will hole up at or near the mouths of Funny and Killey rivers. Additionally, that portion of the Kenai from Skilak Lake downstream to Naptowne Rapids is a major breeding area for late run salmon and these silvers will be available in good numbers through the season closure on October 31.

Upper Kenai River has some fabulous silver action starting with the early run in late August-early September and terminating with the late run in early to mid-October. Anglers here target the traditional holes, runs, and sloughs with the late-run fish providing better and more consistent angling opportunities. Russian River is a major spawning area for early-run fish while the late run is available in decent numbers to anglers throughout the mainstem until November.

Tributaries

With the exception of Moose and Russian rivers, there are relatively few tributaries offering good fishing for silvers. In addition, all of the streams draining into Kenai Lake are closed to salmon fishing year-round. Some isolated opportunities may be found in the lower reaches in a few of the smaller clearwater streams for anglers wishing to experiment. Peak time to look for early-run silvers is from late August to mid-September.

Structure

Silver salmon are flexible fish in terms of holding water and may be found in near-shore water only a foot deep to holes in the main current of mainstem Kenai. Even if many fish during the upstream migration swim close to the river bottom, silvers will more often than not choose their direction of travel through current of least resistance. It is also very common to see fish holding in sloughs or other calm resting areas only inches below the surface with part of their tail fin sticking out of the water.

In the mainstem Kenai, search for fish in back-eddies, behind islands and reefs, and pockets of slower-moving water associated with the mouths of sloughs and side channels as well as behind boulders and jetties. Sometimes, however, schools of salmon may be encountered in non-structure locations, sitting close to the surface in mid-current. Move around and pay careful attention, making sure to hit spots that have ideal holding water, such as the seams of slow or standing water and the main swift current.

Concentrations of early fish are often encountered at the confluence of Kenai River and spawning tributaries as fish are staging prior to entering the smaller streams.

In tributaries, always scout for depressions in the stream bottom between longer stretches of shallow water or riffles. Sharp bends in a stream usually means the current has carved out holes and an undercut bank may be present – perfect structure for cover and rest. In areas with an abundance of slack water, look for a narrowing down of stream width that generally translates into deeper water and faster current. Fallen trees, boulders, and logjams all have the potential for increased depth.

What to Use

Silvers will take just about anything at times but they can also be frustratingly picky. The key is variety and successful anglers carry an arsenal of different types of offerings in select colors or color combinations in order to hopefully match the flavor of the day. A wide range of tackle has proven effective on the Kenai and its tributaries, including spoons, spinners, plugs, attractors, flies, and bait.

Gear

Spin/bait Casting: Seven-and-a-half to eight-and-a-half feet long rod, matching reel containing some 200 yards of 8- to 17-pound test line.

Fly fishing: Eight- to 10-foot, 7- to 8-weight rod, matching reel, floating or sink tip line of 8- to 17-pound test tippet.

Note: Use the lighter weight gear during the early run or in tributaries, the heavier weight being more appropriate for mainstem late-run silvers. Up to 20-pound test is common in strong current or in crowded areas.

Mainstem Lures

As far as hardware goes, very few things can compare to a spinner. The incessant buzz and flash of a size 3 to 5 spinner through an area containing fish is almost assured of getting a strike. Vibrax is the most popular brand and is locally known as the "silver killer," yet the large assortment of Mepps, Panther Martin, and Rooster Tail are deadly too. Chrome is a long-time favorite color but metallic blue, copper, and green are exceptional in many instances. When water is high and somewhat murky, use orange, red, and chartreuse hues.

The slower wobbling of a spoon sometimes work very well, especially when the water is very cold. Sizes from about ½-ounce to 7/8-ounce are best. Suggested brands include Pixee, Krocodile, Hot Rod, and Kastmaster. Blue or green inset is good. The sharper hues do better in dark or murky conditions.

Plugs are at times as effective as spinners. Cast and retrieved or back-trolled take a fair share of silvers every year. Popular brands are Kwikfish, Flatfish, and Wiggle Wart.

Attractors such as Spin-N-Glo's, Corkies, and Cheaters, especially the ones with reflective wings, are good. They can be cast just the same as any other lure but can in addition also be fished stationary or drifted with a small cluster of salmon roe. Some anglers, when fishing a bait combination, prefer attractors with solid colors without reflective wing surfaces.

Tributary Lures

Some of the mainstem Kenai lures also do well in tributaries, except that smaller sizes are employed. Size 3 and possibly 4 Vibrax, Mepps, Panther Martin, and Rooster Tail in chrome, copper, and bronze are quite popular, with metallic blue or green being good colors. In darker water conditions use brighter hues such as red or chartreuse.

Small Spin-N-Glo's, Corkies, and Cheaters in neutral colors do best. Metallic blue, green, purple, chrome, and black are all effective.

Flies

The mainstem Kenai often requires flies with some degree of coloration, unlike clearwater tributaries where darker hues are the game. Size 2 to 6 Flash Fly in silver or purple, Coho in purple or chartreuse, Polar Shrimp, Krystal Bullet, Purple Woolly Bugger, chartreuse Egg-Sucking Leech, and Everglow are just a few of the flies that have a track record on the Kenai River. For less fancy concoctions, pieces of cut Glo Bug yarn tied on a hook is sometimes all that is required.

A trick an adventurous angler may want to try is casting a dry fly such as a Pink Pollywog into calm or clearwater sloughs of the Kenai River and slowly stripping it back across the surface.

But when fishing in clearwater tributaries, though, slightly smaller versions of the flies described above (including Comet and Bunny Leech) are used and preferably in more neutral colors. Purple, brown, olive, blue, green, and black are all attractive hues for silvers. Orange, red, pink, and chartreuse colors are better in the twilight of early morning or late evening or in murky water conditions.

Bait

A small- to medium-sized cluster of fresh salmon roe is definitely on the all-time top menu list for silver salmon. Either fished stationary on the bottom with a small sinker or drifted through holding areas with or without an attractor/sinker setup, roe catches silvers quickly and in fast order. In some locations it makes sense to use a bobber, the bait suspended two to three feet or more on the line below. Again, a sinker may be attached to the line at least 18 inches above the hook. Furthermore, some anglers add scent to bait to create an even stronger concoction. Anise oil and salmon-egg oil are popular.

If using bait, be prepared to catch and keep fish instead of focusing on catch-and-release. Besides trout and char, also silver salmon have a tendency to inhale bait deeply – sometimes even swallowing it. Additionally, fish in intertidal areas suffer a high degree of mortality if caught and released on roe.

How to Fish

All of the techniques briefly discussed in this section are described in more detail in Chapter 4 on page 91.

Back-bouncing

Perhaps the most effective technique employed from a boat is back-bouncing. Unlike fishing for kings, back-bouncing for silvers entails anchoring up and letting the current "walk" the attractor/bait combination along the bottom in fish-holding water.

Drifting

Casting a lure, fly, or chunk of bait out at 45-degree angle, letting it sink and bounce along the bottom every couple of feet or so for some distance is a great technique in many places, particularly in runs with moderate current and depth. A large area is covered on one cast.

Casting

If fishing from an anchored boat or from shore, the straight cast-and-retrieve technique is used in quiet water on the edge of faster current. Proceed to cast lures or flies into the holding area, making slow and steady to erratic retrieves. If there are silvers present, it usually does not take more than a couple of dozen casts to find out. Then again, one may elect to wait for a school of fish to come through, especially if fishing the holes on the lower river.

Flipping

This simple technique is usually employed from the bank on the mainstem Kenai downstream of the mouth of clearwater streams and to holding or migrating fish in clearwater tributaries. Lure or fly is flipped out upstream at 45-degree angle, allowed to sink to the bottom, drifting with the current, and then pulled in at 45-degree angle downstream. This is a superb technique for sight fishing.

> *Tip:* Silvers are highly visual and territorial creatures and much more prone to strike a lure or fly coming directly or from a 45- to 90-degree angle towards it rather than from behind. Take note of which direction the current flows in a hole or pool and adjust casts accordingly.

Hot Spots

The lower mainstem river between Soldotna and Warren Ames Bridge has long been regarded as a silver paradise as waves of fresh fish come in on the tides and a multitude of productive holes are present for salmon to stack up in. Anglers in the middle Kenai do very well in the slow water from Naptowne Rapids to the Skilak Lake outlet as silvers stage here in masses. However, there are many good holes and runs between Naptowne Rapids and Soldotna as well. The stretch of upper river can be exceptional along its entire length.

The lower part of Russian River and its confluence with the upper Kenai provides excellent sight fishing for silvers. Likewise can be said about the middle and upper reaches of Moose River in terms of fast-paced action.

PINK SALMON

Scientific Name: *Oncorhynchus gorbuscha.*
Common Name(s): Humpy and Humpback.

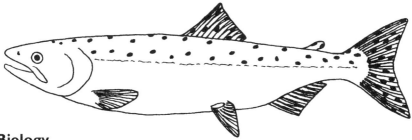

Biology

Description: Faint oval-shaped black spots cover back and tail fin. Back is dark, sides silvery, and belly white. Spawning males develop very distinctive humped back and elongated, hooked snout.
Size: Average 3 to 6 pounds, up to 8 pounds or more. State record is 12 pounds 9 ounces (Moose River, 1974).
Distribution: From mouth of Kenai River to headwaters, including several tributaries.
Abundance: Very heavy run on even-numbered years, population likely numbering in the millions. Largest return in lower and middle river, relatively few in upper river and most tributaries.

Sport Fishing

Regulatory Season: No species-specific regulations in place; general restrictions apply.
Timing: July to September, peak in August.
Gear: Five- to seven-foot rod spin/bait caster; seven- to eight-foot, 6-weight fly rod; 4- to 8-pound test line/tippet.
Tackle: Spoons, spinners, attractors, plugs, and flies.
Methods: Casting, drifting, back-trolling.
Hot Spots: Lower and middle stretches of Kenai River, best downstream of Sterling Highway Bridge in Soldotna.

PINK SALMON in the Kenai River

Life Cycle

All stocks of pink salmon in the Kenai River drainage are anadromous. The fish are born in fresh water, migrate to the sea to feed for a period of one year, and return to the place of birth as is common with all species of Pacific salmon.

Pink salmon may enter the Kenai on any stage of the tide but prefer incoming and high tides. In-migration is primarily in late summer with some fish continuing into early fall. At the time of arrival from sea, pinks are steel blue to blue green on the back, silver on the sides fading to white on the belly. Faint oval-shaped black spots cover back and both lobes of tail fin. The flesh is orange to pink.

Pinks are notorious for maturing rapidly. After only a few days in fresh water, the silvery coloration begins to fade and after ten days the shine has disappeared, replaced by a grayish hue with a light pink lateral band. Faint vertical bars in green may be seen on lower sides. Males begin to take on a ridgeback condition. At two to three weeks in the river, the fish have attained full nuptial coloration; back is dirty brown, sides are yellowish green, and the belly creamy white. Large oval spots are very pronounced on the back, dorsal fin, and both lobes of tail fin. All males display a very characteristic humped back and elongated, hooked snout. Flesh color is white.

It is common for pink salmon to begin changing into spawning colors already at sea and many fish arrive in semi-bright to fairly dark hue, this being especially the case toward the latter part of the run. Some pinks enter the river ready to spawn.

These small salmon select breeding grounds that can be as diverse as the tidal area of the Kenai River upstream into headwater tributaries. The fish are even capable of reproducing in brackish water at the river mouth as pink salmon eggs can withstand a high degree of salinity. Females deposit 800 to 2,000 eggs in the river bottom, the eggs hatching in winter. Three to five weeks after entering the river the pinks have completed spawning and will decease within a week.

Juvenile pinks first consume insects and zooplankton, switching to a diet rich in fish and crustaceans as maturity sets in. The period of time of young pinks in freshwater is very short, the fish migrating to sea almost immediately, this being particularly true if spawning sites are near saltwater.

Early & Late Runs

Unlike other salmon species in the Kenai River, pinks do not exhibit two distinct runs or populations of fish. However, there are indeed differences in timing (and physical size) of the various stocks within the drainage, but they are not as pronounced as numbers of early-arriving pinks are comparatively small to late-arriving fish. And there is also an overlap in timing between the populations. In general, the fish that enters the river first will travel the farthest.

Early pink salmon stocks ascend the Kenai River in mid- to late June with more fish arriving into July. By mid-August there are likely few pinks still coming into the river. These salmon are bound for spawning grounds in small clearwater tributaries of the mainstem Kenai and Kenai Lake. The timing of this population is very similar to that of stocks in systems of upper Cook Inlet.

The main population of pinks in the Kenai is of the late-arriving type. The run commences in mid-July, builds to a peak in early to mid-August, and tapers off into mid-September. Several stocks of fish are represented here, including those of the main tributaries of the lower and middle mainstem as well as the Kenai itself. A small segment of the run will continue upstream into upper Kenai River, but for the most part the majority of the run stays downstream of Skilak Lake. The timing is typical of stocks found on the southern Kenai Peninsula.

Size & Age

The pinks of Kenai River are among the largest in Alaska, which follows the general trend of the river producing trophy and record specimens of several other kinds of game fish. As a matter of fact, the state record pink salmon was taken at the confluence of Moose River and Kenai River in 1974 and weighed 12 pounds, 9 ounces. Several other fish in the 10- to 12-pound category have been documented as well.

The early returns to the river (prior to August) contain salmon that average 3 to 4 pounds with few fish exceeding 6 pounds, which is the typical size of mid-summer pinks throughout Southcentral Alaska. In August, however, as the late-arriving pinks enters the drainage, the average weight increases to 4 to 6 pounds with several trophy specimens between 8 and 9 pounds or more present.

Despite the difference in size, all pink salmon are of the same age but with a slight genetic variation. These fish run on a strict two-year life cycle and thus the populations of odd- and even-numbered years do not mix and therefore considered two separate and distinct stocks of fish. Three-year-old specimens have been reported from waters outside of Alaska but not from the Kenai River.

Abundance Estimates

There are no official documentation on the size of pink salmon runs in the Kenai River, except for weir or field counts done on a few of the clearwater tributaries. Most rivers and creeks in this drainage produce from only a few dozen or a couple of hundred up to several thousand pinks. The mainstem Kenai River population, on the other hand, is estimated at several million fish, making pinks the most abundant species of salmon in the system.

Returns on even-numbered years are very heavy, conforming to other Southcentral pink stocks, and odd-numbered years small and relatively insignificant.

FISHING FOR KENAI PINKS

Very few – if any – species of game fish on the Kenai is able to provide such intensity in action as that of pink salmon. On even-numbered years in August, fish-on-every-cast is not only possible but in many instances the norm. It is a perfect species to introduce young anglers to the art of sport fishing and for more seasoned veterans to relax and just enjoy a time on the water without really thinking too much about technique or giving hours worth of effort to get a strike.

Most anglers that regularly fish on the Kenai for other more sought-after game species do not specifically target pink salmon but the sheer volume of these littlest salmon is difficult to ignore. In fact, the masses of fish and their willingness to strike artificial lures oftentimes make for quite a nuisance. But being such an important part of the ecosystem of the river drainage, enjoy them for what they are and the best way to do that is to use ultra light gear for a terrific fight.

There are no species-specific restrictions for pink salmon in the Kenai River system and standard rules and regulations apply. The bag limit (6 fish) is very liberal.

When & Where

Pink salmon are generally available from the first of July into September with solid action taking place in early to mid-August, but only in even-numbered years. Fishing in odd-numbered years is non-productive for the most part with only a few pinks available. Although these salmon are found scattered throughout the system in vary-ing degrees of abundance, the best locations by far are on the lower river as this is where the fish are freshest and put up the best fight. Additionally, the fish coming in as the run is in progress of building towards a peak are in absolute prime shape for consumption as well as sport.

River Sections

For anglers wanting to experience light action sport for dime bright pink salmon, the lower river from Soldotna downstream is recommended. Many fishers prefer the tidal area above anywhere else as pinks are aggressive coming in from the sea and more often than not are encountered in astonishing numbers.

The middle river between Soldotna and Skilak Lake outlet does harbor a large return of pinks but not all the fish are in equally good condition. Expect huge numbers of semi-bright salmon with only a fair number of fresh ones thrown in. Be prepared to do a lot of catch-and-release for quality.

Anglers on the upper Kenai are not exposed nearly to the number of fish found lower down in the drainage. Relatively few pinks spawn in this section of river and the fish that are here are usually in less than prime condition.

Structure

Pinks can be found migrating or holding just about anywhere in the river during the height of the run in August. However, as they are not very strong swimmers anglers do better focusing in on areas that have only moderate to little current.

Action concentrated around tidal movements is tops. Incoming and outgoing tides offer excellent opportunities. The slack water of high tide can be good but the better option is to proceed to holes and pools just upstream of the high tide mark as there is more current and big schools of pinks are moving through.

Quiet water associated with the downstream side of islands, the mouth of channels and sloughs, and the confluences with clearwater tributaries all represent the perfect structure to find masses of fish. Pinks can actually be finicky at times in these spots if angling pressure is high but if in the right mood no better action can be had.

Top 3 Kenai River Pinks

#	Pounds - Oz.	Inches	Date	Year	Angler
1.	12 – 9	30.0	n/a	1974	Steven Lee
2.	12 – 4	28.25	n/a	1974	Carl Schreiner
3.	11 – 0	30.0	n/a	1984	Joann Lukken

What to Use

When the pinks are really running just about anything with some flash and color will produce fish. Yet there are some things that actually does work better and will increase the odds of hooking more and fresher salmon.

Lures

Medium-sized, half-ounce spoons, spinners, and plugs are most often used on the Kenai River as they provide enough mass to be adequately seen and elicit an aggressive response in the glacially silted water. Standard brands used the most on the Kenai include the ever-popular Pixee as well as Vibrax, Mepps, and Krocodile, not to mentioned the myriad of other lures that are less known but probably just as effective as anything else.

Straight metallic silver or copper hues are good, particularly when fish are finicky and the sun is out, but it is the metallic brass along with certain colors that seem to work on the most consistent basis. Green, blue, red, orange, purple, and chartreuse are all effective in combination with hammered silver. The top producer, though, is almost without a doubt a lure with a silver background and pink inset. Fluorescent orange and pink are deadly under most water conditions.

Flies

A variety of flies work on Kenai pink salmon but be certain to select the more colorful versions for visibility in a river of large volume. Comet, Boss, Polar Shrimp, Flash Fly Kispioux Special, Thor, Alaskabou, and Egg-Sucking Leech are good. Any patterns used are most effective if containing an abundance of silver Krystal Flash along with orange, red, and pink colors.

For proper casting and a good drift, try the tidal zone between Eagle Rock and Warren Ames Bridge.

Gear

Ultra light equipment will provide the most challenge but recognizing that the pinks are very numerous with foul-hooked fish commonplace and the current swift in places, a slightly heavier outfit may be more practical. Six- to seven-and-a-half-foot rods, fast action, with matching reels loaded with four- to eight-pound test line is ideal in areas with slack current and room to play the fish. Heavier line may be need in some locations.

Fly gear would consist of a five- to six-weight rod (eight-and-a-half to nine-and-a-half feet) with matching reel and either floating or sink tip line. Tippets are generally four- to eight-pound test, no more than four feet long for sinking presentations.

How to Fish

There is no particular science to fishing for pinks compared to that of king salmon or rainbow trout. The majority of anglers trying for pinks locate a suitable hole or pool, cast out, and makes a slow retrieve. If in a spot perpendicular to the current, cast slightly upstream, let the lure or fly sink to the bottom, and let the offering tumble downstream. In slack water, retrieve a lure in the direction fish seem to be traveling. However, sometimes a fly stripped or spinner buzzed in the opposite direction is even better.

CHUM SALMON
Scientific Name: *Oncorhynchus keta.*
Common Name(s): Dog.

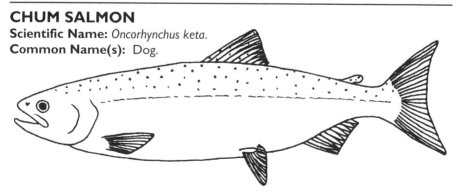

Biology

Description: No obvious or apparent markings. Back is dark, sides silvery, and belly white. Spawning fish are dark on back; crimson markings in red, black, and yellow decorate sides.

Size: Average 6 to 10 pounds, up to 15 pounds or more.

Distribution: May occur throughout Kenai River drainage but established presence only documented in Quartz and Ptarmigan creeks of Kenai Lake.

Abundance: Very small population only numbers a few hundred fish.

Sport Fishing

Regulatory Season: No species-specific regulations in place; general restrictions apply.

Timing: July and August, no peak.

Gear: Six- to seven-foot rod spin/bait caster; eight- to nine-foot, 7-weight fly rod; 10- to 12-pound test line/tippet.

Tackle: Spoons, spinners, attractors, plugs, roe clusters, and flies.

Methods: Casting, flipping, and back-trolling.

Hot Spots: No best places or locations; all fish caught incidentally to fishing for other species.

CHUM SALMON in the Kenai River

Chum salmon in the Kenai River drainage are anadromous. The fish are born in fresh water, migrate to the sea to feed for a period of time ranging from two to five years, and return to the place of birth as is common with all species of Pacific salmon.

Identification of fresh-from-the-sea chums can sometimes be problematic and the fish are commonly mistaken as red or silver salmon. Iris of the eye is large and base of tail thin. A fine dusting of small specks may be visible on back and top of head. Lower fins have distinctive white tips. Back and top of head is dark metallic blue, sides silvery, and belly silvery white. Flesh color is orange to pink.

Chums return to the river on a rising or high tide in mid- to late summer. Most fish are headed to tributaries of Kenai Lake and, due to their small numbers, are very rarely observed or encountered during their migration. The physical changes from the ocean phase to the spawning phase are quite rapid and a few chums will begin turning even before entering the river.

After about three weeks in freshwater, the previously mint-bright chum has developed crimson markings covering the sides in red, black, and dirty yellow. The back is olive green, black, or brown. The pectoral, anal, and pelvic fins have white tips. Males display a hooked jaw with protruding canine-like teeth while females show a dark horizontal band across the sides. The flesh tone is white.

The only documented spawning populations have been located in Quartz and Ptarmigan creeks of the Kenai Lake drainage; however, ripe and spawned-out chums are on occasion spotted along the mainstem Kenai River in late summer and fall, evidence perhaps that at least a few fish may utilize other areas as well for reproductive purposes.

Females deposit somewhere between 2,000 and 4,000 eggs in several gravel redds.

Five to six weeks after entering the river the chums have completed spawning and will decease within a week. The eggs hatch in late winter or spring, the young spending only a few months in the river environment before moving out to sea. Diet early in life is primarily insects and zooplankton, eventually switching to fish in immature adults.

FISHING FOR KENAI CHUMS

The chum salmon is the least abundant of the five salmon species in the Kenai River drainage. The total population only numbers in a few hundred specimens but even so a few fish are caught every season. There are no species-specific regulations for chums other than that the spawning streams in which they may be found are closed to salmon fishing.

Despite the very heavy angling efforts for salmon along the mainstem Kenai River, extremely few catches of chum salmon are ever reported. For the most part this is because the run is so small and the fact that chums are not known as very aggressive sport fish in glacial waters. Another reason, which is well understood from systems with high densities of the species, anglers more often than not misidentify fresh chums as either red or silver salmon. Undoubtedly this also occurs on the Kenai River. Even so, a few dozen chums are reported taken every summer.

Targeting chum salmon in the Kenai would be an exercise in futility taking into consideration the size of the drainage and the fish few that are present. However, it is possible to spot a fish or two amongst schools of spawning reds in late summer on the upper river. The mouth of clearwater tributaries or sloughs can hold fish. But even with intention to find fish anglers must be prepared to spend many hours, perhaps days, in the search. If located, medium-sized spoons and spinners or colorful flies may get a strike. Before setting out, anglers should keep in mind that some people claim to have fished the river a whole lifetime without hooking a single chum. Thus, this elusive salmon will more than likely be rendered to incidental catches only while fishing for other species.

TROUT & CHAR
in the Kenai River

An Introduction

Trout and char represent two groups or families of game fish that are abundant in the Kenai River drainage. They are much sought after by anglers because of the aesthetics involved as well as their sporting qualities. Two species within these groups thrive in the marine environment, one of which displays a true anadromous life cycle. The other are strictly freshwater forms.

The trout family consists of rainbow trout, both of the resident and sea-run kind. Only resident rainbows are truly native to the Kenai system and can be found in varying degrees of abundance in most any tributary lake or stream, including the mainstem river. Without a doubt the rainbow is one of the most popular sport fish in the Kenai next to only king and red salmon. The sea-run version of rainbow trout – steelhead – is not indigenous to the drainage but stray fish from other rivers have established a small but seemingly growing presence. They are very rarely caught, however.

Dolly Varden, arctic char, and lake trout represent the char family. The latter species is not actually a trout but a form of big lake-dwelling char, its distribution being quite minimal. But wherever this lake char is found, anglers do search it out because of its good size and fondness of bait and artificial lures.

The other two species, Dolly Varden and arctic char, are very similar in appearance and considered by some biologists to be one single species, each with some minor morphological characteristics, none of which are really obvious to the untrained eye. Dolly Varden, like rainbow trout, are present throughout the Kenai River and the vast majority of lake and stream tributaries. It is a popular quarry among fly fishers in late summer and fall. Some stocks of Dolly Varden migrate to sea in spring and return to Kenai later on in summer, while others apparently reside in freshwater year-round.

The arctic char is, like the lake trout, a fish that thrive the most in deep, large lakes. Anglers do not target it to any great extent since only a couple of stocks are present within the Kenai River drainage.

Both trout and char are quarried in lakes and streams from spring through fall and remain available even through the winter months in many lakes in the system. They are not particularly difficult to tell apart, the standard rule being that trout have small black spots, char have fairly large spots or blotches in various colors from creamy white to pink.

The following chapter sections describe all of the trout and char species in the Kenai River drainage and details the what, when, where, why, and how's of sport fishing for them, including biological information that can prove very valuable in understanding the nature and behavior of the salmon and the application it has on angling for them.

Chapter Content:

RAINBOW TROUT
Scientific Name: Oncorhynchus mykiss.
Common Name(s): Trout and 'bow.

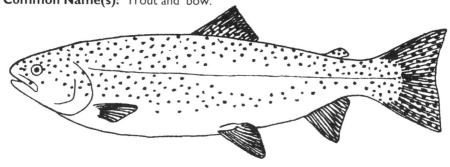

Biology

Description: Numerous black spots on back, sides, tail fin, and top of head. Back is dark, sides silvery, light brown, or olive, belly white. Spawning fish are reddish pink on sides and cheeks. Back is black or dirty dark green. Spots become enlarged.

Size: Average 10 inches to 3 pounds, some fish to 10 pounds, up to 20 pounds or more.

Distribution: Found throughout mainstem river from mouth to headwaters, including all tributaries.

Abundance: Approximately 30,000 in mainstem Kenai River, unknown numbers in tributaries but overall population seems very healthy throughout the system.

Sport Fishing

Regulatory Season: Varying open dates depending on drainage. General restrictions apply.

Timing: Year-round in lakes, May and August through September best bet.

Gear: Five- to seven-foot rod spin/bait caster; seven- to eight-foot, 6-weight fly rod; 4- to 12-pound test line/tippet.

Tackle: Spoons, spinners, attractors, plugs, flies, and bait.

Methods: Casting, drifting, jigging, and stationary.

Hot Spots: Middle and upper stretches of Kenai River; Russian and Moose river drainages.

RAINBOW TROUT in the Kenai River

Characteristics

Rainbow trout in the Kenai River display both a strict freshwater as well as anadromous life history. In this section it is the resident rainbow that will be stressed; the sea-run version, steelhead, is dealt with separately elsewhere in this chapter. Biological details of the rainbow trout on the peninsula are not known to any great extent and therefore the information laid out here is of general reference only, unless noted.

Distribution

Rainbows, along with char, are one of the most widespread game fish species in the Kenai River system. They are present from the upper reaches of the tidal zone and throughout the mainstem Kenai, including Skilak and Kenai lakes, and on into tributary rivers and streams and headwater lakes. There seems to be a healthy abundance of trout in all areas of the range with a notable strong presence in the middle and upper Kenai River and the Moose and Russian River drainages.

Identification

Numerous black spots are present on the back, sides, top of head, and both lobes of caudal (tail) fin. A pink stripe of varying width and pronunciation runs along side of fish from head to tail. General coloration may vary greatly between drainages as described below. Back is black or dark green and flesh color orange in both types.

Spawning fish are often more similar in color range throughout the Kenai drainage, the back and top of head being black or dirty dark green, reddish pink on sides and cheeks, belly grayish or brown. Black spots are enlarged and more pronounced. Flesh color is white.

Reproduction

Rivers and streams with gravel or rock structure are preferred breeding habitat, females depositing somewhere between 200 and 12,700 eggs in a nest on the bottom, primarily from early May to early June in the Kenai drainage. The eggs hatch in late spring and summer. Juvenile trout feed on insects and zooplankton, later switching over to a diet consisting of smaller fish and fish eggs as well as insects.

Size & Age

The common size range for mainstem Kenai River fish is from 10 to 22 inches with a good number of trout reaching 25 inches and 5 to 6 pounds. A trophy fish would be anything over 30 inches and 10 pounds. A few trout will reach weights of between 15 and 20 pounds and specimens up to 25 pounds have been reported from the middle stretch of Kenai River.

Rainbows from isolated stocks in the system seldom grow to any great size. The average fish is in the eight- to 20-inch category with relatively few specimens exceeding 25 inches and 6 pounds. Occasionally trout up to 28 inches and approximately 8 pounds are reported from larger lakes in the upper Moose River drainage, as well as Upper Russian Lake and River.

Rainbows may reproduce several times and live up to 11 years of age.

Stock Description

There are a multitude of trout stocks in the Kenai River and its tributaries. A few stocks within the drainage are distinct in that they do not mix with fish from the mainstem Kenai or even other tributaries. Some stocks, however, has been shown to display a significant overlap with seasonal spawning and/or feeding migrations, often blending with that of rainbows from other drainages. But there seems to be two main populations – or types – of rainbows in the Kenai, one oriented to the mainstem river and the other in tributary lakes and streams.

Mainstem River Type

Kenai River fish are generally silver on the sides and white on the belly, the distinct stripe being light red or pink to barely even visible at times. These fish can be difficult to differentiate from steelhead but bodies are often broader and stouter compared to the more elongated form of their sea-run cousins.

These rainbows spend the winter in Skilak and Kenai lakes, moving into various stretches of Kenai River starting in March and continuing through the spring. The older, larger trout select spawning areas in the mainstem Kenai as well as lower reaches of major tributaries, such as the Russian River, while smaller specimens may move into smaller tributaries. After the reproductive process is completed in late May and June, many of the larger fish will retreat to the mainstem for the rest of the summer and fall.

It is speculated that not all rainbows spawn annually in the Kenai as is perhaps evident by some mainstem fish displaying silvery summer feeding coloration throughout the traditional spawning period.

The migration back to the overwintering areas begins in the latter part of October and continues into December. Some fish, however, will spend the cold months in the deeper far upper sections of the middle and upper Kenai River.

Lake & Stream Type

Trout from tributary lakes and streams influenced by muskeg or tannic waters are typically much darker in hue compared to mainstem Kenai fish, usually copper, light brown, or olive on the sides and back, the stripe on the sides being dark reddish or red, belly tan. Rainbows in clearwater or glacial lakes are much lighter hued, more akin to mainstem Kenai fish.

Come spring (April-May) the annual spawning migration commences, trout moving out of their overwintering grounds in lakes and into small rivers and streams. Some of these streams can be very small and only support fish during the spring spawning period when water flow is sufficient as a result of snowmelt.

After breeding has been completed, many rainbows move back into lakes for the duration of the season until next spring. Other trout elect to feed in larger streams through summer and fall before migrating to their overwintering areas.

FISHING FOR KENAI RAINBOWS

The mainstem Kenai is a fly angler's dream, with approximately 43,000 rainbow trout caught every season. Strict measures of conservancy are in place both by set regulations and angler ethics with some 95% of trout being released.

Rules & Regulations

Along with the multitude of restrictions placed on certain salmon species, rainbow trout has its own set of rules and regulations. Seasonal restrictions to protect spawning fish permeate most of the flowing waters of the Kenai River drainage, including the upper mainstem. This spring closure may also include parts of lakes such as inlets and outlets are concerned. These seasonal closures usually entail a total ban on sport fishing but in some areas the restriction is only applied to rainbow trout since other valuable species, like king salmon, are present in the water.

When & Where

Rainbow trout are present year-round in the Kenai River system but principally available in rivers and streams only from mid-June into November. Although good action can be enjoyed anytime during the year, some of the more consistent and predictable sport occurs after breakup on the many lakes in the drainage and again in fall prior to freezeup. Rainbows in flowing waters, however, are at their best from late summer through fall. Apart from seasonal peaks, successful anglers take notice of the time during the day (morning and evening) as well as timing of important food sources, such as insect hatches and salmon spawn, two of the most important ingredients in catching Kenai trout.

Spring (April-May)

Since most flowing waters are closed to sport fishing or the catching of rainbow trout in spring, this season is then a lake opportunity. As the ice begins to recede from lake surfaces, rainbow trout become active by the infusion of much-need oxygen and light. Aggressive feeding may take place and anglers do well casting forage imitation lures and flies around the ice edges.

Also look for schools of mature trout gathering near inlets or outlets in preparation for the spring spawn. The larger rainbows may take a lot of coaxing to strike an offering, but the smaller fish will typically show no inhibitions whatsoever. These spots are also a focal point for outmigrating juvenile salmon and thus a logical feeding ground.

In the mainstem Kenai River that is open to fishing for rainbows through April, anglers can have some limited success pursuing spawn-bound fish. A few hogs are caught this time of year yet for the better sport wait until the middle of June or later.

Summer (June-August)
By mid-June and the onset of long, warm days, the lake action for rainbows begin to wind down. The fish retreat and disperse into deeper waters and some work and planning becomes necessary to search out structure (see section below). Some very good fishing can still be had, though, in lakes situated in higher alpine country where cooler air and water temperatures prevail through the summer.

As rivers and streams open to sport fishing sometime in the middle of June, anglers take a good number of trout on spoons, spinners, and plugs, as well as forage and insect imitation flies. However, rainbows are opportunistic feeders and will take advantage of food sources as they are presented to them.

But the overall quality of fishing actually improves starting in mid-July with the arrival of spawning king and red salmon. The diet of trout switches rather abruptly over to egg and flesh and that is exactly what anglers should imitate. The whole month of August is considered the zenith of trouting in the Kenai River drainage, including many tributary streams.

Fall (September-October)
The autumn of the year is said to be tops for rainbow trout throughout its range not just in the Kenai system but also in Alaska. Falling temperatures, an abundance of food sources, and highly aggressive fish makes for a perfect combination. Starting in the early part of September and continuing through most of October, anglers will find excellent opportunities in area lakes. The rainbows come into the shallows to actively feed and casting near structure will result in fish.

September is also the month when salmon are in the midst of spawning and the mainstem Kenai is completely inundated with free floating eggs and carcasses, both high on the menu with trout and other fish. Egg and flesh imitation flies and beads still work – sometimes exceptionally well – but a change in strategy sometimes helps if rainbows are finicky. Forage imitation flies and spinners can provide relief.

Winter (November – March)
Come November, most lakes in the Kenai drainage are either frozen over or in the process of doing so. Ice fishing becomes an option in December or January, depending on the weather, with good success using bait and small jigs for anglers willing to brave the elements. Later on in winter the "bite" slows and usually does not improve significantly until spring. For open-water opportunities, anglers should head over to the inlets and outlets of Kenai and Skilak lakes.

The mainstem Kenai and a few of the larger, deeper tributaries still has a smattering of trout present into November and even December in some years. The mid-winter months of January and February are generally, yet not always, dead but a few pre-spawn rainbows traditionally do start to appear on the middle and upper Kenai in March.

Structure – Lakes

Inlet and outlet river and stream mouths are almost always good as these locations concentrate food sources and provide a positive change in water temperature (inlets). Additionally, larger rainbows are often found here in spring as they ready to move into flowing water to breed. Big trout are commonly situated only a couple of feet deep, enjoying the warmer and more oxygenated water. In late summer and fall, it is a possibility that spawning salmon are present and trout will gather here to feast on eggs and associated byproducts.

Areas of submerged vegetation, reeds, weed beds, overhanging foliage, and lily pads are productive throughout the open water season but perhaps especially so in late summer and fall. Rainbows use this location to hunt for aquatic life, including small baitfish. It also provides cover.

Steep dropoffs, points, shoals or reefs, and beach areas around small islands are all locations that attract fish year-round.

Structure – Rivers & Streams

In smaller creeks, look for deep holes, pools, and runs where fish seek cover and spy food articles drifting downstream. Undercut banks are a favorite holdout. In larger streams, the preceding are good spots in addition to overhanging foliage such as trees and brush, weed beds, and behind large rocks and tree trunks.

Rivers, depending on the size and current, provide much the same hot spots as in streams. However, gravel bars, riffles, back-eddies, and the seam behind islands are great as well. Do not overlook logjams in side channels as this provides excellent cover and a trap for food sources.

The fish cleaning stations on the upper Kenai, Russian, and lower Kenai rivers are superb trout magnets. The focus should be on areas immediately downstream of where anglers gut and fillet their salmon. Use egg and flesh imitations.

What to Use

Flies

Early in the season, April into June, forage/smolt imitations are best as they mimic the preferred food source at this time of year – juvenile salmon. The Muddler Minnow in metallic green or blue and the Blue Smolt are both good in the mainstem Kenai as well as tributaries. Additionally, try leech and sculpin patterns.

Dry flies are prime during the summer season on lakes and streams of the Kenai system and work quite well even on the mainstem Kenai. However, it is in clearwater drainages they do best, such as in the Moose and Russian rivers and connecting lakes. Sizes #8 through #14 Elk Hair Caddis, Wulff, Adams, Black Gnat, and Mosquito are responsible for many fish.

When spawning salmon arrive in late summer and fall, flies such as Glo Bug, Polar Shrimp, Babine Special, Battle Creek Special, Woolly Bugger, and Two-Egg Sperm Fly in sizes #2 to #12 and orange to pink colors are the preferred choice. They work best early on in the spawn but tends to decrease in effectiveness later in the season. Refer to beads at this point (see below).

For a change of pace if the action seems slow with millions of real salmon eggs drifting about to compete with, switch over to darker patterns in black, brown, or purple, such as a Woolly Bugger or Egg-Sucking Leech. Oftentimes just adding a different item to the regular menu is enough to spark renewed attention.

In early September as salmon begin dying off and carcasses disintegrating, flesh flies are the mode. In areas of the mainstem Kenai, the Ginger Bunny and Battle Bunny Fly are proven, while in back channels and sloughs and in smaller streams the Sparse Flesh Fly works better. For an improvised version, two pieces of colored "peach" yarn on a single hook does the trick. Flesh patterns are best in fall until November but do attract strikes all winter and into spring in mainstem Kenai.

Beads

This is without a doubt one of the most effective creations for rainbow trout and designed to imitate a single drifting egg. It is usually fished just prior to and during the salmon spawn; however, beads can work most anytime of the year as salmon in the Kenai mainstem are present throughout the winter months.

Anglers can experiment with a multitude of colors and sizes to fit the "hatch" of the day, but beads generally are hued in orange to pink. Present it in likely locations by using a dead drift, preferably with a floating line, a strike indicator, and a small split shot.

Attractors

Small Spin-N-Glo's, Okie Drifters, Corkies, and the alike in orange, pink, and red hues can be productive on aggressive trout early on in the salmon spawn but generally looses their effectiveness as the season progresses and rainbows become wiser. They should be fished as any other egg imitation pattern.

Attractors in darker colors (metallic green and blue), such as the Spin-N-Glo, work early and late in the season when fish are more keyed in on forage rather than eggs.

Lures

Size 3 and smaller spinners and quarter-ounce spoons can be very efficient in providing immediate strikes. They perform well in lakes as well as rivers and streams. The more subdued colors like silver, copper, bronze, and even black are proven, as is the metallic blue variety. These hues are effective early and late in the season on the mainstem Kenai.

Popular brands include Vibrax, Mepps, Little Cleo, Krocodile, Fjord Spoon, and a variety of other forage imitation lures. Silver flash in combination with metallic blue or green is particularly good in late spring and early summer imitating outmigrating juvenile salmon. Use with single hooks only.

Bait

Clusters of salmon roe, single salmon eggs, and shrimp are among top kinds of bait for rainbows. Use it sparingly in lakes if ice fishing in order to take home a fish or two but avoid it altogether in rivers and streams where catch-and-release may become necessary. Targeting rainbow trout with bait is increasingly seen as unethical in nature due to the high degree of mortality associated with this type of offering.

Gear

A good fly outfit for mainstem fish is a seven-weight rod with 8- to 14-pound test tippet. In tributaries, a 5- to 6-weight rod with 4- to 6-pound test tippet is sufficient. As for spinning gear, a seven- to eight-foot rod and reel containing 150 yards of 8- to 14-pound test line is good in the Kenai River while smaller waters command a six- to seven-foot rod and matching reel with 4- to 6-pound test.

How to Fish

Most techniques involving fly and lure fishing stipulates the cast-and-drift method into likely holding areas. Plugs used when back-trolling catch trout, as does bait fished stationary. For more elaborate descriptions, see the chapter on Methods & Techniques, page 91.

Hot Spots

The first few miles of water on the mainstem river downstream of Skilak Lake outlet is recognized as being one of the best spots in the entire drainage, especially for big fish. The upper Kenai, from Skilak Lake inlet to the confluence with Russian River, is excellent in late summer and fall. The canyon section on the upper river has trophy rainbows. The lower river around Soldotna is good but fish are not quite as abundant as further upstream. However, some of the biggest trout (up to 20 pounds plus) on the Kenai have been caught here in mid- to late summer.

Tributaries such as Russian and Moose rivers and Quartz and Ptarmigan creeks are good locations. Within the Russian drainage, the lower river is best in summer while the upper river between the lakes provide increased opportunity throughout summer and fall. Upper Russian Lake can be exceptional when salmon spawn. As for the Moose system, try the narrower sections of the upper river around the forks as well as associated lakes. Juneau and Trout lakes northwest of Cooper Landing are great for more solitude.

STEELHEAD TROUT

Scientific Name: *Oncorhynchus mykiss.*
Common Name(s): Steelie, rainbow, and metalhead.

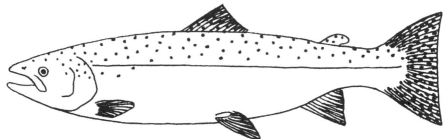

Biology

Description: Small black spots on back, upper sides, tail fin, and top of head. Back is dark, sides silvery, and belly white. Spawning fish are dirty red on cheeks and sides, back and sides greenish yellow or gray.

Size: Average 5 to 8 pounds, up to 15 to 20 pounds or more.

Distribution: Largely unknown but documented to occur in the lower and middle Kenai River. Believed to ascend clearwater tributaries in spring.

Abundance: No abundance estimates available. A small number of fish reported to be present in mainstem Kenai from fall into spring.

Sport Fishing

Regulatory Season: Open season June 11 through May 1. General restrictions apply.

Timing: September to June, fish are usually encountered in fall.

Gear: Seven- to eight-foot rod spin/bait caster; eight- to nine-foot, 8-weight fly rod; 8- to 12-pound test line/tippet.

Tackle: Spinners, attractors, plugs, and flies.

Methods: Casting, drifting, stationary.

Hot Spots: No particular best places. Both lower and middle Kenai River has fish; usually caught incidentally to fishing for other species.

STEELHEAD TROUT in the Kenai River

Steelhead, as a sea-run version of rainbow trout, is not common in the Kenai River drainage. Prior to the late 80s and early 90s stocking program on Crooked Creek, a tributary of Kasilof River, steelhead was a very rare species on the Kenai with reports of fish surfacing only every few years or so. However, the ADF&G stocking efforts resulted in a fair number of trout straying into the Kenai River and concerns arose that the these foreign fish would interbreed with the local population of native rainbow trout. The stocking program was subsequently halted as a result.

Although the number of steelhead present in the river has subsided from those years ago, a small self-sustaining population appears to have taken hold. Very little is known regarding these elusive trout other than that anglers take a few specimens every fall. It is believed some steelhead may spawn in the mainstem Kenai but also in clearwater tributaries such as Funny and Killey rivers, which are quite similar in habitat and stream characteristics compared to the southern peninsula steelhead streams. Remaining to be seen is whether the sea-run trout population will survive and even flourish.

Identification of steelhead can be difficult considering that some of the larger rainbow trout present appear quite similar in coloration. One of the distinguishing factors may be that steelhead are generally longer in body form compared to native trout, especially in the fall as rainbows are often football-shaped from gorging on salmon eggs and flesh. Small black spots are present on back, upper sides, and both lobes of tail fin. Back is almost black; sides are silvery, while belly is white. A very distinct horizontal pinkish band appears on sides after a week or two of freshwater residence. Flesh color is orange. During spawning, black spots become more pronounced, the sides and cheeks are dirty red, and back is greenish yellow or gray. Post-spawn fish return to a silvery shine on the sides, belly turning white and back dark. Flesh color is white.

The life cycle of Kenai steelhead is probably very similar to stocks in nearby streams.

As these trout are anadromous, the migration into freshwater begins in August and peaks in September. The fish overwinter in deep sections of the river until the following spring when a movement commences to the breeding grounds. Where these areas are in the Kenai drainage has not been documented at this time. The reproduction process peaks in May with surviving adults exiting freshwater in June. Females deposit somewhere between 600 and 12,000 eggs in the gravel bottom, the eggs hatching in summer or early fall. Steelhead may spawn up to four times and live to seven years of age.

The diet in young fish consists of insects, fish eggs, and later other small fish. Adults at sea sustain primarily on fish and crustaceans.

Mature steelhead returning to Kenai River have been reported to weigh about six to eight pounds with a few specimens said to weigh as much as 15 to 20 pounds.

FISHING FOR KENAI STEELHEAD

Unless one is intimately familiar with various holes and runs on the river and where trout usually concentrate in numbers, targeting steelhead is not advised. Even experienced anglers do not catch sea-run trout regularly and most have never hooked one at all. Yet a very few people claim that it is possible to land steelhead on a fairly consistent basis in a few locations on the middle Kenai during the fall months.

As for the majority of autumn fishers, steelhead trout are only caught incidentally to casting for other species, such as silver salmon, rainbows, and char. The few specimens that do succumb to angler's offerings are taken on egg imitation flies, small orange or red attractors, size 4 spinners, and clusters of salmon roe (bait not recommended if targeting steelhead). The stretch of river between Sterling and the Skilak Lake outlet has produced a few fish in October. Drift lures and flies through deep holes and runs and do not overlook the confluence of clearwater streams and the mainstem Kenai. Employ similar techniques and methods as for rainbow trout (page 57).

The regulatory season and other restrictions for steelhead are the same as for rainbow trout (consult ADF&G regulations).

LAKE TROUT
Scientific Name: *Salvelinus namaycush.*
Common Name(s): Mackinaw and Laker.

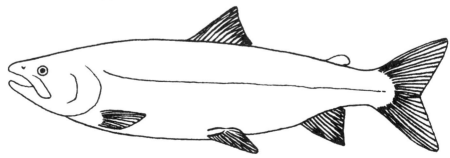

Biology
Description: Distinctly forked tail. Sides and back are dark gray or brown, whitish or yellowish markings scattered throughout body. Spawning fish display dark lateral band on sides, fins a slight orange or reddish hue.
Size: Average 3 to 5 pounds, some larger fish to 15 pounds, up to 25 pounds or more.
Distribution: Found in major lakes of the Kenai drainage but some fish may also be found in parts of Kenai and Trail rivers.
Abundance: No abundance estimates are available but stocks appear to be healthy in all established populations.

Sport Fishing
Regulatory Season: No species-specific regulations in place; general restrictions apply.
Timing: Year-round, best in late winter/early spring and late fall.
Gear: Six- to seven-foot rod spin/bait caster; eight- to nine-foot, 8-weight fly rod; 6- to 12-pound test line/tippet.
Tackle: Spoons, spinners, jigs, plugs, flies, and bait.
Methods: Casting, drifting, trolling, stationary, and ice fishing.
Hot Spots: Hidden, Trout, and Juneau lakes; also some worthwhile action in Skilak and Kenai lakes.

LAKE TROUT in the Kenai River

Lake trout are present in fair to good numbers in several large lakes on the Kenai Peninsula, nearly all of which are within the Kenai River system. The glacial Skilak and Kenai lakes harbor the most significant populations and smaller stocks are situated in clearwater lakes such as Hidden, Juneau, and Trout.

Contrary to what the name seems to imply, lake trout are not actually trout at all but a species of char. Identification clearly sets lake trout apart from the trout genus. The tail is distinctly forked, the mouth extending well beyond the eye. Scales are small. Coloration may vary from watershed to watershed. Sides and back are dark green, grayish, brown, or even almost black while belly is white. Whitish or yellowish markings are scattered throughout body, including the head and some fins. Flesh color is pale, usually light pink to white. Spawning fish display a dark lateral band on the sides of males, back becoming a lighter shade. The pectoral, pelvic, and anal fins may take on a slight orange or reddish hue. Flesh is white.

Lake trout are basically lake dwellers and are found in this environment throughout the year; however, smaller char do exhibit the habit of venturing into larger rivers and feeding in sections with a slower current during the summer and fall months. Parts of middle and upper Kenai River as well as Trail River quite often see immature lake trout.

Biological details of the life cycle of lake trout on the peninsula are not known to any extent and therefore the information laid out here is of general reference only, unless noted.

Reproduction is in autumn, usually from September to the end of November, peaking in October. The char moves into water 10 to 20 feet deep, sometimes much shallower, where females will deposit between 200 and 17,000 eggs in gravel and rock bottom structure. Later in winter and early spring the eggs hatch. As is common with trout and char, fish may spawn several times during a lifetime. But lake trout are among the species with greatest longevity, up to 50 years of age has been documented.

Diet consists of insects and plankton in juvenile char, changing to primarily insects and other fish as adults. Young salmon and whitefish are both high on the menu with Kenai lakers.

Lake trout on the Kenai Peninsula do not generally grow very large compared to fish in other parts of the state and in Canada. The vast majority of the populations are of char in the three- to five-pound range with a fair number of older fish up to eight to 12 pounds. A very large char is anything over 15 pounds. Trophy specimens are rare but lake trout between 20 and 30 pounds are known from Skilak, Kenai, and Hidden lakes.

FISHING FOR KENAI LAKERS

Lake trout are not a particularly abundant species of char within the drainage but can be found in quite dense concentrations in certain places and at certain times of the year. Kenai and Skilak lakes probably support the largest number of fish due to the size of watersheds but the glacial nature of the lakes play a big role in their less than stellar angling performance. Scented lures or bait work throughout the year but artificial lures and flies can be just as effective during improved visibility conditions during the late fall to early spring time period.

For clearwater conditions, Hidden, Juneau, and Trout lakes are the places to be. Although Hidden is a fairly large lake that requires a boat to reach the best action, Juneau and Trout lend themselves better for smaller watercraft or fishing from the bank.

There are currently no species-specific rules and regulations in place within the Kenai River drainage. Fish populations are healthy and stable and angling pressure relatively light. About 3,300 fish are harvested every year.

When & Where
Since lake trout are not known for their great abundance in any waters on the Kenai Peninsula, the key to finding these fish is awareness of seasonal habits and locating proper structure in order to approach likely areas of concentration.

Seasons
As the ice begins to go out in spring, lake char become active in their search of food. Try lake inlets and outlets. In lakes without anadromous species, cast near the edge of receding ice, letting the lure or fly sink ten to 15 feet (or the bottom) before implementing a slow retrieve. Bait is good. Some of the best action of the year can be had during ice-out.

During the warm summer months, larger adults are situated deep, often down to 20 to 60 feet. Casting from shore is often difficult – but not impossible – in achieving success. A boat or some other type of watercraft is recommended in order to reach proper depth and structure. Jigging lures is possible but most often trolling is the preferred technique. Smaller char (2 to 5 pounds) are often caught fairly shallow in early morning or evening and at the mouth of clearwater streams draining into glacial lakes, especially later in summer when spawning salmon are present, as fish are drawn here to consume food items being flushed into the lake by the stream, including salmon eggs.

Autumn is absolutely prime time to pursue lake trout, especially in October. The fish move out of deep water into the shallows (five to 15 feet) to feed and spawn and are relatively easily targeted by anglers from shore and boat. Rocky beaches, shoals and small bays hold fish. Lures and flies both take char, as does properly presented bait.

In early winter, quite a few char are still situated in shallow areas, particularly around lake inlets and outlets. Lures and flies do well in open water, while jigging lures and soaking bait is best from the ice. I mid-winter, however, the fish disperse into deeper water and can be difficult to find unless able to locate good structure. Starting in mid-February and on through March, anglers will yet again see action pick up as lake trout begin to move into lake outlets in preparation for the annual salmon smolt migration.

Structure

Being able to identify proper structure is absolutely necessary in locating lake trout. Lake inlets and outlets are natural fish magnets as these areas draw a variety of potential food sources. In systems containing salmon, smolt and fry will be the main prey and the inlet and outlet of lakes are focal points of juvenile salmon preparing to migrate out to sea, and thus a natural spot to look for lake trout.

Underwater islands, reefs, hilltops, or pinnacles are all reputed hangouts for lake trout throughout much of the year. Without much prior experience these locations can be hard to find. However, the use of a depth sounder is ideal and will give a good idea of what the bottom looks like and the likelihood of fish being present.

As fish commence the fall spawn, success is more likely to be found in areas near shore such as bays and rocky beaches, yet offshore shoals and the immediate surroundings of small islands are good places to try as well.

Steep dropoffs into deep water is another favorite char location. A bathymetric map is very helpful in identifying bottom contours and where such structure is to be found.

What to Use

Lake trout has an infinite appetite for most anything with a flash and a wobble, hence the popularity of certain spoons and plugs. When fish are concentrated in active pursuit of feed, flash in combination with vibration or erratic movement attracts char.

Lures

In late winter and spring, use bright spoons, spinners, and plugs to imitate salmon fry and smolt. Krocodile, Dardevle, Pixee, Mepps, and Vibrax are proven hardware, as are plugs such as Kwikfish, Wiggle Wart, Tadpolly, Rapala, and Flatfish. As most lakers on the peninsula are not very large, lures three to four inches long are best.

In summer, trolling is the best method to use for lake trout and the focus should be on deeper water using slightly larger lures for visibility and inciting reflex response.

Lures four to six inches long are good, suggested brands include Canadian Wonder, Diamond King, Tom Mack, and Apex. Try the plugs mentioned above also.

Come fall and early winter, use the same lures as recommended in spring but in different structure as outlined above. Productive colors throughout the year include silver, gold, silver/blue, silver/chartreuse, silver/green, green/yellow, and white pearl. The more vibrant colors function best in glacial waters such as Kenai and Skilak lakes.

The winter fishery commands more patience in that fish are often sluggish and more difficult to find. Jigging large, flashy spoons and jigs with or without bait is tops.

Flies

While flies can be used anytime there is open water, it is during the spring and fall months that are most practical as lake trout are found in shallower, more accessible areas. Early in the season use smolt, leech, sculpin, and attractor patterns sizes #1/0 to #6, but nymphs are also good at times. In autumn, try Yellow Marabou, Mickey Finn, Smolt, Gray Ghost, Marabou Muddler, and Leech.

Bait

Strong scented bait lure lake trout from a good distance away. Chunks or pieces – even whole parts – of herring and smelt are proven to catch fish all year long. Salmon scraps may be used as well. There are basically three different ways to use bait, including casting, stationary/ice fishing, and trolling.

Gear

Spin fishing requires a light to medium weight rod, six to eight-and-a-half foot of medium action, and a reel with 6- to 12-pound test line. If deep water trolling, use slightly heavier outfit. Fly fishers use eight- to ten-foot, seven- or eight-weight rods with matching reels.

How to Fish

Casting

Anglers fishing in smaller lakes or in areas of good structure sometimes cast lures or flies, letting the offering sink to the bottom while feeding line out, and then engaging a slow jigging or erratic retrieve. This method is productive from boat or shore.

If using bait, shore anglers often attach a piece to a single hook with a lead weight fixed about 18-20 inches up on the line and cast the offering into likely structure according to the season. The setup is usually left on the bottom (especially in glacial waters) for fish to pick up or a retrieve employed as with a lure. Small, whole herring fished along the bottom in clearwater lakes is effective.

Jigging

A method that can be used year-round but particularly effective in ice fishing. After proper structure and concentrations of fish has been located, drop lure or lure/bait combination to correct depth and jig offering with a short and fairly swift motion, letting the setup flutter down after each upstroke. Lake trout usually engulf the lure/bait as it flutters down or right after the motion is completed.

Trolling

This method can be used from most any size watercraft. It usually involves fairly stout rods, downriggers, fish locators, and flashers, this being especially the case in larger bodies of water. A slow but varied speed at depths of 15 to 60 feet is best. However, in smaller lakes or areas of known concentration, simply trolling a lure or plug alone or with minimum weight attached works fine too.

DOLLY VARDEN

Scientific Name: *Salvelinus malma.*
Common Name(s): Char.

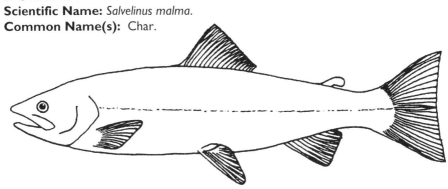

Biology

Description: Black or greenish blue on back, sides silvery with faint white spots, and belly white. Spawning fish are dirty green or dark on back and upper sides, lower sides and belly bright orange or reddish. Large pink spots accent dark sides.
Size: Average 10 inches to 3 pounds, some fish to 10 pounds, up to 15 pounds or more.
Distribution: Found in all tributaries of the Kenai River drainage, including the mainstem from river mouth to headwaters.
Abundance: Moderate to large numbers of fish in all areas of the Kenai system. No abundance estimates available.

Sport Fishing

Regulatory Season: No species-specific restrictions currently in place with the exception of seasonal closures for parts of Quartz Creek and Snow River. General regulations apply.
Timing: Year-round in lakes, best in May and August through September.
Gear: Five- to seven-foot rod spin/bait caster; seven- to nine-foot, 6-weight fly rod; 4- to 12-pound test line/tippet.
Tackle: Spoon, spinners, attractors, plugs, flies and bait.
Methods: Casting, drifting, jigging, and stationary.
Hot Spots: Middle and upper Kenai River, Russian River, Quartz Creek, Ptarmigan Creek.

DOLLY VARDEN in the Kenai River

Characteristics

The Dolly Varden population in the Kenai River system shows a great degree of nuances and traits as can be expected in a watershed of this size as the fish are able to adapt to a multitude of conditions in order to survive and flourish.

It is also is intriguing to discover that some lakes within the Kenai River system support both arctic char and Dolly Varden (two species that are extremely close in appearance and characteristics), with a degree of overlap in distribution and thus creating a dilemma – at least biologically speaking – of species recognition and classification.

Distribution

Dolly Varden is a very abundant game fish with a wide range of distribution in the Kenai River drainage. They are found from the salt chuck off the mouth of the river in Cook Inlet through the mainstem and on up into smaller tributaries and headwater lakes. The greatest concentration of fish is found in the main channel of the Kenai as well as in Kenai and Skilak lakes. Decent stocks also exist in tributaries of Kenai and Trail lakes and in the Moose and Russian River drainages.

Identification

Identification is very similar to arctic char. Fresh from the sea, the Dolly Varden is black to dark greenish or blue on the back and top of head, sides being silvery with faint white spots, the belly white. Flesh color is orange to pink. After a week or more in fresh water spots begin to become more pronounced, a more pink hue, while the sides lose the silvery sheen. Back eventually turns dark brown, green, or black, sides yellowish with pink spots.

Spawning char display some of the most vibrant colors of all game fish in Alaska. Backs and upper sides are dirty green or dark, lower sides and belly turning bright orange or reddish. Large pink or red spots accent dark sides. Males develop an orange kype on lower jaw, while the pectoral, pelvic, anal, and lower caudal fins have clear white edges. Flesh color is yellowish white.

Reproduction & Diet

Dolly Varden are autumn spawners, process taking place between mid-August and late November with peak activity in September and October. Habitat chosen for reproduction may include areas of the mainstem Kenai River and select clearwater tributaries consisting of gravel bottom structure. Female char deposit 350 to 10,000 eggs in a nest, the eggs hatching in spring. Juvenile fish consume insects and plankton, older char mainly other fish, crustaceans, plankton, salmon eggs, and various insect life. Dolly Varden may breed several times and live up to 18 years of age.

Size & Age

The Dolly Varden population in the Kenai River is probably the largest strain of char in Southcentral Alaska. Fish average approximately 10 to 20 inches in the mainstem Kenai with a fair number of char exceeding 25 inches and 6 pounds. Specimens weighing more than 12 pounds are not unheard of with occasional reports of fish to 15 pounds or more. Trophy Dolly Varden to 18 pounds have been confirmed and it is believed that these char can reach 20 pounds.

The landlocked version of char is much less impressive concerning size, seldom reaching 20 inches in length with the average closer to 10 to 15 inches. In protein-rich waters, however, landlocked Dolly Varden may stretch to 24 inches and weigh several pounds.

Stock Description

Dolly Varden lead a very complex life history that is as yet to be completely understood but studies are ongoing. The population in the Kenai River drainage is believed to consist of three somewhat distinct stocks of char that differentiate mostly in seasonal behavior and distribution but also in physical size. A certain segment of the population is anadromous, especially the fish of the lower and middle Kenai River drainage, while char residing in the upper river reaches and tributaries may be a combination of both sea-run and resident Dolly Varden. To make this even more complicated, it appears that some specimens do not migrate to saltwater annually but every two to three years instead, or if at all. And a few stocks are completely landlocked.

However, it is important to note that stock descriptions outlined below are not based on an exact science as the habits of the fish may alter or change for unknown reasons.

Anadromous

Sea-run Dolly Varden spend the winter in lakes or deep rivers, migrating to Cook Inlet in spring (May) to feed in the nutrient-rich ocean environment for a period lasting from only a few weeks up to several months. The majority of char begin returning to Kenai River in July with a few fish still arriving into September. Some Dolly Varden elect to feed through the summer until fall, at which point the fish migrate to certain streams to reproduce. After the process is complete, the spent char move to lakes or deep river sections to feed and overwinter.

Non-mature Dolly Varden that do not engage in the reproductive cycle will, after entering freshwater, feed throughout the summer and fall months and then finally proceed to overwintering areas.

Not all char in the Kenai River are of Kenai origin as anadromous char frequently move about between watersheds. In fact, it is not uncommon for Dolly Varden to outmigrate to sea and swim up a completely different drainage many miles down the coast, occasionally even hundreds of miles or more from water of origin.

Resident

The segment of the Dolly Varden population that resides in freshwater year-round is usually referred to as resident char. These fish differ from landlocked char in that they are found in waters directly connected to the ocean but for some reason elect to remain in freshwater to feed instead of migrating to the sea.

Fish begin moving out of the overwintering grounds in late spring and early summer, feeding in mainstem Kenai and tributaries until the autumn spawning period. Some char, however, will stay in lakes through the summer to feed, only migrating into flowing water in fall to breed. Both types of char then swim back to the lake of origin for the winter.

Landlocked

The true landlocked version of Dolly Varden makes up a very small segment of the overall drainage population. The char are confined to remote lakes that have become barred off from the main Kenai system by natural causes, such as waterfalls or rapids, which prevent fish from moving freely downstream.

Because of low protein food sources available, the size of these Dolly Varden is small compared to fish in other parts of the system. However, if salmon runs are able to negotiate the barriers and reach the lake (as they are stronger swimmers than char), the size range increases substantially. The Dolly Varden overwinter in the lakes, moving into streams in summer to feed or in fall to spawn.

FISHING FOR KENAI DOLLIES

Rules & Regulations

There are relatively few restrictions involving Dolly Varden in the Kenai River system. Size slot limits are in place and there are a couple of streams (upper Quartz Creek and South Fork Snow River) that have seasonal closures in effect to protect spawning fish.

When & Where

Dolly Varden are present year-round in the Kenai River system. The best action is during the open-water season, foremost in spring (May) and late summer through fall (late July into October). Fishing during the winter and mid-summer months can sometimes be quite productive as well. Aside from timing concerns, anglers should also consider lighting conditions and the availability of various important food sources, like the presence of salmon and its byproducts.

Spring (April-May)

The month of May is a good time to be chasing hungry Dolly Varden. Fish that reside in lakes are stirring to life after a long winter and will be actively feeding in ice-free waters, especially around lake outlets, while the middle and lower mainstem Kenai experiences an outmigration of anadromous char.

Forage imitation lures and flies are always best this time of year since the Dolly Varden are keyed in on salmon fry and smolt as well as emerging aquatic insect life.

Summer (June-August)

Starting about mid-July anglers begin to notice an increase in activity after the traditional early summer lull, the lower Kenai turning on first as sea-run char return from Cook Inlet along with the late runs of king and red salmon. By late July, the action on the lower and middle mainstem is excellent and is beginning to pick up significantly in the upper river and its tributaries as the second run of reds advances and the first run begins to spawn.

As with rainbow trout, the month of August is prime for Dolly Varden. From near the tidal region of the Kenai upstream into headwater tributaries, fishing is excellent. The time span from mid-August on into fall has superb potential on the middle and upper mainstem. Egg and flesh imitations are tops on the menu for char.

There exists some fair to good chances for lake char in late summer, particularly so in waters having runs of salmon. Try near inlets and outlets. In mountain lakes with landlocked populations of Dolly Varden and no influx of salmon, expect the bite to improve towards the end of August as the late-season chill sets in.

Fall (September-October)

As an extension of the terrific late summer char fishery, September is another month that promises fast-paced action. In many of the larger clearwater tributaries and in the middle and lower Kenai River, anglers can do exceedingly well using egg and flesh imitations.

October also produces worthwhile angling, the middle and upper river being best during the first half of the month. In smaller tributaries, the char will begin moving downstream to overwintering grounds. The traditional fall tackle stands but forage imitations should not be overlooked.

For Dolly Varden in lakes, autumn is the prime time for anglers to be on the water. Both months can provide good to excellent fishing but perhaps the window right before freezeup offers the most abundant opportunity, as larger fish are concerned.

Winter (November-March)

Most smaller streams have very few char left in them by November with freezeup being imminent. Larger waters, such as the mainstem Kenai, will continue to see decreasing numbers of Dolly Varden through the month and into December. Expect poor to fair success at best.

Clearwater lakes that contain good overwintering populations of char may offer some decent ice fishing opportunities through the winter months, with the early ice season yielding the best catches. Glacial lakes are worth a try, the outlets usually being relative hot spots.

Structure – Lakes

Early on in the open-water season, look for concentrations of char at the inlet and outlet of lakes. Fish that gather near inlets are primarily in search of food until the fall when mature spawners are more prevalent. Outlets is a focal point of Dolly Varden for food as well as migratory preparation, char staging here in schools waiting to exit lake via river or stream to summer feeding grounds. Landlocked populations of fish can be found in these locations from spring into fall.

Areas of submerged vegetation, reeds, weed beds, overhanging foliage, and lily pads are good spots to locate Dolly Varden in late summer and fall. Food supplies are in abundance, such as aquatic insect life.

During the summer and winter months, offshore structure such as steep dropoffs, points, shoals or reefs, and beach areas around small islands, are all prime locations that attract char.

Structure – Rivers & Streams

In larger rivers, search out char in likely holding areas in the form of gravel bars, riffles, back-eddies, and the seam behind islands. Logjams in side channels provide excellent cover and a trap for food sources, such as salmon carcasses.

Fish cleaning stations on the upper Kenai, Russian, and lower Kenai rivers are superb for drawing concentrations of hungry char. The focus should be on areas immediately downstream of where anglers gut and fillet their salmon. Use egg and flesh imitations anytime during the salmon season.

In smaller streams, deep holes, pools, and runs where fish seek cover and intercept food articles are hot spots. Undercut banks are a favorite holdout for food and cover. Overhanging foliage like trees and brush, weed beds, and immediate areas behind large rocks and tree trunks are good.

What to Use

Flies

Early in the season, April into June, forage/smolt offerings are best as they imitate the preferred food source – juvenile salmon – early in the season (April-June). Metallic green or blue Muddler Minnow and Blue Smolt are good early flies in the mainstem Kenai and its tributaries. Leech and sculpin patterns can be deadly as well.

Dry flies work to some degree during the summer season on clearwater lakes and streams but are not that efficient on the mainstem Kenai. Elk Hair Caddis, Wulff, Adams, Black Gnat, and Mosquito in sizes #8 through #14 are recommended.

Egg imitations such as Glo Bug, Polar Shrimp, Babine Special, Battle Creek Special, Woolly Bugger, and Two-Egg Sperm Fly are good choices when salmon arrive to spawn in late summer and fall. Sizes #2 to #12 and orange to pink colors are the best.

Darker patterns in black, brown, or purple, such as an Egg-Sucking Leech or Woolly Bugger, can be extremely effective in fall despite an abundance of salmon eggs and flesh in the water. Do not overlook nymphs.

Flesh flies are associated with the annual die-off of salmon in the Kenai River drainage during the months of September and October. Ginger Bunny and the Battle Bunny Fly have reputations. In smaller clearwater streams or in shallower side channels of mainstem Kenai, the Sparse Flesh Fly works best. Flesh patterns are most effective in fall but do catch char all winter and into spring in mainstem Kenai.

Lures

Smaller spinners and quarter-ounce spoons are very efficient, especially when used in spring and early summer and again in fall. Use them in lakes as well as rivers and streams. Neutral colors in silver, blue, copper, bronze, and black are all good. Popular brands include Vibrax, Mepps, Little Cleo, Krocodile, Fjord Spoon, and a variety of other forage imitation lures. Plain silver and metallic blue or green are good for imitating outmigrating juvenile salmon. Use with single hooks only.

Bait

This is one of the most efficient char-catchers in the Kenai drainage, as well as in the state. Clusters of salmon roe and single salmon eggs are top choices. As when fishing for trout, bait must be used sparingly and only if wanting to take home a fish or two but avoid it altogether in rivers and streams where catch-and-release may become necessary. Targeting Dolly Varden with bait is increasingly seen as unethical in nature due to the high degree of mortality associated with this type of offering.

Gear

Spinning gear usually consists of a seven- to eight-foot rod and reel containing 150 yards of 6- to 10-pound test line is good in the Kenai River while smaller waters command a six- to seven-foot rod and matching reel with 4- to 6-pound test. A perfect fly outfit for mainstem fish is a seven-weight rod with 6- to 10-pound test tippet. In tributaries, a 5- to 6-weight rod with 4- to 6-pound test tippet is good enough.

How to Fish
Most techniques involving fly and lure fishing stipulates the cast-and-drift method into likely holding areas. Plugs used when back-trolling catch char, as does bait fished stationary. For exact description, see the chapter on Methods & Techniques, page 91.

Hot Spots
Almost the entire mainstem Kenai River is very productive for Dolly Varden. The lower river is good during the spring outmigration of sea-run char but improves to excellent in mid- to late summer when salmon spawn. The middle section around Kenai Keys to Skilak Lake outlet is prime in late summer and fall. As for the upper Kenai, superb action is the norm from Skilak Lake inlet upstream to the confluence with Russian River. August and September are the best months.

Quartz Creek has outstanding char action from late July into September and Ptarmigan Creek fishes quite well too approximately during the same time frame. Lower Russian and Trail rivers are good. Upper Russian River and Lake offers very good fishing from mid- to late summer into fall.

ARCTIC CHAR
Scientific Name: *Salvelinus alpinus.*
Common Name(s): Char.

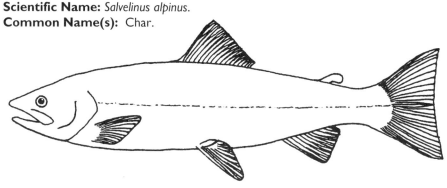

Biology
Description: Pink spots decorate sides. Dark back, upper sides slightly lighter hue, lower sides and belly being white. Spawning fish are orange red to red on lower sides and belly. Spots are larger in bright pink or red. Leading edges of lower fins creamy white.
Size: Average 10 to 20 inches, some fish to 25 inches and 6 pounds, up to 10 pounds or more.
Distribution: Primarily clearwater lakes tributary to the Moose River drainage.
Abundance: No abundance estimates available. The few lakes that char are present in the populations seem to be healthy.

Sport Fishing
Regulatory Season: No species-specific regulations in place; general restrictions

apply.

Timing: Year-round in lakes, peak May and again from September through October.

Gear: Six- to seven-foot rod spin/bait caster; seven- to eight-foot, 6-weight fly rod; 4- to 8-pound test line/tippet.

Tackle: Spoons, jigs, plugs, flies, and bait.

Methods: Casting, jigging, stationary.

Hot Spots: Swan and Silver lakes.

ARCTIC CHAR in the Kenai River

Arctic char is a very closely related species to Dolly Varden and is considered the same species – but with very slight nuances – by many. Not only that but there is a certain overlap of distribution between the two species, making matters even more confusing. On the Kenai Peninsula, these char are non-anadromous and occupy deeper lakes in the northern portion of the peninsula. They are most common in the Swanson River drainage but a few lakes of the Moose River system have stocks of arctic char as well.

Although identification is similar to that of Dolly Varden, arctic char do display some rather unusual colors not so commonly witnessed in its cousin. Back is dark green, blue, or brownish green while the upper sides are tan or yellowish brown. The lower sides and belly are white, spots a light pink hue. Flesh color is light orange. Spawning char are exceptionally colorful, as lower sides and belly become orange red to bright red. The pectoral, pelvic, and anal fins have creamy white leading edges. Spots are pink or red with halos, the ones along the lateral line often larger than the pupil of the eye. The tip of the lower jaw on males may turn orange or reddish brown. Flesh color is yellowish white.

In spring (April-May) as the ice begins to recede, char move from deep water to relatively shallow areas to feed. As temperatures increase in early summer, the fish retreat back into deeper water, often along the bottom of the lake, for the course of the season. Primary food sources include fish, insects, worms, and salmon eggs. Some juvenile char may, however, stay in the shallows and even move into streams in search of sustenance. In September, there is yet again a movement but of more equal distribution as fish can be found suspended at all depths.

Spawning commences in early fall and can continue into mid-winter, with most activity taking place in October and November. Females deposit 200 to 6,000 eggs in suitable bottom structure in water of moderate depth. As is normal with other char species as well as trout, arctic char may reproduce several times. The eggs hatch in spring, the young char feeding on insects, worms, and zooplankton.

FISHING FOR KENAI CHAR

Since access logistics can be a hindrance in fishing for char during the winter months, the information presented here pertains to the open water season from spring through fall. There is currently some effort by anglers reaching the remote lakes of the Moose River drainage that do contain populations of char yet most of it is geared toward the more prolific rainbow trout.

It is primarily tributary lakes of the West and North forks of Moose River that support this species. Anglers experience fair to good action using a variety of offerings, from hardware to flies to bait. The best fishing is without a doubt in spring after breakup and again in fall during the period leading up to freezeup. At that time, casting from shore in areas bordering deep water is possible whereas the rest of the year the fish are suspended in water too deep to be readily accessed unless by canoe or ice. Anglers fishing from a canoe almost always have advantage fishing for char since it affords flexibility in reaching locations where fish concentrate.

Glittery medium-sized (1/4 to half ounce) spoons cast and slowly retrieved in areas containing structure such as steep drop-offs, around submerged islands and reefs, pinnacles, and vegetation mats are all good. Forage imitation flies with sinking lines should be fished much the same way, allowed to settle near the bottom before being stripped back erratically through layers of water. Jigging spoons can be equally productive and is ideal when char are found in deeper sections of a lake.

Bait can be fished with a spoon or small jig as a teaser or alone. Clusters of salmon roe or medium small chunks of herring and smelt all work. In soft bottom or weedy areas, fish it stationary at depths of ten to 20 feet or more, suspended a few feet above the bottom. In shallower locations containing rock or pebble structure bait can also be fished directly on the bottom.

Good lure colors include foundation of silver, copper, and bronze with perhaps a stripe of blue, green, red, or chartreuse. On dark days or in deeper water, fluorescent orange can be exceptional.

OTHER SPECIES
in the Kenai River

An Introduction

There are several other species of game fish that inhabit the Kenai River and its tributaries that are the sole representative of larger groups or families, these being grayling, whitefish, pike, and cod.

The arctic grayling is the only member species of its family not just in the Kenai but also in all of Alaska. It is not native to the Kenai Peninsula but thrives in a few cold, clear lakes in the Chugach Mountains where it was planted many decades ago. It has since spread gradually from these lakes into the general watershed of the Kenai drainage, relating a small yet established presence. Anglers taking the time to explore the waters where this gamester is found in abundance are treated to some of the finest ultra light tackle fishing anywhere. The grayling is typically not finicky at all concerning artificial lures and is a superb fish to chase using fly-fishing gear.

Round whitefish is part of a fairly large group of various whitefish species found throughout Alaska. In the Kenai drainage it shows an abundant population in the Skilak and Kenai lakes much of the year as well as the mainstem river and tributaries during the summer and fall months. Despite the good numbers available, round whitefish are not particularly known as a great game fish. The standard enticements as far as lures and flies go are quite different from other sporting species and therefore require specialized attention for success. But when finally hooked, they are good fighters.

Northern pike is another species not indigenous to the Kenai Peninsula. It was illegally introduced to a few lakes of the Kenai River drainage back in the 50s and has since then spread systematically to many other lakes and streams. Pike are not abundant by any means anywhere it is found but pockets of fish can provide some level of excitement. For the most part, however, it is a fish caught incidentally to fishing for other species.

Burbot is sort of an anomaly in the Kenai drainage, being present in only one lake not just in the system but also on the entire Kenai Peninsula. It is the sole member of the cod family that thrives exclusively in freshwater. Burbot are generally not recognized as being much of a sport fish due to its rather reserved attitude regarding artificial lures and flies and an absence of fighting power when hooked. Yet, on the right equipment and tackle, it does provide some decent action and some anglers in the know argue that what it lacks as a game fish it makes up by far in flavor.

Chapter Content:

ARCTIC GRAYLING
Scientific Name: *Thymallus arcticus.*
Common Name(s): Grayling and Sailfin.

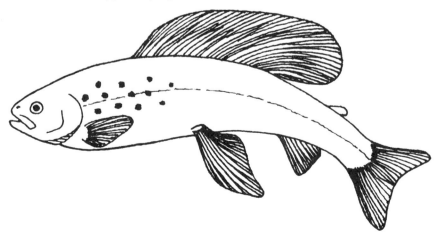

Biology

Description: Exceptionally large dorsal fin. Large, black spots from gills to almost midway down sides of fish. Fins have vague spots or stripes that in spawning fish become pink or red in color. Overall color is silver gray to brown.

Size: Average 7 to 16 inches, some larger fish to 18 inches, up to 20 inches.

Distribution: Found in virtually all tributaries and main sections of Kenai River from Skilak Lake to Kenai Lake and beyond.

Abundance: Not very common in most areas of the Kenai River drainage but are abundant in Crescent, Paradise, and Lower Fuller lakes.

Sport Fishing

Regulatory Season: No species-specific restrictions currently in place with the exception of spring closures on Crescent and Paradise lakes.

Timing: Present year-round in lakes, June through September best.

Gear: Five- to six-foot rod spin/bait caster; six- to seven-foot, 4-weight fly rod; 2- to 4-pound test line/tippet.

Tackle: Spinners and flies.

Methods: Casting.

Hot Spots: Crescent, Paradise, and Lower Fuller lakes.

ARCTIC GRAYLING in the Kenai River

Grayling are not native to the Kenai Peninsula and their current distribution and abundance is credited to stocking efforts dating back to the 50s and 60s. Only a few locations were planted with fish but the artificial populations grew and thrived and today are healthy and self-sustaining. It is because these lakes were not true landlocked waters that the grayling stocks survived as mature fish could use tributary streams for breeding and thus multiply.

But these connecting streams also drained into the Kenai River system, exposing the watershed to a new species previously not found there. A fair number of juvenile grayling and a few adults are flushed out into the Kenai every year, giving the fish ample opportunity to explore a completely new and vast territory. Today, grayling are reported from many parts of the drainage, including Kenai and Trail lakes, upper Kenai River, Quartz Creek, and Russian River. Even though the Kenai system has been infiltrated with these fish for several decades, there are relatively few areas that present suitable habitat for spawning purposes and thus seeing an explosion in numbers of grayling is quite unlikely.

Biological details of the life cycle of grayling on the peninsula are not known and therefore the information laid out here is of general reference only, unless noted.

Identification of grayling is universal and the fish are easily distinguishable from other species. An exceptionally large dorsal fin decorates the back, several pronounced black or dark brown spots can be seen from the gills to almost midway down the sides. Scales are large, mouth is small, and the tail forked. Coloration is silvery gray, light brown, or copper on the sides, back is dark or brown, belly being white. The dorsal and pelvic fins have vague spots or stripes. Flesh color is white. Spawning individuals are darker; deep purple to dark brown on back and sides, red and pink spots and stripes decorate fins, belly is bluish white.

Grayling are found year-round in lakes and deeper parts of large rivers, mature fish moving into streams in May and June to reproduce. Peak breeding activity is during early and mid-June for populations on the peninsula since waters are situated at high altitudes and spring arrives late.

Females deposit 1,700 to 14,000 eggs in bottom gravel, eggs hatching after about three weeks. Juvenile fish subsist on insects and insect larvae, older grayling primarily smaller fish, fish eggs, insects, and insect larvae.

After spawning, grayling either return to the lake or remain in the stream to feed during the summer and fall. A migration back into overwintering lakes takes place starting in September and continuing into October. Fish may reproduce several times and live up to 22 years of age.

The average arctic grayling is only about nine to 15 inches long with some lakes producing a fair number of fish up to 17 inches. Trophy-sized grayling to 20 inches and 3 pounds or more reside in Crescent Lake.

FISHING FOR KENAI GRAYLING

By far the best places to locate grayling are Crescent, Paradise, and Lower Fuller lakes as these waters have the biggest populations and fishing is typically good to excellent. (For full description of the above lakes, see chapters 11 and 13.) Some decent, but often inconsistent, action can be had in connecting streams, such as Quartz and Daves creeks and the Russian River. Anglers fishing side channels and around the mouth of clearwater sloughs on the upper Kenai report catching a few grayling.

Rules & Regulations
There are no existing rules catered specifically for arctic grayling with the possible exception of the Crescent Lake and Paradise Lakes drainages, which has a spring closure to protect spawning fish. Lower Fuller Lake does not have any seasonal restrictions. Otherwise, general restrictions apply.

When & Where to Find Grayling

Lakes
Although grayling are found year-round in lakes, fishing for them is only productive during the open-water season from spring through fall. Ice fishing is possible but action is generally no better than fair at best. Due to the altitude of the peninsula grayling lakes, the main season arrives late and ends early, prompting anglers to focus on the mid-June to mid-September time period for peak catches.

In mid-summer, search out shaded areas during the day or deeper water of at least 10 to 15 feet. Cool runoff streams entering a lake often draw fish like a magnet on hot days. Best time to be on the water is in early morning or evening, preferably near an inlet or outlet stream as these areas attract important food sources. Underwater reefs or vegetation mats hold schools of grayling, some specimens of which can be very large.

In spring (where allowed) and fall, grayling can be found throughout all layers of water most anywhere in the lake. But also this time of year are there hot spots and for two reasons. One is that mature grayling in spring are preparing to move into the streams in preparation for spawning and are found at inlets and outlets. Big schools often circle these locations with excellent fishing possible. Another reason is food availability. Water flowing into and out of a lake is a focal point of activity for insect life and other small organisms that grayling are fond of.

Rivers and Streams

Most streams on the Kenai Peninsula do not offer consistent grayling action for anglers. There may be some fish left in spawning streams adjoining lakes with healthy grayling populations as the season opens in mid-June, thus quite good opportunities abound. Other streams in the Kenai River drainage, including the mainstem Kenai, only have sporadic catches and are usually incidental to fishing for other species. As with fishing in lakes, the best time to find a fish or two is the June through September timeframe. Occasionally a school of fish may be located and the resulting action good.

Search out deep holes and pools early and late in the season, while in mid-summer look for areas with shallower, faster water such as riffles and submerged structure.

What to Use for Grayling

There are two items that catch more grayling than anything else in the state: Flies and spinners. Both imitate the most important food sources of grayling, which are insects and small fish. Wet and dry flies function perfectly in proper circumstances as do small spinners. However, since grayling are not very finicky and can be extremely aggressive to artificial offerings, tiny spoons and plugs can be good as well.

Ultra light gear is how to enjoy the best grayling has to offer. Since most fish caught are in the lower to mid-teens with a "big one" being around the 20-inch mark, use appropriate rod and reel for most enjoyment.

Flies

The standard dry and wet flies all can produce good results, with some of the better ones listed below. Attention should be paid to what conditions are at the water intended to fish. When lake surface is calm and fish are "dimpling," use dry flies to accommodate feeding behavior. If no feeding activity is obvious, try sub-surface wet flies. The latter is also good during or right after rainfall as downpour flushes insects from air and off overhanging brush into water.

Dry flies can work anytime of the open water season but perform best during the June through August time period as this is when flying insect activity is at a peak. Try Mosquito, Adams, Royal Wulff, Light Cahill, Elk Hair Caddis, Humpy, Griffith's Gnat, and Black Gnat in size 10 or smaller.

Wet flies, including forage imitations, are good throughout the summer and fall. Suggested are Woolly Buggers, Muddler Minnows, Black Ant, Hare's Ear Alevin, and Nymph and Stonefly patterns. In streams that contain populations of spawning salmon, small egg sucking leeches (brown, purple, and black) and Glo Bugs can be effective in August and September.

Lures

There is no doubt that lures, especially spinners, are great for grayling and in some instances even outperform flies and catch bigger fish. The sonic vibrations and added flash attract grayling from a good distance away, hence their effectiveness.

Spoons, spinners, and plugs are all good lure types and will undoubtedly draw attention. Dark, natural colors are best with black, brown, blue, green, copper, and bronze hues being best, but metallic silver and gold can often be deadly. Contrast is sometimes the key and lures with a basic dark background with spots or stripes in red, yellow, green, and white have proven to be irresistible in many circumstances.

Spinners such as Vibrax, Mepps, Panther Martin, and Rooster Tail in sizes 0 to 3 are highly recommended.

In salmon spawning streams, small attractors in orange and red imitating salmon eggs catch fish. Use beads or tiny corkies.

Gear

In waters that contain exclusively grayling, fly gear 2- to 3-weight, six- to seven-foot rods are good with a single action reel. Line should be of 4- to 6-foot long tippets with 2- to 4-pound test. If fishing in areas that contain an abundance of other sport fish species such as trout and char, use heavier gear and line, such as a four- to six-weight rod of eight to nine feet long.

As for spinning gear, an ultra light six to seven-and-a-half foot fast action rod with matching reel and 2- to 4-pound test. Again, in waters with other game fish, use slightly heavier rod, reel, and line.

ROUND WHITEFISH

Scientific Name: *Prosopium cylindraceum.*
Common Name(s): Whitefish and Cisco.

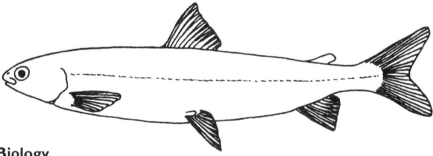

Biology

Description: Body shape tubular, mouth small. Dark back, silvery sides, white belly. Spawning fish slightly more tan or light brownish hue.
Size: Average 10 to 20 inches, up to 5 pounds.
Distribution: Found from mouth of Kenai River to headwater streams and lakes.
Abundance: No abundance estimates available. Fish are locally abundant in late summer and fall, particularly on the upper Kenai and a few tributaries of Kenai Lake.

Sport Fishing

Regulatory Season: No species-specific regulations in place; general restrictions apply.
Timing: Year-round, peak numbers of fish seen from August into November.

Gear: Five- to six-foot rod spin/bait caster; seven- to eight-foot, 4-weight fly rod; 3- to 4-pound test line/tippet.
Tackle: Spoons, spinners, flies, and bait.
Methods: Casting, drifting, stationary.
Hot Spots: Upper Kenai River and Quartz Creek.

ROUND WHITEFISH in the Kenai River

There are two species of the extended whitefish family in the Kenai River drainage, round whitefish and Bering cisco. While round whitefish is most common and a year-round Kenai resident, the Bering cisco is less abundant and portrays an anadromous life cycle. This chapter will focus on round whitefish since it plays a bigger part in the anglers' fauna.

Body shape is elongated and tubular, scales large. The mouth is small with very tiny teeth. Back is dark gray or greenish, sides silvery, and belly silvery white. Spawning fish display a slightly darker hue. Back is dirty brown, sides being grayish silvery, light brown, yellowish, or bronze. The fins may take on an orange coloration.

Whitefish thrive in both glacial and clearwater drainages. During the winter months whitefish are found suspended in lakes and deeper, slow-moving sections of large rivers. In May and June a migration begins into the mainstem Kenai River and mouths of larger tributaries, ascending these waters in July to feed for the summer and fall months. Adult whitefish consume mainly insects and fish eggs. Some whitefish, however, will elect to remain in lakes over the summer, only moving into streams in the fall in preparation for the spawn.

By September, schools of whitefish gather in rivers and streams with suitable spawning habitat. The reproductive process begins in October, peaks in November, and can extend into December. Females deposit up to several thousand eggs in spots with gravel or pebble bottom. After the process has been completed, the spent fish begin a rapid migration to overwintering areas. Whitefish may spawn several times. The eggs hatch in spring, the emerging young sustaining on insect larvae and zooplankton.

Round whitefish are believed to be abundant in the Kenai River drainage with sizable populations also present in the Trail lakes and Moose River systems.

FISHING FOR KENAI WHITEFISH

Anglers do normally not target whitefish and the majority of catches made are incidentally to fishing for trout and char. But considering that whitefish are a more abundant species than grayling in the Kenai drainage – and of matching size – it is a welcome addition to the whole experience. It is important to remember, however, that the real reason whitefish are not caught in the numbers they are is because anglers do not use lures or flies meant to imitate what these fish feed on. What catches rainbows and dollies do not necessarily work effectively on whitefish.

Whitefish are opportunistic feeders and will follow food sources as they become available. In mid-summer when schools of these fish begin arriving in clearwater tributaries, such as Quartz Creek, anglers can do fairly well using small flies and tiny rooster tail spoons and spinners. Proven fly patterns include Midge, Maggot, Black

Gnat, Mosquito, Scud, and Hare's Ear tied on a number 14 or 16 hook. Focus efforts in deeper holes, runs, and pools with structures such as behind fallen trees and bridge pilings and near logjams. These patterns also catch fish in clearwater lakes.

Starting in late summer and continuing into fall as salmon arrive and begin spawning, egg imitations are good. The mainstem sections of the middle and upper Kenai River and the Trail River, because of their glacial content, demand offerings with some visibility, this especially being the case on Trail River (try fluorescent colors). Tiny corkies in orange or red, beads, and Glo Bugs fished in stretches of quiet water do catch fish. Drift them on the edges of faster current or do a very slow retrieve through deep, slack water. Sometimes it helps to just let the offering sit in the current, stripping in small sections of line every minute or so.

As is commonly the case with trout and char, whitefish are also drawn to fish cleaning stations. Tiny flesh flies and egg imitations work here.

One of the absolutely best items on the menu for whitefish is salmon eggs. Where legal, a small single salmon egg on a tiny hook can be deadly. Small clusters of salmon roe fished stationary on the bottom are equally effective. At the inlet and outlet of the glacially influenced Kenai and Skilak lakes, bait is just about the only way to efficiently catch whitefish.

NORTHERN PIKE
Scientific Name: *Esox lucius.*
Common Name(s): Pike.

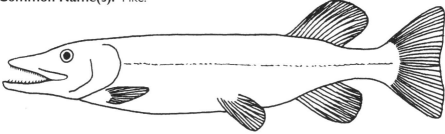

Biology
Description: Dorsal fin placed far back on body. Long, flat duck-billed snout. Dark grayish green to brown on back and sides, numerous yellow spots decorate sides.
Size: Average 3 to 6 pounds, up to 20 pounds or more.
Distribution: Primarily clearwater lakes tributary to middle Kenai River. A few fish reported to be in Skilak Lake and upper river.
Abundance: No abundance estimates available. Very few fish scattered throughout system with the possible exception of the Soldotna Creek drainage where a fair to good population is present.

Sport Fishing
Regulatory Season: No species-specific regulations in place; general restrictions apply.

Timing: Year-round in lakes, most active in April-May and again in September.
Gear: Six- to seven-foot rod spin/bait caster; eight- to nine-foot, 7-weight fly rod; 6- to 12-pound test line/tippet.
Tackle: Spoons, spinners, attractors, plugs, flies, and bait.
Methods: Casting, drifting, stationary, ice fishing.
Hot Spots: There are no readily accessible hot spots within the Kenai River drainage. The few lakes that do harbor sizable populations of fish are surrounded by private property.

NORTHERN PIKE in the Kenai River

Northern pike is not a native species to the Kenai River drainage. Once introduced to a lake in the Soldotna Creek system back in the 50s, the fish has since permeated that watershed and still to this day keep infiltrating new waters for feeding and spawning. Pike are an exceptionally hardy species and can survive under very harsh, inhospitable conditions. It is foremost known as a formidable predator and will consume other fish, including its own species, as well as insects, rodents, and young waterfowl. Pike have a reputation of exterminating other kinds of fish in smaller lakes and ponds, thus proving to be a quite unpopular guest in any waters it infiltrates.

Northern pike are efficiently built for the purpose of launching quick, sudden attacks on its prey. The body is somewhat elongated, the dorsal fin placed far back for speed. Mouth is large and equipped with long, sharp teeth. The head is tapered into a long, flat duck-billed snout. Scales are small. Back and sides are dark grayish green, green, or dark brownish with belly being creamy white or yellowish. Numerous yellow spots in irregular longitudinal rows decorate sides. Fins are green, yellowish, or even orange and marked with dark blotches. Flesh color is white.

The distribution of pike in the Kenai River drainage is fairly widespread but there are very few stocks that are healthy and strong in numbers. It is primarily the Soldotna Creek drainage lakes that have stable populations, including Mackey lakes. Some pike are also known to inhabit the Moose River system and the lower and middle main-stem of Kenai River. These watersheds are prime habitat for pike, which includes an abundance of muskeg lakes and slow-moving streams. It is speculated that pike use the mainstem Kenai primarily as a migration corridor to more suitable waters. The upper Kenai River drainage has very few reports of northerners but one specimen has been documented from the Russian River.

Spawning takes place in the spring and early summer (May-June) in shallow water of lakes, ponds, and sloughs of rivers and streams. Females deposit 2,000 to 600,000 eggs along the bottom, preferably in areas with significant vegetation mats. Eggs hatch a few weeks later, the young feeding mostly on insects and plankton. Pike may reproduce several times and live up to 25 years of age.

After the spawn, the spent pike begin a slow movement into slightly deeper water and disperses throughout the drainage to feed for the summer and fall. With the approach of winter, pike withdraw to ponds and lakes to overwinter.

FISHING FOR KENAI PIKE

Although the opportunity to catch pike has been around for several decades in the Kenai drainage, it is only in the last few years that it has grown into popularity. However, most of the productive pike waters providing public access are not in the Kenai system and the ones within the system are primarily surrounded by private property. In this respect, fishing for pike is poor at best and anglers' exposure to the species remains the incidental catches while trying for other kinds of game fish.

Aside from the Soldotna Creek drainage, anglers may find limited success in the Moose River system. A few pike are taken in this vast waterway from time to time by anglers fishing for salmon and trout. Some decent catches are reported sporadically but none have been officially verified and test netting of various lakes in the system have turned up very little to substantiate the claims. But there is no denying that pike are in the system and that the drainage lakes and streams are perfect habitat for pike to establish a healthy population.

Anglers wanting to explore the idea of catching a Kenai pike should use spoons, spinners, and forage imitation flies with some extra flash. Silver, copper, bronze, and metallic blue and green are proven colors. A touch of red or yellow/chartreuse is great under some water conditions. Top water offerings can work very well. Bait such as whole or part smelt and herring are effective when used with a bobber or fished stationary from a boat. Because pike have an abundance of sharp teeth, a wire or hard plastic leader is a must.

The absolutely best time of year to dredge up a pike is in spring, especially right after the spawn. These fish are extremely territorial right before and during the reproductive process and will often attack anything that moves into its domain. Also, the fish go on a feeding binge after spawning is completed.

Best areas to try are in the shallows in spring, preferably in locations with a fair amount of grass or weed. Two to four feet of water is ideal depth. Hunt for pike along the lake shoreline as well as around islands with proper structure.

BURBOT
Scientific Name: *Lota lota.*
Common Name(s): Ling cod and Cod.

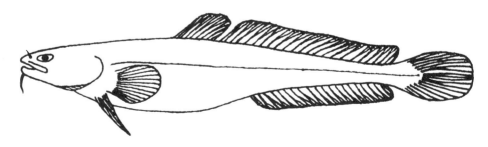

Biology
Description: Body long and slender. Large head and mouth, chin whisker. Color brown.
Size: Average 15 to 22 inches, up to 28 inches and 5-6 pounds.
Distribution: Only documented in Juneau Lake.
Abundance: No abundance estimates are available but population appears healthy.

Sport Fishing
Regulatory Season: No species-specific regulations in place, open year-round.
Timing: Year-round, best March into May and September through December.
Gear: Five- to seven-foot rod spin/bait caster; 4- to 6-pound test line. Set lines.
Tackle: Spoons, jigs, and bait. Most effective is bait such as smelt or herring.
Methods: Casting or stationary; set lines.
Hot Spots: Juneau Lake.

BURBOT in the Kenai River

Burbot is the only member of the codfish family found exclusively in freshwater. It is a species that is considered abundant in many parts of the state but absent from the Kenai Peninsula, with one exception. Juneau Lake, a tributary lake of the upper Kenai River drainage, northwest of Cooper Landing, has a healthy population of burbot.

The burbot's appearance is unusual and not easily confused with any other species. The body is long and slender, head being wide and broad, mouth large. A characteristic barbell adorns tip of lower jaw. The dorsal and anal fins extend from the middle of the body almost to the caudal (tail) fin. The caudal fin is rounded rather than square or forked. Scales are very small, almost microscopic. The back and sides are mottled brown, olive-black, or dark green, the belly a lighter hue. Numerous dirty yellow patches or markings cover the back, sides, and belly in dirty yellow. Flesh color is white.

Although burbot are known to venture into larger streams and rivers to feed and spawn, the population in Juneau lake is confined to the lake proper throughout the year. Adult diet consists primarily of fish, insects, mollusks, snails, and fish eggs. Mature burbot spawn from January into March in areas of suitable bottom structure, females depositing between 600,000 and 3 million eggs that hatch in late winter and spring. Juvenile fish consume insect larvae and plant material. Unlike salmon, burbot may reproduce several times and known to live up to 25 years of age in some populations in Alaska.

FISHING FOR KENAI BURBOT

Of all game fish species on the Kenai Peninsula and the Kenai River drainage, burbot is one of the species anglers are least likely to come into contact with. The reason is foremost a lack of species distribution as burbot can only be caught in one single lake on the whole peninsula. Very small populations or occurrences of burbot may exist elsewhere yet the Juneau Lake stock is the single documented case thus far.

Fishing can be good where the burbot are found, however. A few anglers do target the fish during the spring to fall months using bait. Burbot are also caught incidentally to fishing for other species, such as lake trout. Apart from bait, spoons and jigs both take fish. Small chunks of herring or smelt are a favorite and scraps of salmon parts and other meats work well too.

Burbot are mainly bottom dwellers but will chase properly presented hardware a short distance. Casting from both boat and shore is possible, preferably in deeper water, and retrieves should be slow and methodical, pausing temporarily to jig the lure a few times and let it flutter to the bottom before continuing. Use medium-sized spoons in silver, copper, and bronze with a touch of green or blue. Avoid fluorescent colors.

Bait is best fished stationary on the bottom or suspended slightly above. This can be achieved either by using a normal fishing rod or set lines as is so popular in other burbot fisheries in the state.

Fly fishing is something that has not been tested and tried on burbot to any extent. However, forage patterns should work.

The peak time of the year to locate burbot is during the cooler months of the year when fish are aggressive and situated in more shallow, inshore waters. The warmer months of June, July, and August see cod suspended in deep, cold layers of the lake. The winter months have traditionally been the best time to pursue burbot but logistical concerns may be an issue going into Juneau Lake that time of year. Anglers should take note that during the late winter spawn these codfish go almost completely off the bite. Prior to or after the spawn anglers may enjoy some great action.

The *HIGHWAY ANGLER*
Fishing Alaska's Road System

The best-selling guide to fishing roadside waters on the Kenai Peninsula, the Matanuska/Susitna Valleys, Prince William Sound, the Anchorage and Fairbanks areas, Copper Valley, the Dalton Highway, and Tanana Valley.

- Over 750 locations
- 17 species of game fish
- Detailed access information
- Run timing charts
- Best lures and flies

Available at retail stores throughout Southcentral and Interior Alaska. Can be ordered at *highwayangler.com* and directly from the publisher:

Fishing Alaska Publications
P. O. Box 90557
Anchorage, AK 99509
(907) 346-1177

Signed/personalized copies available upon request.

METHODS &
TECHNIQUES

This chapter contains the very basic applications of sport fishing in the Kenai River with some of the methods and techniques laid out also appropriate for use in tributary streams and lakes. It is written with the novice Kenai fisher in mind but some aspects within the chapter would probably prove useful for higher skill levels as well.

Chapter Contents

FISHING THE KENAI BY BOAT

Back-Trolling

Best used with a plug or attractor/bait combination, this method is a favorite for king salmon. It can be employed both from a powerboat as well as a drift boat. Angler releases line to lure from 15 to 50 feet or more behind the boat. Enough power or rowing should be applied to keep the boat stationary with its bow facing into the current. The boat can be steered from side to side, while slowly dropping back with the current, thus letting the line and lure sweep across a bigger section of river. Allow boat to slip several more feet in the current and repeat procedure. It is a very effective way to provoke a king to strike since the method provides a thorough coverage of bottom structure.

Using a plug: As line tightens, the river current works plug automatically. Water pressure pushes against plug lip and makes plug dive down to inches off the bottom, diving into the riverbed and bouncing back up, creating an action that greatly aggravates territorial kings. Plug is ideally fished alone in medium to slow or fairly shallow water but with a planer in very swift and/or deep water.

Using an attractor: A planer is attached ahead of the lure, catching the current and forcing the rig down towards bottom.

The slow presentation of the lure means that this method is great for all water conditions, from clear to murky. With king salmon, let the fish "chew" on the lure for a second or two before setting hook.

Drifting

Drifting, also known as "drift-fishing" and "dragging bait," is a method that is commonly used for king salmon on the lower Kenai and for trout and char on the middle and upper river. If in a powerboat (or possibly even a raft), it entails positioning the boat sideways to the current – or perpendicular to land – so that the motor is nearer the shore, and drifting downstream. One member of the party near the bow may use an oar or paddle to keep the boat positioned correctly. With the front of the boat pointed out toward mid-river, the motor will react faster in forward gear than in reverse. In a drift boat, the positioning may be different as the bow and stern may be lined with the river current if so desired.

Anglers cast upstream, allowing lure or fly to sink and work along or near the bottom at the speed of the current. As the offering does move quite fast through holes and runs, this method is most effective when the Kenai runs fairly clear and fish can see the lure coming from some distance. It is not a very efficient method in off-colored or muddy water conditions.

Back-Bouncing

Also referred to as bottom-bouncing, this method stipulates the boat be under power and pointed upstream. The boat is then allowed to very slowly back down with the current into holes and runs. Attractors and bait combinations are the lure of choice along with a sinker heavy enough to keep offering in contact with the bottom, this usually being a four- to eight-ounce weight for king salmon and three- to six-ounces for other species. The offering is repeatedly lifted and lowered in a slow jigging motion as the boat slides downstream, the sinker hitting the bottom periodically.

This method is especially good for deep areas, such as Big Eddy, and during the months of July and August when water flow is greatest. In spring, early summer, and fall with cooler temperatures and less glacial melt, current flow is often not swift enough (and too many exposed rocks and snags) to efficiently work this method. Some anglers, however, resort to using lighter gear to compensate.

Anchoring

This used to be a popular method for king salmon years ago but is no longer used as an anchor line in the water is more seen as an obstruction than anything else. It is still very commonly employed when fishing other species, however. The boat is kept stationary in a hole or run simply by dropping an anchor. Anglers may want to use a quick-release set-up on the anchor line along with a stout, highly visible buoy attached to line if wanting to chase down fish, which is in all likelihood quite unnecessary unless it is a king salmon.

Various techniques can be utilized, including casting hardware and flies or just soaking bait stationary on the bottom. Hot Spots for this method is Eagle Rock, Beaver Creek, around Funny River, Big Eddy, Fall In Hole, Bing's Landing, and the mouth of Killey River.

FISHING THE KENAI FROM SHORE

Flipping

This is the most effective and efficient method of presenting a fly to migrating red salmon. Casts (or flips) are short – perhaps 12 to 15 feet – with the angler working water that lies in the arc 45 degrees above to 45 degrees below his or her position. Line is pulled in with one hand through rod guides, rod swinging around in a circular whip, and let loose again. Feel the sinker bounce along the bottom and repeat procedure.

This technique is especially popular and effective in smaller rivers and streams or wherever fish travel close to shore. It is mostly used on red and silver salmon.

"Lining"

This is a method that has proved extremely productive on tight-lipped reds in the Kenai and Russian rivers but works just as well on silver salmon, at least on the Russian. The basic procedure is the same as the "flipping" technique described above. The length of line between fly and sinker is about three to five feet. The fly and sinker create a trap in which the fishing line between the two slides into the mouth of the fish and with the help of the current pulls the fly right into the mouth. Through the drift, the angler keeps the rod tip low, sweeping it downstream with the current, pulling the line with one hand to keep it tight.

Any presentation with a light, streamlined shape can be used to line fish, even just a plain bare hook. Anglers using this method in clearwater streams prefer highly colorful flies to better be able to visually steer their presentation into the mouths of migrating salmon.

Casting

This very basic technique of casting and reeling in can be used in several different ways but usually entails the angler finding water with slow to moderate current, such as the mouth of sloughs, channels, or just in slack water areas like holes and pools of the main current.

Proceed by casting lure or fly into the holding area, making slow and steady retrieves. Try varying speeds until the right depth has been found where fish are resting. Sometimes it is along the bottom, other times the surface, or both. If the fish are on the bite, it usually does not take more than a couple of dozen casts to find out. Then again, one may elect to wait for a school of fish to come through, especially if fishing the holes on the lower river near tidewater. Casting into quiet water draw strikes from silver and pink salmon, trout, char, and grayling.

It sometimes helps to retrieve a lure with the current. Casting upstream and allowing the lure to sink for a second and then starting a quite fast retrieve (but still maintaining lure near bottom) is deadly on king, silver, and pink salmon, rainbow trout, Dolly Varden, and arctic grayling.

Drifting

As a technique expanded on the practice of casting, the lure of fly is allowed to sink to and drift along the bottom without reeling in. The cast should be made 45 degrees upstream of angler position with line reeled in starting about 45 degrees below his or her position. The rule or fly moves approximately with the speed of the current, bumping into the bottom every couple of feet or so. If a series of snags hinder the drift, either change to a lighter lure/sinker or change position up- or downstream.

Drifting from shore is best in areas with moderate current. Anglers use the technique on almost all game fish in the Kenai drainage, even king salmon.

BAIT FISHING

Both salmon roe and shrimp are among top kinds of bait for trout and char, salmon preferring clusters of roe. Use it sparingly in lakes if ice fishing but avoid it altogether in rivers and streams unless trying to catch salmon. For large predatory fish in lakes, such as lake trout, northern pike, and burbot, pieces, chunks, or even whole herring, smelt (hooligan), and sardines are best.

For salmon, use roe alone or with an attractor and fish it sitting stationary on the bottom or drift it with the current. When ice fishing, use bait such as roe, single salmon eggs, shrimp, and fish parts by itself, perhaps with a flasher, or in combination with a jig or spoon. Some anglers put a weight on the line and bait a single hook and leave it on the bottom.

There is no doubt that bait is extremely effective on many types of fish and in some areas of the Kenai River drainage it is illegal to use. Restrictions involving bait usually arise out of concerns that it can kill fish to a much greater extent than artificial offerings, even if careful catch-and-release techniques are employed. Fish have a tendency to take bait deep in the throat, sometimes even swallowing it, creating a dilemma if it is to be released. Therefore, targeting trout and char with bait in flowing water is increasingly seen as unethical in nature due to the high degree of mortality associated with this type of offering. And with strict size restrictions in place, the situation can become unpleasant.

FLY FISHING TIPS & PATTERNS

Selecting A Fly

The general category of flies provide anglers with the most flexible enticement for salmon, trout, char, and grayling more so than any other offering. Flies can be made to imitate just about anything fish eat, from smaller fish and emerging insect life to salmon eggs and even pieces of rotting salmon carcass. They are great for triggering a range of behavioral reflexes from past and present feeding patterns to generating territorial responses. Understanding the life history or cycle of fish is the key to successfully target the various species, especially predatory ones like trout and char.

It should also be noted that insect emergences do not drive Kenai River's seasonal feeding trends to any great degree among resident fish, unlike in some tributary lakes. As in all fishing the key to success is to match the natural food source.

Forage Imitation Flies

Species: Red, silver, and pink salmon, rainbow and lake trout, arctic char, Dolly Varden, northern pike, and arctic grayling.
Timing: April to mid-July and mid-September into October (for species other than salmon), year-round in some areas.

Summary: This covers a very broad category of food imitations, ranging from aquatic insects to salmon smolt to a combination of forage species and salmon eggs. In lakes and streams with limited or no salmon production, forage patterns can be used effectively throughout the open water season, including the winter months where ice is not a hindrance. In the mainstem Kenai and tributaries, these patterns are most effective prior to and after the salmon runs. However, some char and trout may respond favorably even during the presence of spawning salmon as a change of diet to something completely different than eggs is warranted for an improved bite.

Patterns that are proven effective in the Kenai River and its tributaries include Egg Sucking Leech, Muddler Minnow, Woolhead Sculpin, and Woolly Bugger in dark colors (black, chartreuse, purple, brown, olive), the latter two being best in the main current. Larger patterns bring success before salmon show. The Hare's Ear Alevin is tops in braided river areas and side channels and sloughs. Nymph and Stonefly patterns are best fished in clearwater tributaries.

Early in the season, fish the above flies deep on sinking-tip line or with a split shot. Later in summer and fall, experiment with various depths.

Egg Imitation Flies

Species: Red and silver salmon, rainbow trout, Dolly Varden. Also king and pink salmon, grayling, and whitefish.

Timing: Late July to mid-September but into November or later on some species. Use anytime during salmon runs.

Summary: The vast majority of egg imitations are based on salmon spawn and since salmon drive much of the Kenai system in terms of food sources, it is only natural that they would be effective on predatory resident fish. Yet it is recognized that some larger imitations also attract various species of salmon. Orange, pink, red, and various other similar shades of color work best.

Early in the salmon spawning season, traditional egg imitation flies like Battle Creek Special, Polar Shrimp, Two-Egg Sperm Fly perform as well as anything else. However, as the season progresses and fish – notably trout – become wiser, Glo Bug and Iliamna Pinkie are the patterns to try. Eventually, anglers must come up with something that looks virtually identical to the real thing: beads (see section below). Remember, there are literally millions of eggs in a river or stream and any fly has to compete with them. The experienced angler will bring a variety of fly and bead colors to match water and weather conditions and mood of fish.

Although char and grayling are not too particular many times how precise a pattern is presented, rainbow trout may be very finicky and refuse to take egg imitations that are dragged and not free floated. Present egg imitations like you would a bead; using a dead drift with floating line, strike indicator, and split shot.

As for salmon, the traditional patterns mentioned above are effective throughout the season with red and silver salmon being likely candidates.

Beads

Species: Rainbow trout and Dolly Varden. Also grayling and whitefish.

Timing: Late July to mid-September but into November or later on some species.

Summary: Although technically not a fly, beads are almost exclusively used by fly fishers. It is designed to imitate a single drifting egg (preferably salmon) and without a doubt one of the most effective creations for rainbow trout and Dolly Varden. Beads are usually fished just prior to and during the salmon spawn and would ideally reflect the current appearance of most eggs in the water. In other words, color and size changes in beads according to the species, as king salmon eggs are different than that of reds and silvers and so forth. Additionally, color changes in beads during the season.

Anglers can experiment with a multitude of colors and sizes to fit the "hatch" of the day, but beads generally are hued in orange to pink. Unless one finds particular enjoyment out of it, the perceived necessity to memorize or study in depth all the various color schemes of beads and their nuances is really not practical. Stick to a fair assortment of colors and sizes and leave the scientific aspect of it to the professionals – the river guides.

Present a bead in likely locations by using a dead drift, preferably with a floating line, a strike indicator, and a small split shot.

Flesh Imitation Flies

Species: Rainbow trout and Dolly Varden. Also silver salmon and lake trout.
Timing: Early August through October in most locations, through winter into spring in mainstem Kenai.
Summary: Flesh pattern flies are meant to imitate pieces of disintegrating carcass drifting with the current. Starting in August in some tributaries with kings and early run reds, flesh flies become good as the salmon begin to die off. However, in the mainstem Kenai and other streams this may not happen until early September as the late-run reds begin to fade away. Snags, top portion of converging seams, eddies, logjams, sweepers or wherever current deposits salmon carcasses are good locations to cast flesh flies.

Popular flesh patterns in the mainstem Kenai and in larger tributaries include Flesh Bunny, Ginger Bunny, and Battle Bunny. For best effect, these imitations are fished with sinking-tip line. Since the upper and middle river receives late-spawning salmon throughout the winter months, flesh patterns work continuously from fall until spring.

In smaller, clearwater tributaries, the Sparse Flesh Fly on floating line and long leader is recommended.

Dry Flies

Species: Rainbow trout, Dolly Varden, and arctic grayling.
Timing: Mid-June to early August on mainstem Kenai, as late as end of September in clearwater lakes and streams.
Summary: Surface-conditioned flies are most often used in clearwater tributaries of the Kenai River, as insect hatches are perhaps most prolific and salmon byproducts not the most common source of food. Misconceptions is that these patterns do not work on the mainstem Kenai, yet they do and sometimes very well. However, fish feeding off the surface are generally smaller in size than sub-surface or bottom feeders.

Popular patterns for all species mentioned above include Elk Hair Caddis, Humpy, Wulff, Adams, Cahill, Gnat, and Mosquito. The Mouse fished near cover in deep water can result in some surprisingly big trout and char.

Salmon "Swing"

This technique is commonly used when in pursuit of red and silver salmon on the mainstem Kenai River as well as in some of the larger tributaries in areas with at least moderate current flow. Except for when fish are staged in calm holes and pools, fish moving through fairly swift current do not move up or down more than a few inches in the water column to intercept a fly drifting by.

The "swing" itself is all in the line supported by matching current and depth. A floating line creates the most efficient sweep and with the angler keeping the line tight by moving the rod downstream ahead of the drift, the take of a fish can easily be felt and the hook set in the direction of the current, the rod horizontal to the water.

In order for the fly to be presented in the line of vision of the fish consistently and continuously, an angler needs to approach the situation either using a sinking or floating line. Many prefer the advantage of fishing a floating line with a small sinker since it lends more to flexibility in adjusting for current speed and depth by increasing or decreasing the weight of the sinker and leader length. A 12-foot leader with a split shot is a common setup.

Sinking lines, however, often prove less ideal as the water conditions must fit the line density for a proper drift to take place, thus potentially limiting the angler to only casting in certain locations unless he or she has acquired enough skill and experience to counter the situation. A 300- or 400-grain sinking line is common on the Kenai for this purpose. Another consideration is that the mainstem Kenai has lots of big rocks and boulders to grab sink lines, preventing a natural drift.

FISHING TIPS

This chapter was written with the novice angler in mind but may also prove helpful with the intermediate and advanced not familiar with fishing the Kenai River drainage. Many of the tips also apply to Alaskan waters as a whole. It briefly touches on some of the general aspects regarding where to locate fish in various types of water and conditions and a few points to further assist the angling experience.

LOCATING THE FISH

It is well known that fish do have special preferences for the environment they choose to rest and feed in and migrate through. Knowing where and at what time in a river, stream, or lake to look for fish is at least as important – if not more so – as having the right gear and skill. Although angling for any species of fish can be productive at any time of the day or year, there are definitely times when the action is better and more predictable. The most common factors to consider are lighting conditions, available structure, current flow, depth, seasonal behavior, and water temperature. Being able to "read" the water, or in other words, having sufficient information on fish habits to know exactly where a fish is most likely to be found is the key and, if mastered, can bring much success.

The following points illustrate the very basics in locating fish in the various types of water and the factors involved.

RIVERS & STREAMS

1. Locate deep holes, pools, and eddies. Many species have a tendency to congregate in such areas as they find security there while either feeding or migrating to or from the spawning grounds. This applies to the mainstem Kenai River as well as tributaries. In very large or deep sections, look for fish at the head or tail and around the edges of these areas.

2. Try moderate- to slow-flowing water. A more passive flow attracts fish since they do not have to fight strong current and burn energy unnecessarily. Avoid very fast-flowing, white-water stretches of rivers and streams as fish only pass through these areas on the way to calmer sections. Take note, however, that a few species bite better in faster current than slack (red salmon, for example).

3. Concentrate on river and stream confluences. The mixing area of larger rivers and smaller streams is a superb location to find all species of fish and serves as a resting and feeding area. Salmon very often stack up here in large numbers prior to moving up the tributary to spawn and other game fish may hold for the same reasons or to simply use the area to locate food sources.

4. Fish the tides. In the lower Kenai River the fishing can vary greatly according to tidal movements. Work the area starting a few miles upstream of the mouth on an incoming tide as salmon and other sea-run species migrate into fresh water. Also try deep holes and runs as the tide recedes or upstream areas during or after mean high tide. Both salmon and sea-run char will be present.

5. Fish the low light hours. The best action is generally experienced in early morning and evening and on cloudy days. Trout, char, grayling, and other species feed most heavily then, and salmon respond with more enthusiasm to anglers' offerings. Avoid bright sunshine as shadows cast on the water has a tendency to spook fish.

LAKES & PONDS

1. Fish according to the seasons. Late spring, fall, and early winter are probably the best times to fish lakes and ponds because of ideal water temperatures and high oxygen levels. Fish are often lethargic in mid-summer and late winter due to low oxygen levels and too warm or cold water temperatures.

2. Fish after break-up. Trout, char, grayling, and pike are often concentrated fairly close to shore in shallow water as they prepare to spawn, engage in a feeding frenzy, or migrate to summer feeding areas.

3. Try before and after freeze-up. All resident species are very active at this time, feeding heavily near shore in shallow water. The cool and oxygen-rich water in late fall and early winter sparks the energy level of fish, subsequently resulting in anglers experiencing some of the best fishing of the season.

4. Concentrate on feeding areas. Fish thrive best in areas of the lake where there is an abundance of feed. Inlets and outlets, vegetated shorelines, and submerged structures such as shoals, pinnacles and tree trunks are very productive places. During windy conditions, avoid protected areas and focus effort where wave activity is greatest. The waves wash food particles out into the lake from shore.

5. Fish the low light hours. All species are most active during early morning and evening or on cloudy days, especially in summer. Avoid bright, mid-day sunshine as fish become shy and move into deep water. Additionally, the upper layer of water is often too warm for fish and they will thus seek out the cooler water at mid-depth or bottom of lake or pond.

FOOD SOURCES

1. Spawning salmon. Resident species such as trout, char, grayling and others depend largely on salmon eggs and flesh to supplement their diet and are often found within a few feet of spawning fish. Follow the trend of what and where the various salmon species are doing within their life cycle and choose locations and tackle based on those conclusions. Gain knowledge of when salmon are spawning in what streams and rivers. The basics are that when the salmon are in the midst of spawning, use egg imitations, and when the fish are dying off flesh imitations are better suited.

2. Fish cleaning stations. A unique circumstance takes place around these stations as normally bits of salmon and eggs would not be available naturally to fish until later in the season. Scraps of protein-rich meat flooding into the rivers as a result of anglers cleaning their catch by the water are a natural magnet for trout and char and other forage species. This is an "artificial" food source of sorts, with fish acting on an opportunity created by anglers filleting their fish and throwing the remains into the water. These stations are located on the Russian River and similar situations also occur on the lower and middle Kenai where people clean their fish consistently in one place. Action can be hot near or just downstream of fish cleaning stations using egg imitation and flesh flies.

3. Juvenile salmon. All predatory species in the Kenai drainage feed heavily on salmon fry and smolt. The young salmon will often choose areas with plenty of cover during the day, usually in side channels or sloughs away from the main current. In late spring and summer, the smolt migration headed for the ocean peak their downstream movements along the mainstem Kenai and tributary streams at night and this is when trout and char are most active. Smolt or forage imitations work best and can be used anytime during the early part of the season.

4. Insect hatches. The Kenai River is not a huge producer of various insect hatches during the open water season. The mainstem river has relatively few insects and therefore the seasonal highlights are not driven by insect emergences. The drainage clearwater streams and lakes are probably the better option in locating hatches as the non-glacial habitat is more suitable for insect activity. However, caddis flies are abundant in late June and early July and mayflies through the month of July. Matching these hatches can be effective along parts of the mainstem Kenai but usually more so in clearwater tributaries.

LURE TIPS

1. Keep lure close to or near the bottom. Species such as salmon, large trout and char, and whitefish commonly "hug" the bottom and will seldom move much of a distance to intercept a lure or fly floating above their head. In the mainstem Kenai, it is usually the smaller fish that pick food items off the surface.

2. Try high-visibility lures in glacially fed waters. Lures and flies in fluorescent red, orange, and chartreuse are best. Sometimes a touch of chrome combination works well. Water color such as greenish-gray or greenish-blue produce fish. Avoid dark brown or gray (milky) waters. Use bait or bait-scented lures if legal and fish lure slowly or stationary.

3. Use flashy or colorful lures in murky conditions. Visibility is important and even more so in glacial waters or during low-light conditions such as rain, heavy clouds, and between dusk and dawn. Deep drainages often command bright lures and flies. Main colors are red, orange, chartreuse, pink, yellow, and silver.

4. Use dark or neutral colored lures in bright conditions. Too much flash can spook fish, especially in bright sunshine and in crystal clear water. Also, fish respond better to less colorful lures in shallow drainages and when angler pressure is high. Main colors include green, brown, black, copper, purple, blue, and bronze.

5. Match lure size and color with mood of fish. If fish appear spooked or skittish, try small and/or neutral-colored lures and flies; if aggressive, use something larger and more colorful.

MISCELLANEOUS TIPS

1. Many of the lakes in the Kenai River drainage offer good fishing but may be some-what tricky to fish from shore due to very shallow, weedy shorelines. Such areas are

best tackled by boat, canoe, inflatable raft, or float tube. The latter is gaining popularity with the hike-in crowd, as the lightweight material is perfect for carrying over long distances.

2. If you are serious about catching fish, it is a good idea to invest in some hip boots or chest waders. The boots or waders will allow you to move freely around the fishing area, through shallow channels or into deeper waters of a lake or river.

3. Polarized glasses are ideal when sight fishing for individual fish or schools of fish in clearwater rivers and streams, as well as for salmon migrating close to shore in mainstem Kenai. They also protect your eyes from the intense glare of the sun's rays reflecting off the surface of the water. And they serve as effective shields from flying lures with sharp hooks.

4. Some roadside waters attract considerable crowds, especially during the peak of salmon runs. One way to counter the presence of other anglers is to hike up- or downstream a few hundred yards. Often, just a little distance from the highway or an access point makes a tremendous difference in the rewards you will reap – usually less company and more fish.

5. Always prior to pursuing a particular type of fish, take some time to learn the life cycle and other pertinent information concerning the species. Having at least some degree of knowledge of the habits and nuances of the fish will assist tremendously in gathering a more in-depth understanding of why the species does what it does and how to apply it to an advantage using a rod and reel and proper methods and techniques.

FISHING KENAI RIVER FROM SHORE

One of the leading problems concerning anglers fishing along the banks of the mainstem Kenai River is the issue of bank degradation and private property. During the immensely popular red salmon fishery in July and early August, hordes of anglers line the banks of the river creating gradual erosion of critical habitat for juvenile salmon. The thick vegetation along the shoreline serves two purposes; one to provide cover for smolt and fry, and two, an area that attracts insects and other aquatic life forms that the fish feed on. If the vegetation is trampled enough, it dies and eventually gets washed away by the river current, leaving rock and gravel behind which is of little value to growing salmon.

The Alaska Department of Fish & Game has assumed regulatory authority to help mitigate potential negative impacts to shoreline habitats from bank angling. This means that the department closes off certain sections of the river to fishing from the bank during the red salmon season when foot traffic is at a peak.

Another issue is private property. Much of the lower river especially is under private ownership, thus limiting shore access for the common angler.

To assist in providing alternative points of access to the Kenai, the list below are some of the more popular places anglers go to catch fish from shore on the lower, middle, and upper river. Additionally, the locations that are closed to all shore fishing (including wading) from July 1 through August 15 are noted.

Lower Kenai River: Mouth to Soldotna Bridge

Suggested Areas to Fish
1. Mouth of the Kenai River (RM 0)
2. Kenai Flats State Recreation Site (RM 5)
3. Cunningham Park (RM 6.5)
4. Eagle Rock (RM 10)
5. Pipeline State Recreation Site (RM 17)
6. Slikok Creek State Recreation Site (RM 19)
7. Centennial Park Campground (RM 20.5)
8. Visitor Information Center (RM 21)

Areas Closed to Shore Fishing
1. Cunningham Park (RM 6.6 – 6.8) North Bank.
2. Eagle Rock (RM 10.7 – 12) South Bank.
3. State-Owned Islands (RM 11 – 14 and RM 17 – 17.3)
4. The Pillars (RM 12.4 – 12.6) North Bank.
5. Honeymoon Cove (RM 12.5 – 13) South Bank.
6. East Bank (RM 13.2 – 13.5)
7. West Bank (RM 14 – 14.4)
8. Big Eddy Road (RM 14.4 – 14.6)
9. State-Owned Islands (RM 17 – 17.3)
10. Poacher's Cove (RM 17.5 – 18)
11. North Bank (RM 18.6 – 18.8)
12. North Bank (RM 18.9 – 20.2)
13. South Bank (RM 20.9 – 21)
14. Soldotna Creek Park (RM 22) North Bank.

Middle Kenai River: Soldotna Bridge to Skilak Lake

Suggested Areas to Fish
1. Swiftwater Campground (RM 23) North Bank.
2. Airport Property (RM 23) South Bank.
3. Morgan's Landing State Recreation Site (RM 29.5 – 31) North Bank.
4. Funny River State Recreation Site (RM 30.5) South Bank
5. Izaak Walton State Recreation Site (RM 36.5) North Bank.
6. Bing's Landing State Recreation Site (RM 39.5) North Bank.
7. Kenai Keys State Recreation Site (RM 44.5 – 46) North Bank.

Areas Closed to Shore Fishing
1. Soldotna Airport (RM 22.7 – 23.5) South Bank.
2. South Bank (RM 26.4 – 30)
3. Keystone Drive (RM 27.3 – 28)
4. Funny River (RM 29.5 – 30) South Bank.
5. Caymas Subdivision (RM 31.8 – 32.3) North Bank.
6. Nilnunqa (RM 36 – 36.6) South Bank.
7. North Bank (RM 44.6)
8. Thompson's Hole (RM 45.8 – 46.3) North Bank.

Upper River: Skilak Lake to Kenai Lake

Suggested Areas to Fish
1. Mile 57 Pullout (RM 71) North Bank.
2. Kenai & Russian River Confluence (RM 73.5)
3. Russian River Campground (MP 52.7 Sterling Highway)
4. Cooper Creek Campground (RM 79)

Areas Closed to Shore Fishing
5. Jim's Landing (RM 69.7) North Bank.
6. Sportsman's Lodge (RM 73.5 – 73.6) North Bank.
7. Sterling Highway Bridge (RM 82) South Bank.

LOWER KENAI RIVER

Description

The lower Kenai River is defined as the section of water from the Sterling Highway Bridge in Soldotna downstream to its terminus at Cook Inlet outside the city of Kenai. This is by far the most populated portion of the river; private and commercial land are spread throughout the length as the cities of Soldotna and Kenai surround the waterway. Yet there is still an abundance of vegetation to be found, recreational parkland and wooded parcels of land are commonplace, and being on the river does not give the impression of fishing in an area of fairly dense settlement.

The Kenai flows swiftly from the highway bridge downstream to approximately Beaver Creek with numerous mid-river islands and famed angling spots along the way. As the river flows out onto the Kenai River Flats and the intertidal area, the current becomes slack, and the banks of the river a combination of rock and mud as a sign of large tidal fluctuations of many feet.

Although the Kenai is quite wide and deep in many places, there are spots where large rocks or boulders and sandbars can be a hazard to boaters, this being particularly the case in spring when water levels are very low. Unless having a fair amount of experience navigating the river, a high level of caution is a must. Additionally, watch out for boat traffic, which can be a problem during the peak of the king salmon runs.

The average stream gradient from Soldotna to the river mouth is 2.6 feet per mile, a distance of 21 miles total.

Wildlife is a possibility even in this section of the Kenai. Moose are a common sight and a few bears amble along the river in summer and fall. Caribou are not unusual on the Kenai River Flats and eagles frequent the river mouth. Beluga whales and seals often swim up the lower river on high tides in pursuit of salmon.

Access

There are many roads along both sides of the lower river with a variety of access points to choose from. Some points are privately owned; the municipality of Soldotna or Kenai operates others. The Sterling Highway, as the main artery, passes through Soldotna with further access off Kenai Spur Highway and Kalifornsky Beach Road.

The main mode of access up and down the river is by boat. As some sections of the riverbanks are privately owned, anglers have almost complete access to various holes and runs by the use of either a powerboat or drift boat. Developed boat launches are present in several of the river access points.

Commercial airports are present in both Kenai and Soldotna.

Fishing

It is the lower Kenai that placed the river on the map with its run of giant king salmon. The entire area buzzes with activity starting in late May and continues right through July and even into August as anglers and guides plow the turquoise-colored water in search of trophy kings and filling the cooler with red salmon fillets. The best time for kings is June and July, the latter month also being prime for reds. August and September belongs to the silver salmon and trout and char action is good as well.

The majority of the Kenai River guides that fish for king salmon do so on the lower river with many heading straight down to the better holes between the mouth of Beaver Creek and the bridge in Soldotna. This stretch of water harbors legendary hot spots, such as Eagle Rock, The Pillars, Big Eddy, Poacher's Cove, and Sunken Island, all of which may be very congested with boats during the peak of the king runs and on weekends.

Likewise, congestion is an issue along the banks of the Kenai the second half of July when the late run of reds come busting through. Anglers often fish elbow-to-elbow in some of the better places. The silvers, however, see far less effort than kings and reds but still attract a good amount of attention. For trout and char, anglers do experience some very good fishing in late summer and fall.

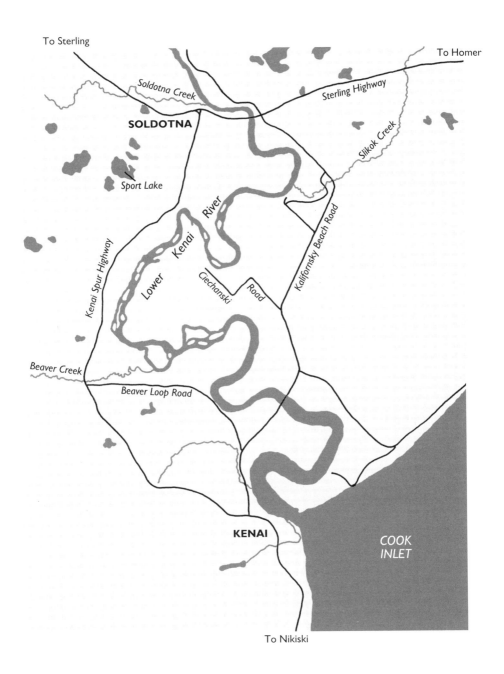

Chapter Contents

The following are the game fish present, the various sections of the Lower Kenai River drainage, and the page number in which more detailed information can be found.

TIMING:

Lower Kenai River

SPECIES INFORMATION

Salmon

Fishing opportunities for salmon is available in profusion as all of the Kenai's salmon species are found in abundance and at a peak in both numbers and physical condition. Excellent fishing for king, red, silver, and pink salmon can be had in this stretch of the Kenai. This is arguably the best place on the river for kings in terms of hookups and the enormous schools of red salmon can be staggering to the mind.

Since tidal movement influences the area heavily, anglers are advised to consult a tide table for times. The most productive time to be on the river is during an incoming or outgoing tide, yet a slack low tide can be good as well during run peaks. Many anglers calculate the estimated migration time salmon use swimming upstream and manage to stay in front of the school to enjoy peak action. Tidal influence on the lower Kenai typically can be observed up to River Mile 12.

Although all salmon destined for the entire Kenai River drainage swim through this stretch of water, fishing for them can be highly variable. That portion of the river upstream of Warren Ames Bridge offers superb potential as holes and runs are well defined and the migratory patterns of fish somewhat predictable. Some of the most productive spots on all the Kenai can be found here.

Downstream of the bridge, however, the Kenai is unpredictable. Flat water and minimal current coupled with drastic tidal changes and somewhat turbid visibility hampers activity. Yet an increasing number of anglers – even guides – are venturing into this part of the Kenai to avoid the heavy congestion associated with king salmon fishing and results have been mixed. The predominantly slack current on most any tide level does not lend well to very productive salmon fishing but at least action can be hot for pinks.

King Salmon

As far as the lower Kenai goes, the Warren Ames Bridge marks the downstream boundary of productive king fishing. Some anglers have done fair when the water conditions are right yet the majority of kings do not hold much in this section of the river, prompting anyone searching for a decent chance of a hookup to head upstream to at least the Cunningham Park area and above where concentrations of kings can be found with predictability.

This river section represents the highlight of king salmon fishing on the Kenai. Fish moving in from Cook Inlet more often than not school up in holes, pools, and deep runs following high tide, resulting in a concentrated mass of kings. And as kings do not have a tendency to engage in a rapid upstream migration pattern which is so common with reds and silvers, the majority of arriving fish in both the early and late runs will be available to anglers for up to several weeks as they linger waiting to mature or for the right water conditions before resuming movement up the river.

Several methods are employed, such as back-trolling, drifting, and back-bouncing with some methods being more effective during certain times of the year in certain holes due to current flow, depth, water visibility, and migratory habit of the specific run. Due to the low and relatively clear water levels in May and most of June, anglers do better generally using smaller plugs in neutral or darker metallic colors. Chrome-bodied plugs with either a chartreuse head or tail are also effective. Drifting and back-trolling is popular this time of year. Back-bouncing works better when water volume increases current flow in late June and July. Fluorescent hues become more effective during the late run of kings.

The following are the most productive locations to find kings. Other holding areas certainly exist as well.

Hot Spots

The Pasture (RM 7) to **The Bluffs** (RM 9): Back-troll or drift on incoming tides, keeping ahead of the rising water as the tide advances.

Beaver Creek Hole (RM 10.2): This is a fairly small, but deep, hole that has a short drift. Fishing, however, can be excellent since the hole concentrates fish as the tide goes out.

Eagle Rock (RM 10.5 – 12): Drift along the left bank on incoming and outgoing tide. It is particularly good during the late run.

The Pillars (RM 12.5): Back-trolling and drifting are best methods here. The state/world record king salmon was caught in this area.

Fall In Hole to **Honeymoon Cove** (RM 13 – 13.4): Back-troll or drift from top of Fall In Hole to just below Honeymoon Cove. If tides are small, this area is productive.

Big Eddy Jetty (RM 14): Best spot is from boat launch area upstream about ¼ mile. Back-trolling is preferred. During very high tides, focus on this stretch of water.

Big Eddy Hole (RM 14.5): Hit the edge of current in deep water by back-bouncing. In chute just above Big Eddy, back-trolling is best. This is one of the deepest holes on the river and a significant number of kings in both runs will stage here.

Little Eddy Hole (RM 14.5): Located across from Big Eddy, this is a popular spot for early kings.

Airplane Hole (RM 15.5): This is not a deep hole (4-5 feet) but can be very productive, particularly early on in the season. Drift or back-troll.

Upper Bluffs (RM 16.5): Another very deep hole; back-bounce or back-troll.

Poacher's Cove (RM 17 – 17.5): Along the left bank opposite of the cove has good water for drifting. For late-run kings, the stretch of water below the first island upstream of cove is productive by back-bouncing.

Sunken Island (RM 18): Back-trolling – and sometimes drifting – here is good for kings.

College Hole (RM 18.9): The uppermost hole for good king fishing on the lower river. Back-troll or drift.

Early Run Kings: A few scouts may show up in the tidewater holes as soon as the third week of April but anglers generally do not connect with fish until the first week of May in any given year. By May 15 there will be fair numbers of kings coming in on the tides, with some impressive early catches into the mid-50s range or heavier not unusual, and action improving steadily through the month into June. Peak in-migration occurs the second week of June with good numbers available through mid-month. In areas near the Sterling Highway Bridge in Soldotna, however, may not see many kings at all until after the first of June at least. A large portion of early-run fish have a habit of waiting in deep holes and runs on the lower river before proceeding upstream toward the spawning grounds in the middle Kenai. Water levels are typically very low in May and the first half of June, thus only a relatively few kings will venture into the shallow stretches of river beyond Soldotna prior to June 15. Productivity slows considerably in late June as the fish move into the middle Kenai. Some blushed early kings remain in the area through most of July.

A seasonal closure is in effect for the mouth of Slikok Creek to protect early-run fish staging there.

Late Run Kings: The transition from the early run to the late run occurs on July 1 by regulation; however, mainstem fish are frequently available in the tidal area starting in late June. Fishing stays mediocre until about July 5 to 10 when the run starts to build rapidly with in-migration peaking about a week later. A good portion of these kings will hold low in the river, downstream of the Sterling Highway Bridge, for at least two weeks before proceeding up the Kenai. Large numbers of kings continue to move up from the tidal zone into late July with action typically being very productive until the season closure on August 1.

There is a very good reason why so many anglers (and guides) focus on this section of the river for king salmon. The Kenai River from Soldotna downstream to Beaver Creek is a major spawning area for these fish and as they come in from the salt they stack up here more so than anywhere else in the drainage. In good years, fish often pile up by the hundreds in various holes and runs, yielding excellent action for anglers using plugs or attractor/bait combinations. As the season wraps up, there could potentially be tens of thousands of kings scattered between Soldotna and the river mouth.

The biggest salmon of the year are usually caught in this part of the Kenai, with most trophies being brought in sometime during the middle of July, as this is when the run is at a peak and fish bright and fat.

In years when runs are very strong and/or late, the portion of river from *Eagle Rock* downstream to the mouth may remain open for kings into early August by emergency order. The fishing is usually fair to good this late in the season but bright fish will still be available among a larger number of blushing ones. Anglers trying for silvers occasionally encounter fresh kings through the month and even into September.

Back-trolling and drifting are the preferred methods in this section of river and with bait being permitted in July the action is generally better than what it is for early-run fish. Back-bouncing is employed in certain spots in the upper part of the tidal zone as current permits. Casting large spinners can be effective too.

Red Salmon

There are two distinct runs of red salmon that migrate through this portion of the Kenai River, one in June and the other in July-August. The latter run is by far the larger of the two and consists of mainstem Kenai as well as tributary fish and should be the run anglers focus on. The early run is comprised primarily of Russian River stock and contributes very little to the lower Kenai fishery due to the much lower number of fish available.

It is imperative that anglers time their efforts according to tidal movements. Starting at about the area between *Cunningham Park* and *Eagle Rock*, anglers do well on outgoing and low tides when river current is strongest. Some two to three hours after high tide all the way to and through low tide is traditionally best. "Lining" is a popular method at low tide level when fish travel only a few feet from shore. Upstream of *The Pillars*, action is best following high tides but can be productive at any time if the run is strong and fish are entering *en masse* at all tide levels.

Keep abreast of how many fish are entering river (through local media reports) and time efforts accordingly. The reds move quickly through this portion of the Kenai, creating a situation of "hit and miss," even during the height of the run. Search out narrow channels around islands or the top of deep holes and runs for concentrations of fish. If the run is not at its peak, head somewhere else.

Successful fishers use a wide array of flies in various color combinations but it seems that orange, fluorescent red, pink, and chartreuse are the top choices. Flipping is the most popular technique, many anglers incorporating "lining" as a way of increasing yield. The reds travel close to shore, usually no more than a few feet from the bank, so long casts are not necessary. A few anglers even resort to using small clusters of salmon roe fished stationary on the bottom with decent results.

Although it may seem tempting, avoid fishing in slack water such as sloughs and pools. The reds may stack up here like cordwood but will seldom bite. Present the fly in stretches of river that has some moderate to fast current and action should be no less than excellent.

The migratory pattern of red salmon in this part of the Kenai is precise and ex-pedient. At times it can be likened to turning a faucet on and off, with fish coming through in enormous schools. The salmon will move from the mouth of the river to the Soldotna area in a matter of hours with each pulse of fish lasting perhaps three to four days followed by several days of relative quiet before the next big push begins. The local media outlets and retail stores will usually have last-minute information on the numbers of reds coming into the river.

Early Run Reds: A few scouts enter the river starting the second week in May with fish continuing to arrive until mid-July. Historically, the run peaks in this area about the second week of June. The early run is miniscule in comparison to the late run and in some years the low number of fish present may not even warrant an attempt. However, fish can still be caught with some time and patience in the traditional slots. In years when the run looks strong it is not unusual for anglers to bring in a limit of fish in a few hours of fishing. Action can never be described as much better than fair and unpredictable is probably more like it. Be prepared to put in some time on the water. A few fish are caught incidentally to king salmon fishing.

Late Run Reds: Although the lower Kenai is famous for its giant kings, it is the late run of red salmon that draws thousands of anglers to the riverbanks. Beginning in late June and early July a trickle of fish comes into the Kenai with fair numbers available by July 10. Right about July 15, give or take a couple of days, the first big push of salmon storms out of Cook Inlet and into the river. Typically the action goes from slow or lukewarm at best to phenomenal in a matter of just a day or so as the throng of reds move as a mass upstream. Fishing often stays very productive through the month of July and can be good even into the first ten days of August.

The August fishery, however, is not as consistent with more days being "misses" than "hits" and quite a few of the salmon present starting to show hints of spawning colors. By mid-month, the run is down to a trickle with small schools of fresh reds pushing into the Kenai only every now and then. As autumn rolls around, catches of reds is sporadic and the run considered over for the season. A very few bright salmon will, however, be present through September and even into October in some years.

The Kenai around *Eagle Rock* and above has more potential in many ways since the river is narrower and current flow better suited for red fishing but angling in holes further downstream carry merit as well.

Silver Salmon

After kings and reds, it is the silver salmon that is the most pursued sport fish on the lower Kenai. The lower holes and channels near tidewater are responsible for a great percentage of salmon caught and retained drainage-wide since the guide and local fleet operate mainly out of Soldotna. Unlike some sections of the middle Kenai, this part of the river has a good number of typical silver salmon lies such as calm sloughs and backwater that attract schools of fish.

Two runs of salmon are available during the season, one in July-August and another in September-October. Activity is not consistent in every month with some lull to be expected between runs or on days when the number of fish coming in is somewhat low, yet a few silvers always seem to be available.

Shore fishers here usually resort to using salmon roe clusters for maximum yield, the offering set stationary on the bottom about 10 to 15 feet from the riverbank. Small attractors can be combined with the bait for added effect. In addition, hardware such as spoons, spinners, and plugs take fish on regular basis, spinners probably outperforming anything else by a solid margin. Colorful streamers do catch some fish on outgoing and even low tides, preferably in the narrower portions of the river upstream of *Eagle Rock*.

Boaters have more freedom of choice and usually drift or anchor up in holes and runs using attractors with bait or casting spinners. Small- to medium-sized plugs either cast and retrieved or back-trolled can be deadly at times, a few anglers wrapping a fillet of sardine to the plugs' underside for added scent and effect.

The king hot spots earlier in the summer also produce their fair share of silvers, such as *Big Eddy*, but just about anywhere there is a portion of slow water on the edge of faster current can be productive. The stretch of river between *The Pillars* (RM 12.5) and *Poachers Cove* (RM 17.5) is popular. Additionally, *Cunningham Park* is a long-time favorite with shore anglers.

Early Run Silvers: An occasional silver is picked up incidentally starting as early as the second week of July by anglers targeting king salmon. By late month, the run is well on the way with each tide bringing in fish. As the king season ends, the guide fleet and pleasure boats will focus on these early silvers in detail with anglers usually finding good action or better by August 10. The traditional holes near tidewater turns on first, followed by locations upstream near the highway bridge a few days later. With the onset of September, the run quickly tapers off at which time the bulk of the run has advanced beyond the Soldotna area.

As is the case all over the lower Kenai River in even-numbered years, pink salmon can be a nuisance if targeting silvers. Try bait fished alone or with an attractor. Hardware such as spoons, spinners, and plugs are guaranteed plagued by pinks, at least during the month of August, but large, chrome spinners may attract less pinks and more silvers. Some anglers have become quite adept at catching silvers on a fly in likely holding areas and even sight fishing is possible to some degree, especially in quiet water such as sloughs and side channels or at the mouths of clearwater tributaries.

Late Run Silvers: This is the stronger of the two silver runs and also yields, on average, the largest fish. A few salmon arrive as early as late August or the first week of September yet it isn't until mid-September that anglers can expect to catch fish consistently. By October, anglers should pursue the bulk of the run farther upstream.

Fish continue to arrive on the tides through October and the season closure, with some bright specimens being in this part of the river even through December.

While bait and spinners are responsible for most catches, some fish may be enticed by large, colorful flies fished on an incoming or outgoing tide.

Many silver enthusiasts prefer fishing for these late-run fish, as the summer crowds are a thing of the past and the salmon abundant and big. Autumn silvers are broad and heavy, especially so coming in straight from the salt, and can even be confused with a small king salmon due to their sheer size. Weights of 12 to 16 pounds are very common with enough 18-pounders to make it interesting.

Pink Salmon

This portion of the Kenai lends perfectly for intercepting these fish in their prime, as they are only a few short miles from the ocean, the habitat perfect for multiple hookups, and the abundance factor definitely in favor of the angler. Fish on every cast is not only possible but also commonplace during the peak of the run on even-numbered years.

A small contingent of fish trickles through the lower river starting as early as in the latter part of June and stays subdued in numbers through most of July, seldom drawing any streak of attention at all. However, this changes around the last week of July as the pink run begins to build strength and by August 5 to 10 the water is completely immersed with hundreds of thousands of fish. Although the run stays heavy through the month and into early September, the number of fresh pinks diminishes rapidly after the 20th or 25th of August. A few semi-bright specimens are present until late September but are heavily outnumbered by their spawning brethren and thus almost impossible to catch.

Fish can be caught on any tide level though the best fishing is usually on a falling tide using medium to large sized spoons and spinners in combination of fluorescent orange or pink and metallic silver. Flies in the same colors are also very effective. Look for slightly calmer water than for reds, checking out sloughs, backwater channels, and the seams behind islands for concentrations of fish. Try more neutral colors if fish appear finicky.

Chum Salmon

A small run passes through area in July and August. Catches are very rare.

Trout/Char

Both rainbow trout and Dolly Varden are abundant in this section of the Kenai with the better fishing taking place upstream of the tidal zone in summer and early fall. There are relatively few rainbow trout downstream of *The Pillars* due to the influence of salt water and less than ideal conditions for feeding but are quite plentiful from the highway bridge in Soldotna and a few miles downstream. Anadromous Dolly Varden are far more common and considered abundant during the spring outmigration and again in mid-summer as fish return from the sea.

Rainbow Trout

A few specimens are present in late winter and early spring and anglers report catching trout incidentally to fishing for king salmon in May and June. The number of fish increases as the summer progresses and by July angler's success rate is good with the best catches in the river section nearest Soldotna. The bite remains steady through August and into early fall before diminishing as rainbows leave the area in pursuit of spawning salmon elsewhere in the Kenai.

As always, use egg imitations when salmon are running, switching to smolt and forage patterns early and late in the season.

Dolly Varden

As with trout not many anglers pursue char to any extent given the prolific runs of salmon simultaneously inhabiting the river. But unlike rainbows, there are good numbers of Dolly Varden to be found during two specific appearances; one in spring as the fish out-migrate to Cook Inlet, and another in mid-summer and fall as the char return from sea.

In late winter and early spring the first few char of the season move into the lower Kenai. The action for these out-migrating fish is fairly decent in May using smolt and forage imitation lures and flies; however, the better sport can be had in early to mid-July as the char return to the river after feeding at sea for several weeks. Some very good fishing for Dollies can be experienced starting in mid-summer and continuing into fall as the fish move in from Cook Inlet and begin to concentrate in areas where salmon tend to hold. July and August are both exceptional months using egg imitation flies and attractors (even flesh patterns) as the char focus on the spawn of late-run kings and pinks.

Come September, many Dolly Varden begin to move toward spawning areas in tributaries or in the middle reaches of the Kenai. Some decent action can still be had on the lower river but the farther upstream the better. By October the productivity for char in this area drops markedly before dying off with the onset of winter. A few specimens may be picked up late in the season using egg and flesh imitations as well as forage patterns.

Other

Occurrences of **round whitefish** and other species (except for salmon, trout, and char) are relatively rare. Non-sporting fish, such as smelt – or hooligan, are very abundant in the Kenai in May and early June and swim along the riverbank for easy harvest if so desired. Dip net is the preferred tool.

KENAI RIVER (RM 0 – 5)

Area: River mouth to Warren Ames Bridge.

Main Species: King, red, silver, and pink salmon and Dolly Varden.

Summary: This part of the lower Kenai is not particularly known as a very productive area to fish, the reputation probably owed to the fact that the water is often off-colored with silt from the muddy riverbanks, the slack or still nature of the current, and a lack of pronounced holes and runs for concentrating fish. However, at the peak of the respective salmon runs, anglers are able to find some worthwhile activity in an area predominantly utilized by dip netters. Fishing for pinks can be superb and silvers quite good on incoming and outgoing tides.

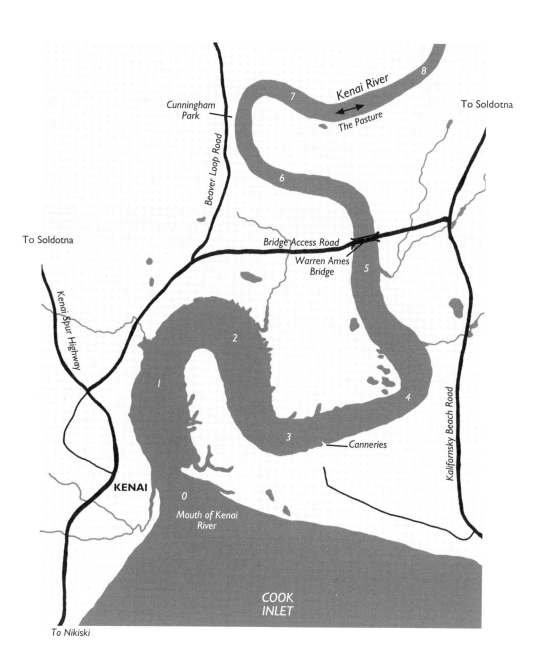

Description: At the terminus of Kenai River and Cook Inlet the river is approximately a quarter of a mile wide at high tide. Strong tidal movements influence this very last portion of river and the difference between high and low tide can be as much as 15 feet or more. When the tides are not pushing water in or out of the river, the current is minimal to almost completely still like a lake. Typically the water is not as clear as it is further upstream.

Surrounding area is quite developed, especially near the mouth at the city of Kenai, but there is still enough grassland and woods to negate an urban presence.

General Access: By road and boat. Bridge Access Road, which runs between Beaver Loop Road and Kalifornsky Beach Road, is the primary way to reach lower end of river. Boats can be launched from here or in locations further upstream.

Access Point A: *Warren Ames Bridge* is one mile S of Beaver Loop Road or 0.5 mile north of Kalifornsky Beach Road on Bridge Access Road. Parking and restrooms.

Access Point B: Access road heading west to river located approximately 0.25 mile south of the junction of Beaver Loop Road and Bridge Access Road. Kenai City boat launch, parking, and restrooms available. Launch is in tidal area and can be unusable during very low tides.

Fishing Opportunities

Restrictions: Species-specific restrictions are in effect (consult ADF&G regulations).

King Salmon

Rating: Poor to fair at best.

Regulatory Season: January 1 – July 31.

Timing: April 20 – July 31, peak June 1 – 10 (early run) and July 10 – 25 (late run).

Size: Average 20 to 40 pounds (early run) and 30 to 50 pounds (late run), kings in the 80- to 100-pound range a possibility.

Tip: Only try for kings in this area if the run is at a peak and sonar counts are indicating good number of fish heading upstream. Attempt to find schools of kings moving in and out with the tides, hitting the run peak.

Red Salmon

Rating: Poor (early run), fair to good (late run).

Timing: May 10 – October 5, peak June 5 – 15 (early run) and July 15 – 31 (late run).

Size: Average 6 to 7 pounds, some larger fish up to 11 pounds (early run); 6 to 8 pounds, some larger fish to 12 pounds. Catches of reds up to 14 pounds or more possible.

Tip: One or two fish may be hooked during peak of run as the tide goes out. Use large, colorful flies. Try only if there are signs of fish being present in good numbers. Large orange, chartreuse, or pink yarn flies work as tide goes out. Some anglers have experienced luck using small clusters of roe fished stationary on the bottom about 10 to 15 feet from shore.

Silver Salmon
Rating: Fair to good.
Regulatory Season: July 1 – October 31.
Timing: July 5 – October 31, peak August 10 – 25 (early run), September 10 – 25 (late run).
Size: Average 6 to 10 pounds, some larger fish to 14 pounds (early run); 8 to 14 pounds, to 18 pounds not unusual. A very few trophy specimens up to 22 pounds or more may be present in September.
Tip: Clusters of salmon roe fished on the bottom catch the majority of fish. Large flashy spinners with fluorescent colors and clusters of salmon roe fished alone or with an attractor on the bottom catch fish.

Pink Salmon
Rating: Excellent on even-numbered years, poor on odd.
Timing: June 15 – September 25, peak August 5 – 25.
Size: Average 3 to 6 pounds, some fish to 8-9 pounds. Trophy specimens up to 10-11 pounds or more possible.
Tip: Pinks can be taken anywhere on the river from the bridge downstream to the mouth. Place lure or fly into the green band of mid-river, avoiding the silt along the shoreline.

Dolly Varden
Rating: Good.
Timing: Late March – mid-October, peak month of May and early July – mid-August.
Size: Average 10 to 20 inches, some larger fish to 30 inches and 10-12 pounds. Trophy specimens up to 15 pounds possible in this area in July and August.
Tip: If using hardware, employ lures and flies with chrome and fluorescent colors. Bait is most effective.

Other Species: (CS,RT,RW).

KENAI RIVER (RM 5 – 12.5)
Area: Warren Ames Bridge to below The Pillars.

Main Species: King, red, silver, and pink salmon, rainbow trout, and Dolly Varden.

Summary: This is the river section that fishing really begins to pick up. Salmon fishing is excellent in these parts, especially upstream of Cunningham Park, and sea-run Dolly Varden are plentiful in mid-summer. Some of the best spots on the whole river for incoming kings (in June and July) and silvers (August and September) can be found here. Red salmon action can be phenomenal in July, pink salmon likewise in August in even-numbered years. During the peak in-migrations of reds and pinks it is possible to observe hundreds of fish porpoising all at the same time in the slack water of high tide. Guided activity is busy during the whole season and many local anglers fish this area extensively.

The best fishing often coincide with the tides but salmon and char may enter the river at any flood stage. Kings have a tendency to follow the main center channel, while

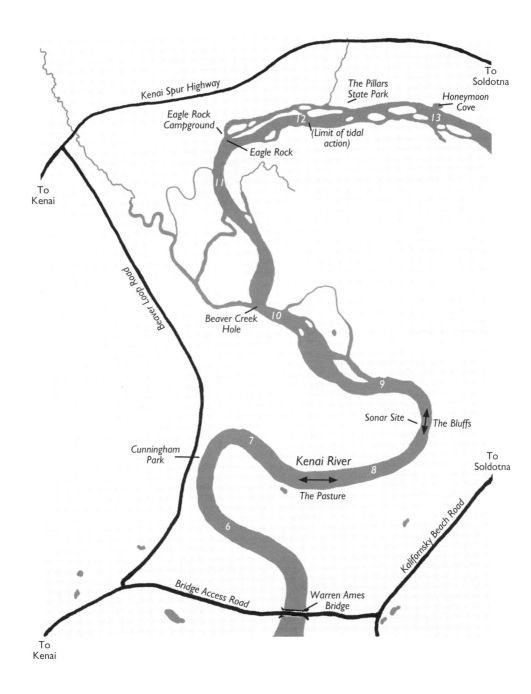

To
Soldotna

Kenai Spur Highway

*The Pillars
State Park*

*Eagle Rock
Campground*

12

*Honeymoon
Cove*

13

*(Limit of tidal
action)*

Eagle Rock

To
Kenai

11

Beaver Loop Road

*Beaver Creek
Hole*

10

9

Sonar Site *The Bluffs*

*Cunningham
Park*

7

Kenai River

To
Soldotna

8

The Pasture

6

Kalifornsky Beach Road

Bridge Access Road

*Warren Ames
Bridge*

To
Kenai

other salmon species spread out more depending on the water level. On incoming, high, and outgoing tides, salmon may be found distributed throughout the water column from a few feet of the bank to mid-river. On low tide, the fish (except for kings) begin to concentrate slightly more along the shoreline.

Description: The tidal range varies from some 10 feet at the Warren Ames Bridge to mere inches at river mile 12.5. Several classic holes and runs are located between the latter and the mouth of Beaver Creek at river mile 10.2. The riverbanks, in particular from Eagle Creek down, consist of clay and leaches out during tidal movements, creating streaks of mud in the shallows along the shore that can hamper the fishing somewhat. High tides create substantial slack water throughout much of area.

There are some private properties along the north shore of the Kenai, on the bluffs overlooking the river. The south shore is largely grassland and brush, known as the Kenai River Flats. Caribou are frequently spotted.

General Access: By road and boat. The Kenai Spur Highway, along with offshoot Beaver Loop Road, are the main arteries of access for both boat and/or shore anglers. Most anglers using boats put in at Eagle Rock (RM 11.4) or drift/motor down from points further upstream.

Access Point A: *Cunningham Park* – access via Beaver Loop Road from Kenai Spur Highway or Bridge Access Road. South on gravel road leading to City of Kenai park area and river. Developed parking, picnic tables, and restrooms.

Access Point B: *Eagle Rock Campground* – MP 5.1 Kenai Spur Highway. West on Eagle Rock Drive 0.4 mile to river. Parking, limited camping, boat launch, and restrooms.

Fishing Opportunities

Restrictions: Species-specific restrictions are in effect (consult ADF&G regulations).

King Salmon
Rating: Good (early run) and good to excellent (late run).
Regulatory Season: January 1 – July 31.
Timing: April 20 – July 31, peak June 5 – 15 (early run) and July 10 – 25 (late run).
Size: Average 20 to 40 pounds (early run) and 30 to 50 pounds (late run), kings in the 80- to 100-pound range a possibility.
Tip: Prior to mid-June, avoid lures with too much chrome, as kings are largely immune to the flash as the river is filled with millions of silvery smelt. Anglers trying large attractors in combination with salmon roe clusters do best.

Red Salmon
Rating: Poor (early run) and good to excellent (late run).
Timing: May 10 – October 5, peak June 5 – 15 (early run) and July 15 – 31 (late run).
Size: Average 6 to 7 pounds, some larger fish up to 11 pounds (early run); 6 to 8 pounds, some larger fish to 12 pounds. Catches of reds up to 14 pounds or more possible.
Tip: Use large, colorful flies in spots that provide for fish concentration. Expect good fishing on days when 20,000 or more reds head upstream with excellent action on

40,000 fish days.

Silver Salmon

Rating: Excellent.

Regulatory Season: July 1 – October 31.

Timing: July 5 – October 31, peak August 10 – 25 (early run) and September 10 – 25 (late run).

Size: Average 6 to 10 pounds, some larger fish to 14 pounds (early run); 8 to 14 pounds, to 18 pounds not unusual. A very few trophy specimens up to 22 pounds or more may be present in September.

Tip: Clusters of salmon roe fished on or along the bottom catch the majority of fish. Large flashy spinners with fluorescent colors and clusters of salmon roe fished alone or with an attractor on the bottom catch fish.

Pink Salmon

Rating: Excellent on even-numbered years, poor on odd.

Timing: June 15 – September 25, peak August 5 – 25.

Size: Average 3 to 6 pounds, some fish to 8-9 pounds. Trophy specimens up to 10-11 pounds or more possible.

Tip: Make long casts on all tide levels except low tide when fish are close to shore.

Rainbow Trout

Rating: Fair.

Regulatory Season: June 11 – May 1.

Timing: Mid-March – mid-October, peak mid-July – early September.

Size: Average 10 to 20 inches, up to 15 pounds or more.

Tip: Try small chrome spoons and spinners and forage pattern flies early in the season, egg imitations later on.

Dolly Varden

Rating: Good.

Timing: Late March – mid-October, peak month of May and early July – late August.

Size: Average 10 to 20 inches, some larger fish to 30 inches and 10-12 pounds. Trophy specimens up to 15 pounds possible in this area in July and August.

Tip: Fish the slack water on the tides from May into July, moving upstream into more current in August and September.

Other Species: (CS,RW).

KENAI RIVER (RM 12.5 – 21)

Area: The Pillars to Sterling Highway Bridge in Soldotna.

Main Species: King, red, silver, and pink salmon, rainbow trout, and Dolly Varden.

Summary: This is the most famed stretch of the Kenai for salmon fishing. Excellent king, red, silver, and pink salmon action is the norm from June to October and a great many guides on the river focus their efforts here. Expect crowds of boats on the

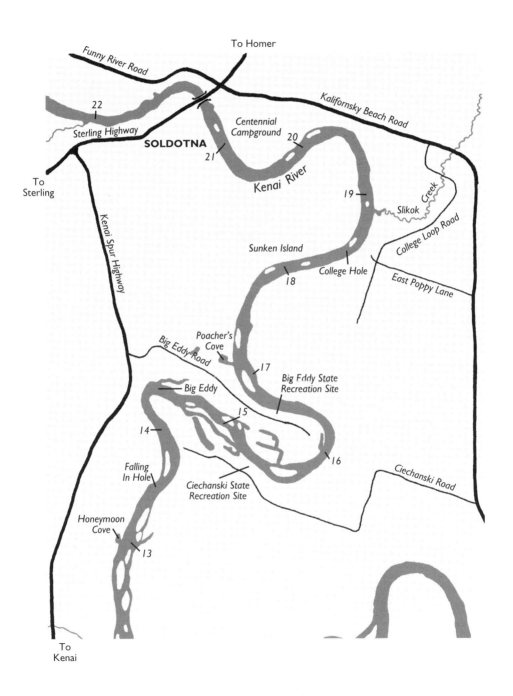

To Homer

Funny River Road

Kalifornsky Beach Road

22

Sterling Highway

Centennial
Campground

SOLDOTNA

20

21

To
Sterling

Kenai River

Slikok Creek

19

Kenai Spur Highway

College Loop Road

Sunken Island

East Poppy Lane

College Hole

18

Poacher's
Cove

Big Eddy Road

17

Big Eddy State
Recreation Site

Big Eddy

15

14

16

Falling
In Hole

Ciechanski State
Recreation Site

Ciechanski Road

Honeymoon
Cove

13

To
Kenai

weekends and whenever the salmon are running thick, this being especially true during the king season in June and July. Coinciding with the king runs is the huge showing of late-run red salmon and, later in the summer and fall, a large number of silvers stack up in holes and runs throughout the lower river.

Their salmon counterparts often overshadow rainbow trout and Dolly Varden, yet do provide some good to excellent angling opportunities in mid- to late summer.

Description: The Kenai meanders to a fair degree in this stretch with numerous deep holes and runs from the highway bridge in Soldotna downstream to tidewater. Despite settlements along the river, there is still an abundance of vegetation and several islands are situated in the main current.

Boaters need to be careful in this section of river in spring and early summer as low water levels often partially expose big rocks or boulders and sandbars that would otherwise be well under water later in the season.

Of the entire mainstem Kenai River, this area is without a doubt the most populated. Private and commercial properties line the banks in many places with a good portion of the river's sport fishing guides located here. There are also a number of private campgrounds and lodges to be found.

General Access: By road and boat. Both the Kenai Spur Highway and Kalifornsky Beach Road off the Sterling Highway offer many great access points for boaters as well as shore anglers.

Kenai Spur Highway

The Kenai Spur Highway begins at the intersection at MP 94.1 Sterling Highway in Soldotna.

Access Point A: The Pillars State Park – MP 4.2 Kenai Spur Highway. West on Silver Salmon Drive 0.5 mile to river. Parking, limited camping, boat launch, and restrooms.

Access Point B: Big Eddy State Recreation Site – MP 1.8 Kenai Spur Highway. West on Big Eddy Road 1.4 mile to recreation site on left. Parking, restrooms.

Sterling Highway

Highway crosses river in Soldotna.

Access Point C: Kenai River Bridge – MP 96.0 Sterling Highway. Northwest on short access road to Soldotna Visitor Information Center and large parking area. Trail leads 200 yards to river. Developed boardwalk present.

Kalifornsky Beach Road

The Kalifornsky Beach Road begins at MP 96.1 Sterling Highway at the intersection just south of the Soldotna Bridge.

Access Point D: Centennial Campground – MP 22.1 Kalifornsky Beach Road. North on access road at sign 0.8 mile to campground and river. Developed campground, parking, boat launch, and restrooms.

Access Point E: Slikok Creek State Recreation Site – MP 20.5 Kalifornsky Beach Road. North on College Loop Road 0.5 mile, right on West Chugach Drive 0.4 mile, left on South Katmai Street 0.3 mile to access road on left and recreation site. Parking, picnic tables, restrooms. Trail leads 0.25 mile to mouth of Slikok Creek and the Kenai River.

Access Point F: Ciechanski State Recreation Site – MP 17.5 Kalifornsky Beach Road. East on Ciechanski Road 2.6 miles to split in road, continue right on Porter Road 0.4

mile to access road on right, 0.2 mile to recreation site on right. Parking, picnic tables, restrooms, and boat docks.

Fishing Opportunities

Restrictions: Species-specific restrictions are in effect. Seasonal and area closures concerning fishing from boats are in place for the following locations: Centennial (approximately RM 20 to Sterling Hwy. Bridge) and mouth of Slikok Creek (consult ADF&G regulations).

King Salmon

Rating: Good (early run) and good to excellent (late run).
Regulatory Season: January 1 – July 31.
Timing: April 25 – July 31, peak June 10 – 20 (early run) and July 15 – 31 (late run).
Size: Average 20 to 40 pounds (early run) and 30 to 50 pounds (late run), kings in the 80- to 100-pound range a possibility. The state/world record of 97 pounds came from the early run on May 17.
Tip: Back-trolling medium-sized plugs in the tidewater holes is best early in the run, hitting upstream holes closer to Soldotna starting in mid-June. Attractors with a cluster of roe is the number one king killer on the Kenai, followed by large plugs in various fluorescent/metallic hues.

Red Salmon

Rating: Poor to fair (early run) and excellent (late run).
Timing: May 10 – October 5, peak June 5 – 15 (early run) and peak July 15 – 31 (late run).
Size: Average 6 to 7 pounds, some larger fish up to 11 pounds (early run); 6 to 8 pounds, some larger fish to 12 pounds. Catches of reds up to 14 pounds or more possible.
Tip: Work holes and runs just upstream of tidewater following high tides and scout areas further up towards bridge later on. Expect good fishing or better on days when 20,000 or more reds head upstream.

Silver Salmon

Rating: Excellent.
Regulatory Season: July 1 – October 31.
Timing: July 5 – October 31, peak August 10 – 25 (early run) and September 10 – 25 (late run).
Size: Average 6 to 10 pounds, some larger fish to 14 pounds (early run); 8 to 14 pounds, to 18 pounds not unusual. A very few trophy specimens up to 22 pounds or more may be present in September.
Tip: Hit the water at daybreak or coinciding with tidal movements. Best action is at dawn but can be good during mid-day following a high tide if skies are overcast.

Pink Salmon

Rating: Excellent on even-numbered years, poor on odd.
Timing: June 15 – September 25, peak August 5 – 25.
Size: Average 3 to 6 pounds, some fish to 8-9 pounds. Trophy specimens up to 10-11 pounds or more possible.
Tip: Tying into a fish on every cast in common at peak of run. Use single hooks.

Rainbow Trout

Rating: Good.
Regulatory Season: June 11 – May 1.
Timing: Mid-March – mid-October, peak mid-July – early September.
Size: Average 10 to 20 inches, up to 15 pounds or more.
Tip: Some fish are available all the way downstream to The Pillars but most rainbows stick to river mile 15 or above.

Dolly Varden

Rating: Good to excellent.
Timing: Late March – mid-November, peak May and mid-July – early September.
Size: Average 10 to 20 inches, some larger fish to 30 inches and 10-12 pounds. Trophy specimens up to 15 pounds possible in this area in July and August.
Tip: Fish above tidewater in May and July, moving upstream closer to Soldotna in August and September.

Other Species: RW,(CS).

MIDDLE KENAI RIVER

Description

The middle section of Kenai River is accounted for being from the outlet of Skilak Lake downstream to the Sterling Highway Bridge in Soldotna. Parts of the south bank and the first few miles of river below the lake is believed to be the most remote area of the mainstem Kenai with very few access roads, little to no settlement (outside the communities of Soldotna and Sterling), and not too many other anglers even during the height of the fishing season. The stream gradient between the lake and Naptowne Rapids near Sterling (10.5 river miles) is 3.3 feet per mile, which translates to minimal current.

The 19.4-mile portion of the Kenai from Naptowne Rapids to the Sterling Highway Bridge in Soldotna is much different in characteristics. Apart from being more populated, the river does not meander nearly as much and the speed of the current picks up substantially, with stream gradient being 5.4 feet per mile.

Wildlife such as moose, eagles, bears, waterfowl, and other animal species are a common sight along this stretch of river, primarily along the south bank and areas of Kenai Keys to Skilak Lake outlet. The largest concentration of bald eagle in Southcentral Alaska can be observed here in late fall and winter as several hundred birds feed on a late run of silver salmon.

Early in the season (May into June), the Kenai River usually flows very low with many spots that can make boat travel difficult. By July the volume increases dramatically and peaks in August. Water levels drop again toward the end of September and October.

Access

There are some points of access on the middle Kenai, most being privately owned, but at least five are state/government run. Many guide and lodge outfits on the river have land in this area and launch trips from their properties at least part of the season, yet will allow invited guests to fish off the banks of their land as well. Fishing from shore is possible in many areas but public roadside access to them is mostly limited to locations in and around the communities of Soldotna and Sterling.

Boat access is by far the most convenient choice when exploring the middle section, with launches anywhere between Soldotna and the lower campground near the Skilak Lake outlet. Some of the best holes on this part of the river are only accessible by boat.

Fishing

The fishing on the middle section of the river can be superb for salmon and other species such as trout and char. Angling pressure is only moderate and cannot be compared to the intense fisheries taking place on the Russian River or lower Kenai River during the height of the salmon runs. There is also significantly less guided activity here because of remote logistics.

Silver and red salmon fishing is often fantastic and the rainbow trout and Dolly Varden in this river section provide some of the best action anywhere on the Kenai. As a matter of fact, the stretch of river between Naptowne Rapids and Skilak Lake is known for producing the largest trophy trout and char in the drainage and can compete, pound for pound, even with the remote fly-in fisheries of southwestern Alaska.

Chapter Contents

The following are the game fish present, the various sections of the Middle Kenai River drainage, and the page number in which more detailed information can be found.

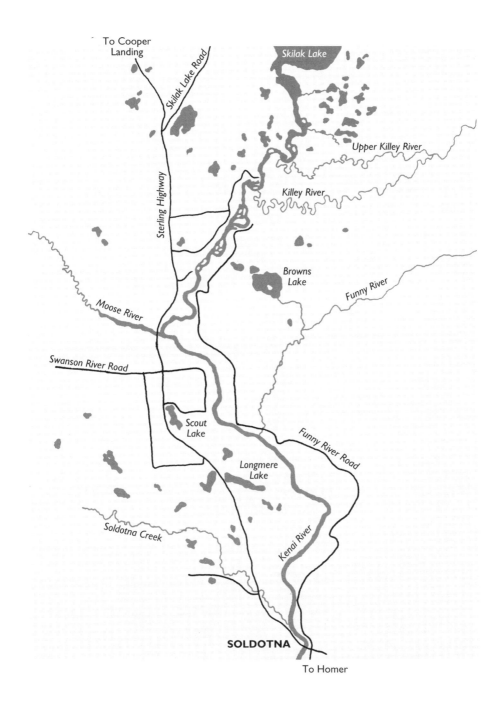

Trout/Char

Rainbow Trout	138
Dolly Varden	138

Other Species 139

Sections	*Species*	
Kenai River (River Mile 21 – 24)	KS,RS,SS,PS,RT,DV	139
Kenai River (River Mile 27 – 39)	KS,RS,SS,PS,RT,DV	142
Kenai River (River Mile 39 – 45.9)	KS,RS,SS,PS,RT,DV	147
Kenai River (River Mile 45.9 – 50)	KS,RS,SS,PS,RT,DV	150

TIMING:

Middle Kenai River

FISH	JAN	FEB	MAR	APR	MAY	JUN	JUL	AUG	SEP	OCT	NOV	DEC
KS												
RS												
SS												
PS												
CS												
RT												
DV												
RW												

Species Information

Salmon

King, red, silver, and pink salmon are all available in large numbers during the season from June into October. Boat anglers mainly target kings and silvers, while reds and pinks principally constitute a riverbank fishery. Multiple runs of each species (except pinks) yield opportunity that lasts for months.

King Salmon

Far fewer anglers look for kings in this part of the river compared to the lower section; however, action can still be great if possessing the knowledge of where concentrations of fish may be found consistently. Some locals and guides operate here later in the season when salmon are more plentiful and crowds not nearly as dense as in the more famous hot spots such as *The Pillars* and *Eagle Rock*. This stretch of the Kenai can probably be described as the most relaxed king water within the drainage in terms of angler participation.

Anglers fishing from the riverbank for kings report sporadic success at *Swiftwater*, *Morgan's Hole*, and the mouth of *Moose River* (see chapter 1, page 24).

The king fishery here is quite different from that of the lower river as the river meanders far less, making holes and runs less pronounced.

Early Run Kings: A few scouts will enter the area in early May, the run slowly building strength into June. The bulk of fish arrives when water flows increase substantially (about the third week of June), thus aiding upstream migration. Compared to the lower river where fish are available in abundance for several weeks, this section of water has a much more condensed window of opportunity based on when the peak number of kings finally comes through and the physical condition of the fish. Many fish in the latter part of June and July are blushing rapidly since they have been in the river for quite some time but there will be some bright ones present as well. A good portion of the early run continues to hold in the mainstem Kenai until ripe (in mid-July) before moving into tributary streams to spawn.

A large number of early-run kings traditionally stage in or near the mouths of Funny River and Killey River (important spawning streams), especially from late June to mid-July, hence the current regulatory closure of the immediate areas (consult ADF&G regulations) in order to protect these fish from being targeted during the coinciding late-run king fishery.

Late Run Kings: The late run will trickle slowly into the middle Kenai, starting in early July, overlapping partially with the early return of kings. The really productive season is highly abbreviated as much of the run will hold in the lower river before ascending into the middle stretch of the Kenai. Anglers enjoy the best action in mid- and late July, giving about two weeks of worthwhile opportunity before the season closes on August 1. As is the case with early-run fish, a good portion of the late run will be stained upon arriving in this area.

King fishers should also be aware that during the month of July – although designated a late-run month by regulation – there are still many salmon present from the first run and voluntary catch-and-release is encouraged. A good number of second run fish will continue to be present through August but this portion of the Kenai is not subjugated to emergency openings extending the fishery beyond the current closure date. Anglers trying for silvers in late summer and fall occasionally hook kings as the middle river represents a main spawning area for the species.

The best stretch of water to hook late-run kings is between Soldotna and Naptowne Rapids.

Red Salmon

The relatively fast current of the middle Kenai lends perfectly to top-notch fishing conditions for red salmon. Despite limited shore access, except for in the Soldotna area, many anglers use a boat to reach ideal locations. The early run does not provide nearly as much excitement as the later run in terms of salmon available and the number of anglers reflects this. Without a doubt, July is the prime month to be fishing here for reds.

Colorful streamers and yarn flies are preferred tackle. The reds here, as anywhere else on the Kenai, travel close to shore and thus long casts are not necessary. Orange and red are good colors, as is chartreuse.

Popular hot spots to try for reds include the area just upstream of the *Kenai River Bridge* in Soldotna, including *Swiftwater*, the *Ball Fields*, *Soldotna Creek Park*, and behind the *Kenai River Science Center*. Higher up in the drainage, *Morgan's Landing* and the mouth of *Moose River* are both good bets. The braided channels around Kenai Keys between Naptowne Rapids and Skilak Lake can be fantastic fishing, such as upper and lower *Torpedo Hole*.

Early Run Reds: A smattering of fish begin arriving in the latter half of May with the bulk of the early run rapidly passing through in mid-June. Anglers able to locate good structure often walk away with a limit of fish but it usually takes time and experience for consistent success. Most anywhere that produces good catches of red salmon later in the season will also hold fish in early summer but because the first run of reds is so small compared to the July run, action is usually spotty at best. Some early fish continue to appear into July and are eventually overtaken by the late run.

Late Run Reds: The area from about a mile downstream of the Sterling Highway bridge in Soldotna to approximately the Kenai Keys is considered to be the best water in the entire drainage for late-run red salmon. It is estimated that tens of thousands of fish are caught every year in this stretch of the Kenai River, most of them during a short span of time in July.

The late run begins around the first of July but stays largely subdued until around mid-month when the bulk of the run charges into the river. Action typically is superb through July and may in some years be very good into the first week of August. Relatively few fish will spawn downstream of Naptowne Rapids and thus most salmon are passing through headed for the outlet of Skilak Lake and upper reaches of the Kenai and clearwater tributaries. As sudden as the fishery began it ends; however, a decreasing number of fresh reds will be present during the remainder of August and into September.

The run is comprised of several big pulses of salmon and a sonar unit on the lower river monitors these pulses. At least 20,000 fish per day into the Kenai are needed for the fishing to be good or better. Fishing may be slow on some days between pulses, even during what otherwise would be the peak time of the run. Anglers are advised to tune in to local media outlets for latest updates in run strength.

Silver Salmon

The stretch of water from Soldotna up to Naptowne Rapids has a multitude of holding water for silvers yet very few of them have any official names. There are, however, a few landmark locations worth noting that produce excellent opportunity, such as the *Funny River* confluence, *Morgan's Hole*, and the mouth of *Moose River*, and a great many additional "pockets" of river are present where salmon stack up.

Upstream of Naptowne Rapids, the river begins to change appearance and take on more ideal structural conditions for finding big schools of silvers. Sloughs, backwater channels, and islands are prevalent for several miles up to the mouth of Upper Killey River. Also, the confluence area of main Killey River is exceptional for salmon.

There are two runs of silvers in the middle Kenai, the first in July-August and the second in September-October. Both provide superb action during the peak of the runs.

Boaters definitely have the edge over anglers fishing from the riverbank as the majority of really productive silver holes and runs are not accessible from the road. Spinners in chrome with blue, green, or chartreuse accents are used extensively while clusters of salmon roe fished in a variety of ways such as stationary on the bottom or drifted along with slack current is just as effective. During the late run, lures with sharper colors in orange and red also work very well. Some anglers prefer to use smaller plugs.

Sight fishing is sometimes possible and presenting a fly to individual fish is a challenge. Near Soldotna where the current is strong, silvers often travel close to shore and salmon can be spotted holding near structure. Higher up in the drainage, above Naptowne Rapids into the Kenai Keys, silvers become very concentrated and water conditions conducive to fishing for them.

Early Run Silvers: Only a couple of weeks after the mass of late-run red salmon have passed through the area, the early run of silvers arrive in force. Having been present in very small numbers ever since around mid-July or so, the second week of August promises the first good push of salmon accompanied by activity that traditionally lasts through most of the month. By Labor Day, however, the run is beginning to wane yet a significant number of fish can still be located near the mouths of Killey and Upper Killey rivers. Some stragglers from this run will continue to arrive well into autumn but are eventually overtaken in numbers by the late silver run.

It can be argued that the zenith of silver fishing takes place on odd-numbered years, the reason being the deluge of pink salmon that completely flood the river on even-numbered years, snapping at any piece of offering tossed into the water. When pinks are present, use salmon roe clusters (pinks do not hit bait with any vigor). If no pinks are to be found, the use of spinners and flies become a reliable option.

Late Run Silvers: The mainstem silvers begin to arrive in late August, in-migration peaking during the second half of September, with decent numbers of fish available into October in waters upstream of Sterling. Persistent fishers will still be able to find a good number of bright silvers until the season closure on November 1, particularly in the Kenai Keys area and near the outlet of Skilak Lake. A few fresh specimens are known to trickle in through December and January or even later but remain inaccessible to anglers by regulation.

Salmon in the 15- to 18-pound range are not unusual and on some days anglers are able to land several such fish during an outing. An exceptional silver is a fish over 20 pounds and record-class specimens (up to 24 pounds) are a possibility.

The habits of these salmon are slightly different from those of the early-run. While early fish often hug the shoreline the second run of silvers are often more spread out and may occupy the main current as well. Yet the best autumn holes are usually the same ones as earlier in the season.

Pink Salmon

Excellent potential exists on the middle Kenai for pink salmon. Although the river flows a little too swift in some places for productive angling, there are many spots that contain huge numbers of holding fish. Some fish come through in July or even earlier but the run essentially does not begin in earnest until the first week of August. By mid-month the salmon are distributed throughout much of the river and catching them is not a problem. Some parts of the Kenai may appear clogged with spawning fish in September yet there always seems to be a few semi-bright specimens mixed in this late in the season.

Popular locations include *Swiftwater*, *Soldotna Creek Park*, the mouth of *Funny River*, *Morgan's Hole*, and the *Moose River* confluence. Excellent action may be had in countless other areas as well.

Chum Salmon

Very rare species in the Kenai. Known to pass through the middle river in July and August.

Trout/Char

Though some fish are available in spring and early summer, things really do not get going until July when the late runs of king and red salmon move into the area. Rainbow trout and Dolly Varden are abundant and some specimens reach trophy proportions, particularly in the upper reaches above Naptowne Rapids. While the former two species are numerous, another species – **lake trout** – is not a common catch, except at the outlet of the lake. Smaller specimens of these char may be hooked in the first couple of miles of river downstream of Skilak Lake. Rare encounters of **steelhead trout** are reported here in late fall.

Rainbow Trout

A very large component of the total Kenai population of rainbow trout migrates out of Skilak Lake into the middle river in spring, destined for spawning tributaries such as Killey, Funny, and Moose rivers. A few trout may be available to anglers before the spring closure on May 2 but the better bet would be to focus on the species later on in the season.

Fishing is productive after the June 11 opener upstream of the Funny River but usually does not turn on fully until July further downstream near Soldotna. With a lack of angling pressure for so long and the fish just having completed reproduction and ready to engage in the seasonal feeding frenzy, the action can be very good. With the advent of salmon arriving, the action spikes and stays hot through late summer into fall.

Arguably one of the best portions of water in the Kenai drainage for trophy trout action is located in the ensuing four miles downstream of Skilak Lake to the confluence area of Upper Killey River. A fair number of rainbows weighing 15 to 18 pounds have been caught and released here with notable specimens exceeding 20 pounds present.

Dry flies can yield fish at the mouths of clearwater tributaries and in calmer areas of the mainstem but the standard fare for catching trout consistently in the Kenai would be to use egg imitation flies and attractors, changing to flesh patterns later in the season. In spring and again from late fall through winter, forage patterns work best. Spinners and plugs meant for kings and silvers sometimes catch very large rainbows.

The fishing starts to slow down in October and is essentially over for the year by December, except for the stretch of river just downstream of Skilak Lake where trout are available in limited numbers all winter into spring feeding on a late-spawning run of silver salmon.

Dolly Varden

Superb char fishing is possible in this portion of the Kenai. Many anglers tend to focus their efforts on Dolly Varden with the influx of salmon into the area but some decent action may be had even before then.

Anadromous char migrate downstream in May, bound for feeding grounds in Cook Inlet, yet a portion of the population will remain in freshwater through summer. Smolt and forage patterns lures and flies work well at this time, but as the fish return to the Kenai and salmon begin to arrive and spawn, egg imitations are superior. The usual lies are good for char, including where anglers clean fish in the river. In fall, flesh patterns are good. Forage imitations do well in September and October and later. Spinners can be deadly, especially the more monotone, metallic ones.

The majority of Dolly Varden has vacated the middle Kenai by December, over-wintering in Skilak Lake and the first few miles of river below.

The Soldotna to Sterling area is very productive early in the season and as long as salmon can be found in abundance. Later on, and for trophy-sized char, the river section upstream of Naptowne Rapids is popular. The Kenai Keys is known to produce Dollies upward of 5 to 10 pounds on a consistent basis with a few specimens in the 15-pound range (20-pound char have been reported).

Other Species
A fair population of **round whitefish** is present during summer and fall. **Northern pike** reported to be in the area and a very few specimens have been confirmed caught.

MIDDLE KENAI RIVER
Includes all waters of the mainstem Kenai River from the outlet of Skilak Lake downstream to the Sterling Highway Bridge in Soldotna.

KENAI RIVER (RM 21 – 24)
Area: Soldotna.

Main Species: KS,RS,SS,PS,RT,DV.

Summary: The peak month of angling activity is July when some one million red salmon stream through the area. Some guides operate here for kings and silvers but the main fishery is directed toward reds, of which awesome opportunities abound. Hot spots are easily accessible from the road in and around the town of Soldotna, the fast river current lending perfectly to catching migrating red salmon. Wherever some piece of slack water can be found, expect large concentrations of other salmon species and fish such as trout and char. These calmer spots are often hot for silvers and pinks and even a few kings may be taken from shore.

Description: This small portion of Kenai River flows relatively fast with very few pronounced holes or pools to speak of. Expect very heavy crowds of anglers in all of the road-accessible locations during the peak of the late run of red salmon in mid-late July.

General Access: By road and boat. There are about half a dozen points of public river access in this area with several more private institutions available as well.
Access Point A: Kenai River Bridge – MP 95.9 Sterling Highway. Private campground on east side of bridge has bank access to river.
Access Point B: The Ball Fields – MP 94.4 Sterling Highway. Southeast on access road next to State of Alaska Maintenance Station short distance to parking area on right. Trails lead down to river.

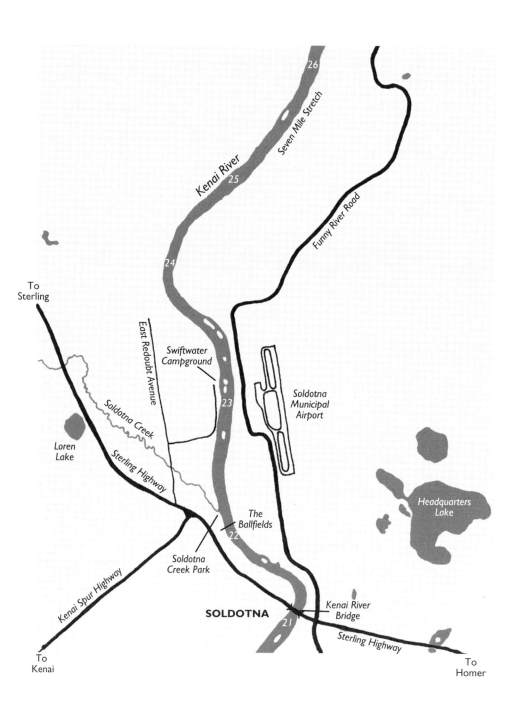

Access Point C: *Soldotna Creek Park* – MP 94.4 Sterling Highway. Southeast on access road next to State of Alaska Maintenance Station and proceed to the left 0.2 mile to park. Parking, picnic tables, and restrooms. Trails lead 200 yards to river and mouth of Soldotna Creek. Developed boardwalk present.

Access Point D: *Swiftwater Campground* – MP 94.1 Sterling Highway. East on Redoubt Avenue 0.6 mile, right on Griffin Avenue 0.8 mile, right on access road leading to campground and river. Parking, camping, and restrooms. Trails lead to river. Developed boardwalk present.

Funny River Road

The Funny River Road begins at MP 96.1 Sterling Highway at the intersection just south of the Soldotna Bridge.

Access Point E: *Kenai River Science Center* – MP 1.7 Funny River Road. Left on access road to science center parking lot. Trail leads 150 yards to river. Camping available just west of center.

Fishing Opportunities

Restrictions: King salmon fishing prohibited August 1 – December 31, silver salmon November 1 – June 30, and rainbow trout May 2 – June 10. Additional restrictions are in effect (consult ADF&G regulations).

King Salmon

Rating: Good.

Regulatory Season: January 1 – July 31.

Timing: May 1 – July 31, peak June 15 – 30 (early run) and July 15 – 31 (late run).

Size: Average 20 to 40 pounds (early run) and 30 to 50 pounds (late run), kings in the 80- to 100-pound range a possibility.

Tip: Drifting, back-trolling, and back-bouncing are all effective techniques here. Back-bouncing attractors with bait is very effective.

Red Salmon

Rating: Fair (early run) to excellent (late run).

Timing: May 10 – October 5, peak June 5 – 15 (early run) and July 15 – August 5 (late run).

Size: Average 6 to 7 pounds, some larger fish up to 11 pounds (early run); 6 to 8 pounds, up to 14 pounds (late run). Catches of reds up to 15 pounds or more possible.

Tip: Try during peak of run only, scouting suitable spots for signs of fish. Look for activity such as breaching or jumping fish. Do not waste time in water that appears void of life.

Silver Salmon

Rating: Good to excellent.

Regulatory Season: July 1 – October 31.

Timing: July 10 – October 31, peak August 15 – 31 (early run), September 15 – 30 (late run).

Size: Average 6 to 10 pounds, some larger fish to 14 pounds (early run); 8 to 14 pounds, up to 18 pounds not unusual (late run). A very few trophy specimens exceeding 22 pounds may be present in late September.

Tip: Look for salmon close to shore in fast-moving sections of river, search out calmer portions for schooling silvers.

Pink Salmon

Rating: Good to excellent (even years); poor (odd years).
Timing: June 25 – September 25, peak August 10 – 25.
Size: Average 3 to 6 pounds, some fish to 8-9 pounds. Trophy specimens up to 10-11 pounds or more possible.
Tip: Pinks usually give themselves away by breaching the surface, this being particularly the case in spots where many fish are schooling up.

Rainbow Trout

Rating: Good.
Regulatory Season: June 11 – May 1.
Timing: Mid-March – late November, peak mid-July – late September.
Size: Average 10 to 20 inches, some larger fish to 32 inches and 12 pounds. Trophy specimens up to 15 to 18 pounds or more possible in late summer and fall.
Tip: Seek out spots where spawning salmon are present. Also, try stretches of water just downstream of fish cleaning stations or where anglers gut their salmon.

Dolly Varden

Rating: Good to excellent.
Timing: Mid-March – late November, peak mid-July – late September.
Size: Average 10 to 20 inches, some larger fish to 30 inches and 10 pounds. Trophy specimens up to 15 pounds possible in this area in late summer and fall.
Tip: Avoid heavy current and try mouth of tributary streams and calmer portions of water where salmon concentrate.

Other Species: RW,(CS,NP).

KENAI RIVER (RM 24 – 39.5)
Area: Soldotna to Naptowne Rapids.

Main Species: King, red, silver, and pink salmon, rainbow trout, and Dolly Varden.

Summary: Expect good to excellent opportunity for salmon overall with boat traffic often considerably lighter in this section of the Kenai than on the lower and upper river. The most successful fishers are the ones with at least several years worth of experience as the river here is less pronounced in characteristics and intimate knowledge of available holding structure is required. However, fishing from the bank can be exceptional in many places for schools of migrating reds and silvers.

Description: There is far less meandering of the river, the Kenai flowing more or less straight between Sterling and Soldotna with very few islands, backwater channels, and sloughs for salmon and other species to use as obvious holding structures. The so-called *Seven Mile Stretch* of the Kenai from river mile 24 to 31 alludes to this fact. Safe boat navigation can be an issue in places during low water flows that are typically prevalent during the spring, early summer, and late fall months as partially submerged rocks and boulders and other obstructions may pose a problem for props.

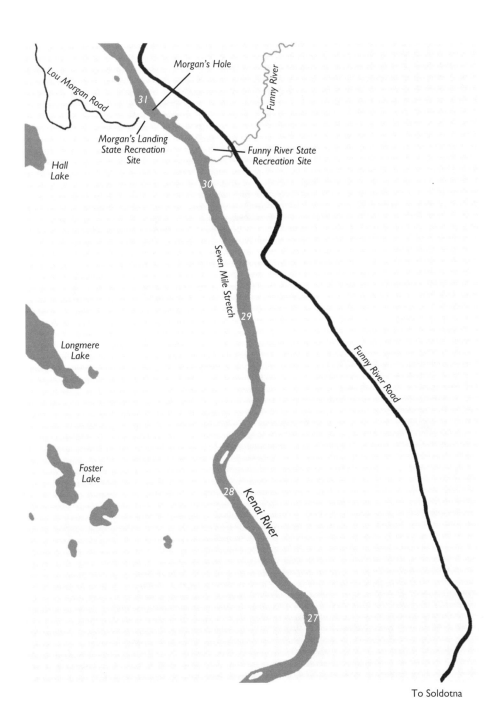

Lou Morgan Road

Morgan's Hole

Funny River

31

Morgan's Landing
State Recreation
Site

Funny River State
Recreation Site

Hall
Lake

30

Seven Mile Stretch

29

Longmere
Lake

Funny River Road

Foster
Lake

28

Kenai River

27

To Soldotna

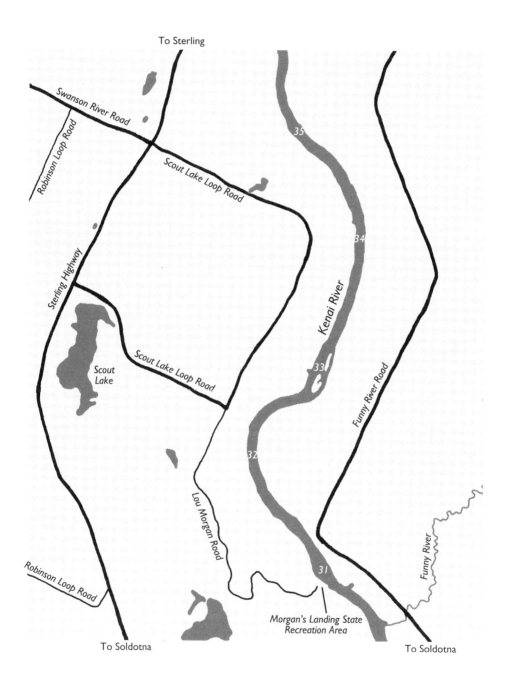

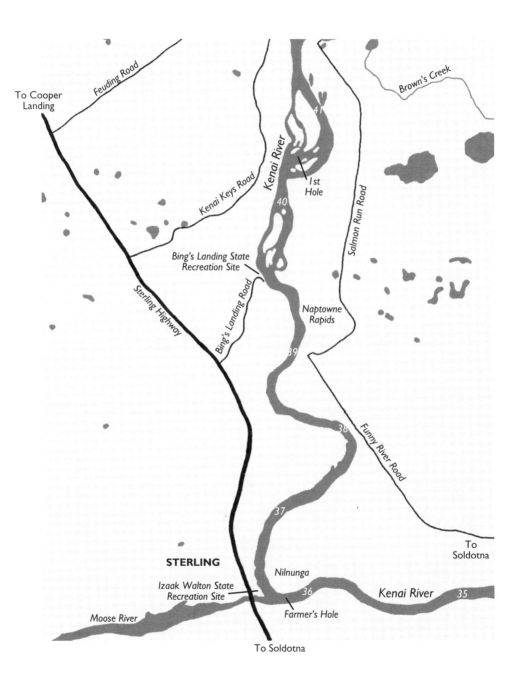

General Access: By road and boat. There are a few roadside access points between Naptowne Rapids and Soldotna via the Sterling Highway or Funny River Road but the vast majority of the river is only reached by boat.

Funny River Road

The Funny River Road begins at MP 96.1 Sterling Highway at the intersection just south of the Soldotna Bridge.

Access Point A: Funny River Campground – MP 11.5 Funny River Road. Left on access road to campground. Parking, camping, and restrooms. Trail leads short distance to river and confluence area.

Sterling Highway

Access Point B: Morgan's Landing – MP 84.9 Sterling Highway. South on Scout Lake Loop Road 1.6 mile to a "T," right on Lou Morgan Road 2.4 miles, right on access road 1.5 mile to campground and parking area. Parking, camping, boat launch, and restrooms. Trails lead from parking and camping areas to and along river.

Access Point C: Izaak Walton Campground – MP 82.3 Sterling Highway. South on access road short distance to campground and Kenai River / Moose River confluence. Parking, camping, boat launch, and restrooms. Trails lead to mouth of Moose River and the banks of the Kenai.

Fishing Opportunities

Restrictions: King salmon fishing prohibited August 1 – December 31, silver salmon November 1 – June 30, and rainbow trout May 2 – June 10. *Kenai River / Funny River Confluence:* Closed to king salmon fishing January 1 – July 14. Additional restrictions are in effect (consult ADF&G regulations).

King Salmon

Rating: Good.

Regulatory Season: January 1 – July 31.

Timing: May 5 – July 31, peak June 15 – 30 (early run) and July 15 – 31 (late run).

Size: Average 20 to 40 pounds (early run) and 30 to 50 pounds (late run), kings in the 80- to 100-pound range a possibility.

Tip: Scout for holding water and fish breaching surface.

Red Salmon

Rating: Fair (early run) and excellent (late run).

Timing: May 10 – October 5, peak June 5 – 15 (early run) and July 15 – August 5 (late run).

Size: Average 6 to 7 pounds, some larger fish up to 11 pounds (early run); 6 to 8 pounds, up to 14 pounds (late run). Catches of reds up to 15 pounds or more possible.

Tip: Look for fast to moderate current just upstream of holes and eddies.

Silver Salmon

Rating: Good to excellent.

Regulatory Season: July 1 – October 31.

Timing: July 10 – October 31, peak August 15 – 31 (early run), September 20 – October 5 (late run).

Size: Average 6 to 10 pounds, some larger fish to 14 pounds (early run); 8 to 14 pounds, to 18 pounds not unusual. A very few trophy specimens up to 22 pounds or more may be present in late September.

Tip: Early-run fish often travel close to shore; late-run silvers are more prevalent in deep, slow-water areas.

Pink Salmon

Rating: Good to excellent (even years); poor (odd years).

Timing: June 25 – September 25, peak August 10 – 25.

Size: Average 3 to 6 pounds, some fish to 8-9 pounds. Trophy specimens up to 10-11 pounds or more possible.

Tip: Avoid fast current and focus on slower river sections.

Rainbow Trout

Rating: Good.

Regulatory Season: June 11 – May 1.

Timing: Mid-March – late November, peak mid-July – late September.

Size: Average 10 to 20 inches, some larger fish to 32 inches and 12 pounds. Trophy specimens up to 15 to 18 pounds or more possible in late summer and fall.

Tip: Early in season, try deep holes and pockets of water; later on, scout for concentrations of spawning salmon and cast in immediate area.

Dolly Varden

Rating: Good to excellent.

Timing: Mid-March – late November, peak mid-July – late September.

Size: Average 10 to 20 inches, some larger fish to 30 inches and 10-12 pounds. Trophy specimens up to 15 pounds possible in this area during late summer and fall.

Tip: Fair to good opportunities in May, better starting in July when salmon are abundant. Look for slow water early on and then search for spawning salmon as the season progresses.

Other Species: RW,(CS,NP).

KENAI RIVER (RM 39.5 – 45.9)

Area: Naptowne Rapids to Upper Killey River.

Main Species: King, red, silver, and pink salmon, rainbow trout, and Dolly Varden.

Summary: This area of the Kenai River promises some of the most abundant opportunities for red and silver salmon on the middle river and a good portion of the late runs of these species spawn here. Excellent action is the norm and sight fishing can be awesome in a multitude of locations. Many early-run kings stage in this stretch of water, waiting to run up the Killey River to spawn, and late-run salmon can be very numerous the last week to ten days of July.

Upper and Lower Torpedo Hole, Wally's Hole, Stump Hole, and 1st, 2nd, and 3rd holes are all popular for salmon, trout, and char.

Description: The Kenai flows relatively smooth and calm throughout much of the stretch of water from approximately river mile 46 until Naptowne Rapids, a quarter of a mile long set of rapids. There are some parts that are fairly braided, complete

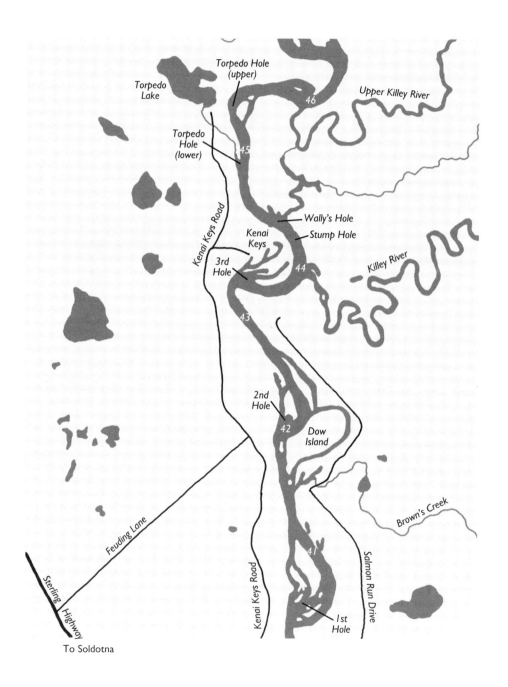

with islands, channels, and sloughs.

General Access: By road and boat. The Sterling Highway provides only one direct public access point but there are several private campgrounds/lodges or guide services in the Kenai Keys area that offer additional river use for a fee.

Sterling Highway

Access Point A: Bing's Landing – MP 80.2 Sterling Highway. South on Bing's Landing Road by sign 0.8 mile to parking area and river. Parking, camping, boat launch, and restrooms.

Access Point B: Dot's Kenai River Camp (Private) – MP 78.2 Sterling Highway. South on Feuding Lane 2 miles, left on Kenai Keys Road 1.6 mile, right on access road by sign 0.3 mile to camp and river. Parking, camping, boat launch, restrooms.

Access Point C: *Torpedo Lake* – MP 78.2 Sterling Highway. South on Feuding Lane 2 miles, left on Kenai Keys Road 1.5 mile, continue left 1.2 mile to end of road. Parking. Trails lead 0.2 mile to river.

Skilak Lake Road

Access Point D: Lower Skilak Lake Campground – MP 13.8 Skilak Lake Road. South on access road 0.9 mile to campground and lake. Parking, camping, boat launch, and restrooms. Proceed by boat due west approximately 1.25 mile to lake outlet and Kenai River; continue downstream 2.5 miles to the Kenai Keys area.

Fishing Opportunities

Restrictions: King salmon fishing prohibited August 1 – December 31, silver salmon November 1 – June 30, and rainbow trout May 2 – June 10. Additional restrictions are in effect (consult ADF&G regulations).

King Salmon
Rating: Good.
Regulatory Season: January 1 – July 31.
Timing: May 10 – July 31, peak June 20 – July 5 (early run) and July 20 – 31 (late run).
Size: Average 20 to 40 pounds (early run) and 30 to 50 pounds (late run), kings in the 80- to 100-pound range a possibility.
Tip: All methods (drifting/back-trolling/back-bouncing) works, including anchoring up in suitable holes and runs.

Red Salmon
Rating: Fair (early run) and excellent (late run).
Timing: May 10 – October 15, peak June 5 – 15 (early run) and July 15 – August 10 (late run).
Size: Average 6 to 7 pounds, some larger fish up to 11 pounds (early run); 6 to 8 pounds, up to 14 pounds (late run). Catches of reds up to 15 pounds or more possible.
Tip: Search out shallow/moderately shallow water areas near shore, such as around islands and in channels.

Silver Salmon
Rating: Good to excellent.

Regulatory Season: July 1 – October 31.

Timing: July 10 – October 31, peak August 20 – September 5 (early run), September 25 – October 15 (late run).

Size: Average 6 to 10 pounds, some larger fish to 14 pounds (early run); 8 to 14 pounds, to 18 pounds not unusual. A very few trophy specimens up to 22 pounds or more may be present in October.

Tip: Look for silvers at the edges of fast current and slow water, such as in sloughs, backwater channels, or the head of holes and pools. Fish often travel close to shore.

Pink Salmon

Rating: Good to excellent (even years); poor (odd years).

Timing: July 1 – September 25, peak August 15 – 25.

Size: Average 3 to 6 pounds, some fish to 8-9 pounds. Trophy specimens up to 10-11 pounds or more possible.

Tip: For brightest fish, try early in run. Majority of salmon will be turning color.

Rainbow Trout

Rating: Excellent.

Regulatory Season: June 11 – May 1.

Timing: June 11 – May 1, peak mid-July – mid-October.

Size: Average 10 to 20 inches, some larger fish to 32 inches and 12 pounds. Trophy specimens up to 18-20 pounds or more possible in fall.

Tip: Look for salmon spawning beds. A few trout are present through the winter.

Dolly Varden

Rating: Excellent.

Timing: Year-round, peak mid-July – mid-October.

Size: Average 10 to 20 inches, some larger fish to 30 inches and 10-12 pounds. Trophy specimens up to 15 pounds possible in this area in late summer and fall.

Tip: Focus effort around spawning salmon. A few char are available through winter.

Other Species: RW,(CS,NP).

KENAI RIVER (RM 45.9 – 50)

Area: Upper Killey River to Skilak Lake outlet.

Main Species: King, red, silver, and pink salmon, rainbow trout, and Dolly Varden.

Summary: This area is a major spawning ground for several species of salmon, especially reds and silvers, and thus one of the most productive stretches of water for rainbow trout and Dolly Varden in the entire Kenai River drainage. The part from just below Lower Olson Creek to the mouth of Killey River and beyond is exceptional for big trout and char with many trophy-sized specimens having been taken here. Rainbows of 20-22 pounds or more and 40 inches are known from this location.

Description: The first few miles of water downstream to river mile 47 is very slow and somewhat shallow and may be up to a quarter of a mile wide in places.

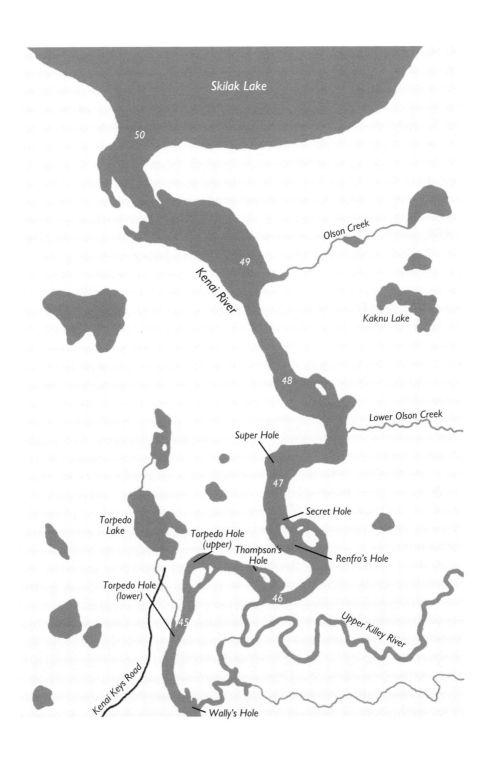

General Access: By road and boat. The Sterling Highway provides no direct road access to the upper portion of the middle Kenai but boats are frequently launched from here. Skilak Lake Road (from either MP 58.0 or MP 75.2 Sterling Highway) provides easy boat access to the river and is a popular launch location for anglers.

Sterling Highway

Access Point A: Bing's Landing – MP 80.2 Sterling Highway. South on Bing's Landing Road by sign 0.8 mile to parking area and river. Parking, camping, boat launch, and restrooms. Head upstream about 6.5 miles (mouth of Upper Killey River).

Access Point B: Dot's Kenai River Camp (Private) – MP 78.2 Sterling Highway. South on Feuding Lane 2 miles, left on Kenai Keys Road 1.6 mile, right on access road by sign 0.3 mile to camp and river. Parking, camping, boat launch, and restrooms. Head upstream 2 miles (mouth of Upper Killey River).

Skilak Lake Road

Access Point C: Lower Skilak Lake Campground – MP 13.8 Skilak Lake Road. South on access road 0.9 mile to campground and lake. Parking, camping, boat launch, and restrooms. Proceed by boat due west approximately 1.25 mile to lake outlet and Kenai River.

Fishing Opportunities

Restrictions: King salmon fishing prohibited August 1 – December 31, silver salmon November 1 – June 30, and rainbow trout May 2 – June 10. Designated a seasonal drift area only (no motor use allowed) between river mile 47 and 50 from March 15 through June 14. Additional restrictions are in effect (consult ADF&G regulations).

King Salmon

Rating: Fair to good.

Regulatory Season: January 1 – July 31.

Timing: May 10 – July 31, peak June 20 – July 5 (early run) and July 20 – 31 (late run).

Size: Average 20 to 40 pounds (early run) and 30 to 50 pounds (late run), kings in the 80- to 100-pound range a possibility.

Tip: Fishing is best near the confluence with Upper Killey River up to river mile 47.

Red Salmon

Rating: Fair (early run) and excellent (late run).

Timing: May 10 – October 15, peak June 5 – 15 (early run) and July 15 – August 10 (late run).

Size: Average 6 to 7 pounds, some larger fish up to 11 pounds (early run); 6 to 8 pounds, up to 14 pounds (late run). Catches of reds up to 15 pounds or more possible.

Tip: Best action starts about three miles downstream of Skilak Lake outlet.

Silver Salmon

Rating: Good to excellent.

Regulatory Season: July 1 – October 31.

Timing: July 10 – October 31, peak August 20 – September 5 (early run), September

25 – October 20 (late run).

Size: Average 6 to 10 pounds, some larger fish to 14 pounds (early run); 8 to 14 pounds, to 18 pounds not unusual. A very few trophy specimens up to 22 pounds or more may be present in October.

Tip: Very productive fishery from mouth of Upper Killey to river mile 47.

Pink Salmon

Rating: Good to excellent (even years); poor (odd years).

Timing: July 1 – September 25, peak August 15 – 25.

Size: Average 3 to 6 pounds, some fish to 8-9 pounds. Trophy specimens up to 10-11 pounds or more possible.

Tip: Try deep holes between river mile 46 and 47. Most fish show some spawning colors.

Rainbow Trout

Rating: Excellent.

Regulatory Season: June 11 – May 1.

Timing: June 11 – May 1, peak mid-July – late October.

Size: Average 10 to 20 inches, some larger fish to 32 inches and 12 pounds. Trophy specimens up to 22 pounds or more possible.

Tip: Hot spots include Super Hole, Secret Hole, and Renfro's Hole, these being very productive for big rainbows from August into October.

Dolly Varden

Rating: Excellent.

Timing: Year-round, peak mid-July – late October.

Size: Average 10 to 20 inches, some larger fish to 30 inches and 10-12 pounds. Trophy specimens up to 15 pounds possible in this area in late summer and fall.

Tip: The deep holes between river mile 46 and 47 can be superb for big char.

Other Species: RW,(CS,NP).

ALASKA FISHING
The Ultimate Angler's Guide

The most comprehensive "insiders" guide on Alaska fishing, revised, updated, and expanded in this new deluxe, full color 3rd Edition. Written by the state's top fishing experts, this latest version now covers all 17 major Alaska sport species (fresh and salt water), all methods (fly, spin, and bait), and all six regions of the state, with details on over 300 of the most productive Alaska fishing locations.

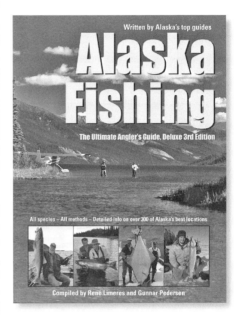

Includes information on regional climate/conditions, run timing, visitor services costs, trophy and record fishes, USGS map references, guides' tips, fishing regulations, trip planner, and best flies in Alaska. Beautifully illustrated, *Alaska Fishing* has over 500 color photos, maps, charts, diagrams, and drawings.

Available at retail stores throughout Southcentral and Interior Alaska. Can be ordered at *highwayangler.com* and directly from the publisher: Fishing Alaska Publications, P. O. Box 90557, Anchorage, AK 99509, (907) 346-1177.

Autographed/personalized copies available upon request.

SKILAK LAKE
& Tributaries

Description

Skilak Lake is a quite expansive body of water, one of the largest on Kenai Peninsula. Several tributaries empty into it, including the upper Kenai River. Skilak is a true glacial lake, much of the fine silt coloring the water owing credit to Skilak River as well as the upper Kenai. The only clearwater streams of any size are tiny compared to area rivers but still do harbor runs of fish in season.

Hidden Lake is a fairly large and deep lake connected to Skilak Lake through Hidden Lake Creek. It is an attractive destination for several reasons but mainly due to the scenery and crystal clear waters. Engineer Lake is part of the Hidden Lake drainage. Upper and Lower Ohmer lakes are just south of Hidden but flow directly into Skilak by a small stream.

Rolling hills and mountains dominate the scenery, forests of spruce, birch, cottonwood, and other tree growth blanketing the landscape. Ice fields and glaciers can be seen in the far distance southeast of Skilak Lake.

Wildlife is, as anywhere in this region of the peninsula, abundant. Bear, moose, eagle, beaver, and wolf are but some of the animal species that frequent Skilak Lake and its tributaries.

Access

All traffic into the area is from the Sterling Highway, although it is possible to fly into Skilak Lake and land on the water. The Skilak Lake Road begins at MP 58.0 (east entrance) and ends at MP 75.2 (west entrance) of the Sterling. This road accesses much of the productive angling locations and trails are present to expand opportunities even further.

Fishing

The angling in Skilak Lake and adjoining waters can hardly be described as fantastic by any stretch of the imagination but can be good during the height of the season, primarily in spring and fall. The open-water period offers productive trout and char fishing and even salmon can excite the moment when passing through from July through October and beyond. For many anglers, the presence of salmon is the key in locating the best action for resident species.

Ice fishing opportunities abound during the winter months with fishers laying down most effort on the outlet of Skilak Lake and various hot spots on Hidden Lake. Lake trout is the most common catch but many rainbows hit as well.

Chapter Contents

The following are the game fish present, various waters of the Skilak Lake drainage, and the page number in which more detailed information can be found.

TIMING:

Skilak Lake & Tributaries

FISH	JAN	FEB	MAR	APR	MAY	JUN	JUL	AUG	SEP	OCT	NOV	DEC
RS												
KO												
SS												
PS												
CS												
RT												
LT												
DV												
RW												

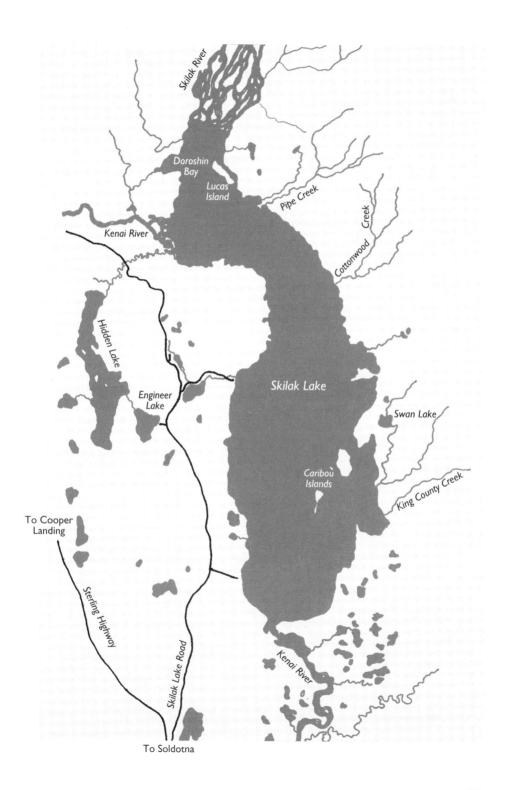

SPECIES INFORMATION

Salmon
All five species of salmon can be found in Skilak Lake. The lake also has the unique distinction of hosting an anadromous population of one type of salmon or another every month of the year, starting with a few kings in May and culminating with silvers in April. But as is typical of large lakes, in particular glacial ones, fishing for salmon is rather difficult unless the angler manages to locate concentrations of fish. As for the rest of the drainage, salmon are locally abundant yet not quite as dispersed.

King salmon migrate through Skilak Lake on the way to the upper section of Kenai River. The appearance consists of both early and late runs with fish present from June into September. A few specimens may occur in tributaries of Skilak but no established runs exist. Fishing for kings is prohibited in this area.

Red salmon are present almost continuously from mid-May to November in one stage or another within the life cycle. Two runs move through Skilak Lake with the late run being by far the largest with many of these fish also spawning in areas of the lake as well as in tributaries. Reds often gather in schools in Skilak and Hidden lakes waiting to reach full nuptial maturity, frustrating anglers with their finicky attitude toward lures and flies. Some success is reported on occasion but usually appears to be an exercise in futility.

Landlocked red salmon, or **kokanee**, are available year-round in Hidden Lake.

Silver salmon are also present in two distinct runs in Skilak Lake, but tributaries of the lake only experience small numbers of early-run fish in August and September. The late run (October-November) is headed for upper Kenai River. A very unique naturally occurring landlocked population of silvers can be found in Engineer Lake.

Pink salmon are abundant near the outlet of Skilak Lake where the middle section of Kenai River begins and a fair number of these fish will traverse the lake destined for spawning ground in the upper Kenai River drainage. May be encountered from July into September.

Chum salmon are very rare in Skilak Lake and absent in its tributaries. The few fish that do come into the lake (in July-August) are headed for tributaries of Kenai Lake.

Trout/Char
Both trout and char inhabit Skilak Lake and its tributary lakes throughout the year and are available in streams during the summer and fall months. This area of the Kenai constitutes predominantly a lake fishery since many of the streams are quite small and shallow with minimal structure or water volume necessary for productive angling. In addition, all flowing waters of the Skilak Lake drainage are closed to fishing from April 15 through June 14 to protect spawning trout.

Rainbow trout populate Skilak, Hidden, and Ohmer lakes to one degree or another but overall are not considered particularly prolific in terms of abundance. Some decent action can generally be had in spring after breakup and again in fall before freezeup, however.

Dolly Varden are active in Skilak Lake, especially at the inlet and outlet, yet are conspicuously low-key in presence as well as angling importance in the various tributaries. As with rainbows, spring and fall are best times of the year.

For rainbows and Dollies, small spoons and spinners and flies representing juvenile salmon and other forage items are good.

Lake trout are available in Skilak and Hidden lakes with some very large specimens showing up occasionally. Smolt and forage imitations are good in late winter/early spring and in fall but many anglers prefer to use certain type of bait for added attraction.

Other Species

A few **arctic grayling** are reportedly in Skilak Lake and may be found in tributary waters as well. **Round whitefish** are abundant in Skilak and mainstem of Kenai River but much less common elsewhere. Fishing for them, however, is difficult. Although no catches of **northern pike** have been confirmed in this area, they are believed to be present.

SKILAK LAKE

Main Species: Silver salmon, rainbow trout, lake trout, and Dolly Varden.

Summary: Skilak Lake, as one of the main bodies of water on Kenai Peninsula, has a huge population of game fish but as is so common with systems loaded with silt, catching these fish effectively and consistently poses a serious problem. Anglers are learning to cope with this issue, taking advantage of salmon runs and recognizing potential feeding areas to maximize their results. The use of strong-scented bait and visibility-enhanced lures are recommended wherever and whenever regulations allow.

Concentrations of ripe salmon and the clearwater inlets of tributaries carrying food sources into Skilak means trout and char are nearby. Also, the east end of the lake where Upper Kenai River dumps in is a focal point for fish waiting to head upstream into the river. The outlet at the west end of Skilak is a major staging and spawning area for salmon and thus attracts forage species as well.

Description: Like Kenai Lake, Skilak is heavily stained with glacial sediment, primarily from the Skilak River on the far western end, but the Upper Kenai River also adds to the distinct turquoise hue. It is fairly deep in places. Ice conditions can be unstable and caution is advised. In some years, the lake may be partially or even completely ice-free. However, a normal winter does see ice at least a few inches thick.
Note: Due to the size of Skilak, boating of any kind (especially in spring and fall) demands caution. Very strong winds can paralyze travel.

General Access: By road, boat, and floatplane. Roadside anglers access the lake via Skilak Lake Road off Sterling Highway; MP 58.0 (east entrance) and MP 75.2 (west entrance). Boats can be launched at the lake or Kenai River to access remote bays, tributary mouths, and lake inlet and outlet. Aircraft can land anywhere but beware strong winds in area.
Access Point A: Upper Skilak Lake Campground – MP 8.5 Skilak Lake Road. South on access road by sign 1.9 mile to campground and the lake. Developed parking, camping, and boat launch, restrooms.
Access Point B: Lower Skilak Lake Campground – MP 13.8 Skilak Lake Road. South on access road by sign 0.9 mile to campground and the lake. Developed parking, camping, and boat launch, restrooms.

Fishing Opportunities

Restrictions: King salmon fishing prohibited. Seasonal restrictions for other species may apply (consult ADF&G regulations).

Silver Salmon
Rating: Fair.
Regulatory Season: July 1 – October 31.
Timing: July 15 – October 31, peak August 15-30 (early run) and September 25 – October 15 (Late run).
Size: Average 7 to 12 pounds, some larger fish to 18 pounds. Specimens up to 22 pounds or more are known from the Kenai drainage.
Tip: Although a few silvers may be taken just about anywhere along or in the lake, by far the better bets are the inlet (where upper Kenai flows in) and the outlet (where the lower Kenai begins) where fish can be encountered in schools.

Rainbow Trout
Rating: Fair.
Regulatory Season: June 11 – May 1.
Timing: June 11 – May 1, peak mid-March – mid-April and mid-July – late October.
Size: Average 8 to 20 inches, some larger fish to 25 inches and 5-6 pounds.
Tip: The lake outlet is a local favorite in late winter and spring. In summer and fall, focus activity on the mouths of tributary streams and both the inlet and outlet, or anywhere a concentration of spawning salmon can be found.

Lake Trout
Rating: Fair.
Timing: Year-round, peak mid-February – mid-April and mid-August – early December.
Size: Average 2 to 5 pounds, some larger fish to 15 pounds. Trophy char up to 25 pounds have been caught in this lake.
Tip: Outlet of lake is productive in late winter and spring as well as in late summer into winter. Some smaller char often available at mouth of tributary streams and at lake inlet.

Dolly Varden
Rating: Fair.
Timing: Year-round, peak mid-May – mid-June and late July – late October.
Size: Average 10 to 20 inches, some larger fish to 25 inches and 5-6 pounds. In fall, look for a few char to approach 30 inches and 10-12 pounds.
Tip: Small concentrations of fish may be found at the lake inlet and outlet in spring and again in the fall when salmon spawn.

Other Species: RS,PS,RW,(KS,CS,AG,NP).

SKILAK LAKE TRIBUTARIES

Includes Hidden Lake, Engineer Lake, and Ohmer lakes.

HIDDEN LAKE

Main Species: Kokanee, rainbow trout, lake trout, and Dolly Varden.

Summary: Hidden Lake is one of the most popular lakes on the Kenai Peninsula, well known for its good action for salmon, trout, and char. Both shore anglers as well as boaters can take advantage of the good fishing opportunities according to the seasons. Ice fishing here is equally productive from mid-winter to early spring. Lake trout is the top draw with several trophy specimens having been taken here. Additionally, Hidden is one of only three lakes on the peninsula supporting a population of kokanee, or landlocked/resident red salmon. The lake also has a good run of anadromous red salmon in late July and early August but they can be difficult to catch.

Hidden Lake Creek, a small stream emptying Hidden Lake, serves for the most part the role of providing passage of migratory fish to and from Skilak Lake yet several species also use it as a spawning area. Anglers may find some smaller trout and char in summer and fall.

Description: Large and deep clearwater lake, down to 150 feet or more in places.

General Access: By road and floatplane. Hidden is reached from Skilak Lake Road, off MP 58.0 (east entrance) and MP 75.2 (west entrance) of the Sterling Highway. Boats can be launched to access remote bays, stream mouths, and deeper water from spring through fall.
Access Point: Hidden Lake Campground – MP 3.6 Skilak Lake Road. North on paved access road 0.7 mile to Hidden Lake Campground and the lake. Developed parking, camping, boat launch, and trail system, restrooms.

Fishing Opportunities

Restrictions: Burbot fishing prohibited. Hidden Lake Creek is closed to salmon fishing and closed to all fishing April 15 – June 14 (consult ADF&G regulations).

Kokanee

Rating: Good.
Timing: Year-round, peak mid-May – late June and mid-September – mid-October.
Size: Average 8 to 14 inches, some specimens up to 18 inches and 2 pounds.
Tip: The best action seems to be in late spring and early in summer as the salmon are feeding aggressively but productive fishing can be experienced throughout the open water season.

Rainbow Trout

Rating: Fair to good.
Timing: Year-round, peak mid-May – mid-June and mid-September – late October.
Size: Average 10 to 16 inches, some larger fish to 22 inches and 3 pounds. Occasional catches of trout up to 25 inches and 5-6 pounds or more have been reported.

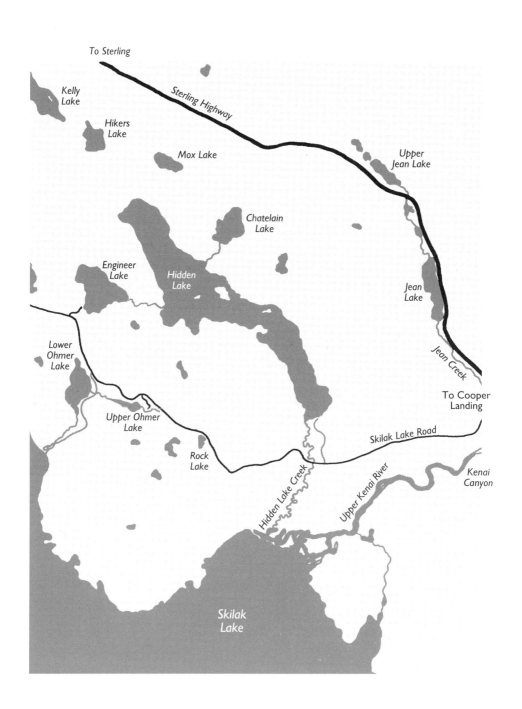

Tip: The lake outlet can be productive in spring. In fall, check out weed beds along the shoreline and in bays (especially those in the middle and western section of the lake), areas around islands, the mouth of inlet streams.

Lake Trout
Rating: Good.
Timing: Year-round, peak mid-May – mid-June and late August – mid-November.
Size: Average 2 to 6 pounds, some larger fish to 15 pounds. Trophy specimens up to 20-25 pounds are known to reside in this lake.
Tip: Action from shore is good in spring as ice goes out and may stay productive into early summer from boat. The char are suspended deep during the warm summer months. In fall and early winter, the fish come fairly close to shore in shallower water. Ice fishing is fair to good.

Dolly Varden
Rating: Fair.
Timing: Year-round, peak mid-May – mid-June and mid-September – mid-November.
Size: Average 10 to 18 inches, some larger fish to 22 inches and 3 pounds. A few char may reach 25 inches and 5-6 pounds.
Tip: The lake outlet is worth some effort in spring and fall and may yield larger than average char. Areas around islands, off stream mouths, and near weed beds in shallow bays seem to show best results.

Other Species: RS,SS,RW.

ENGINEER LAKE

Main Species: Landlocked silver salmon.

Summary: Engineer Lake has some decent opportunities for resident silver salmon. Access is easy with productive fishing off the bank in spring and fall, making Engineer a fairly popular angling destination. A canoe or other watercraft is quite useful in reaching more remote areas of the lake as well as deeper water.

Description: Shallow clearwater lake with a slight tannic stain.

General Access: By road. Lake is reached from Skilak Lake Road, off MP 58.0 (east entrance) and MP 75.2 (west entrance) Sterling Highway.
Access Point: Engineer Lake Campground – MP 9.5 Skilak Lake Road. North on access road 0.4 mile to campground and lake. Parking and camping, restrooms.

Fishing Opportunities
Restrictions: None (consult ADF&G regulations).

Silver Salmon (landlocked)
Rating: Fair.
Timing: Year-round, peak mid-May – mid-June and mid-September – late December.
Size: Average 7 to 16 inches, a few specimens up to 20 inches.
Tip: Try the lake outlet in spring and early summer, moving to other likely feeding areas

later in the season. Ice fishing can be productive through the winter months.

Other Species: RT,DV.

OHMER LAKES

Main Species: Rainbow trout and Dolly Varden.

Summary: Ohmer Lakes (Upper and Lower) contains healthy populations of trout and char. Action is often good with ice fishing being a popular activity here in early winter and early spring as well. A canoe or other type of watercraft is ideal to reach more promising locations around the lakes, especially deeper water away from shore.

Description: Small clearwater lakes connected to each other and Skilak Lake through a stream. Water is clear and of moderate depth.

General Access: By road. Both lakes are reached from Skilak Lake Road, off MP 58.0 (east entrance) and MP 75.2 (west entrance) Sterling Highway.
Upper Ohmer Lake
Access Point: MP 7.7 Skilak Lake Road. South on access road 0.2 mile to lake. Limited Parking.
Lower Ohmer Lake
Access Point: MP 8.6 Skilak Lake Road. South on gravel road by sign short distance to lake. Developed parking and camping.

Fishing Opportunities
Restrictions: None (consult ADF&G regulations).

Rainbow Trout
Rating: Good, best in Lower Ohmer Lake.
Timing: Year-round, peak early May – early June and mid-September – late December.
Size: Average 10 to 16 inches, a few larger fish up to 22 inches and 3 pounds. Lower Ohmer Lake may see heavier specimens on occasion.
Tip: Concentrations of trout are encountered near lake inlets and outlets in spring.

Dolly Varden
Rating: Fair to good, best in Lower Ohmer Lake.
Timing: Year-round, peak early May – early June and mid-September – late December.
Size: Average 10 to 16 inches, some larger fish up to 20-22 inches and 3 pounds or more.
Tip: The lake inlets and outlets are productive in spring and fall; look for deeper offshore water in winter.

MOOSE RIVER
& Tributaries

Description

The Moose River drainage represents the typical lowland watershed of central Kenai Peninsula and situated in the Kenai National Wildlife Refuge. It is a quite extensive system comprising nearly a couple of dozen lakes and ponds, some of them of respectable size. In actuality there are three regions of the Moose, each region being supported by a branch – or fork – of the main river. The West Fork drains an area near the Swanson River Road, while the main river, also known as North Fork, ties into a couple of the larger lakes in the system south of Swan Lake Road and several runoff streams. The East Fork supports six smaller lakes near the Sterling Highway east of the community of Sterling.

Several lakes of the West and North forks are in the Swan Lake Canoe Route with additional access to waters of the Swanson River drainage.

These lakes and streams are mostly all tannic drainages stained with bog residue, displaying a slight brownish tan tint, yet a few lakes that are nestled in-between forest-clad hills do contain clear water. Marshlands are common throughout the Moose River system along with growths of spruce and birch.

Wildlife comprises mainly of moose, beaver, and waterfowl but eagles and a few bears are present in the drainage as well.

Access

The only practical way of accessing lakes and streams within the Moose River system is by canoe. The Sterling Highway serves as a gateway for the mainstem Moose with Swanson River and Swan Lake roads providing additional access to lakes of the West and North forks, respectively. Most every lake of the East Fork drainage is road accessible via the Sterling Highway or has trails present. As this region is a refuge, no aircraft are allowed to land on the lakes.

Fishing

If not seeking trophy trout and char on the mainstem Kenai, canoeists paddling into the Moose River system are welcomed by a healthy population of lure- and fly-happy rainbow trout averaging in the high teens. Good to excellent fishing can be had in most lakes in late spring and fall, while the autumn bite on the upper Swanson River in late summer and lasting into the autumn is sometimes equal to the action found most anywhere else on the Kenai River.

Silver salmon are abundant in the mainstem Moose and the middle and upper portions around the forks are a hot spot for the species. Very few other anglers and big schools of fresh and aggressive salmon make for a worthwhile trip. Other salmon species include red and kokanee, of which only the latter is present in any numbers to be pursued successfully. There are only a few lakes on the peninsula that has kokanee and one of them is located in this system.

Arctic char and Dolly Varden are both available but in lesser numbers than trout. Anglers trying early and late in the season should be able to get in on some good action.

Solitude is a big plus since relatively few anglers go through the lengths of mode of access in order to experience the quietness and eager fish.

The mouth of Moose River where it joins the Kenai River has more variety concerning salmon fishing. Red and pink salmon both are plentiful here and there are even some limited opportunities to catch a king salmon. But this spot is also heavily crowded with other anglers during the peak of the runs.

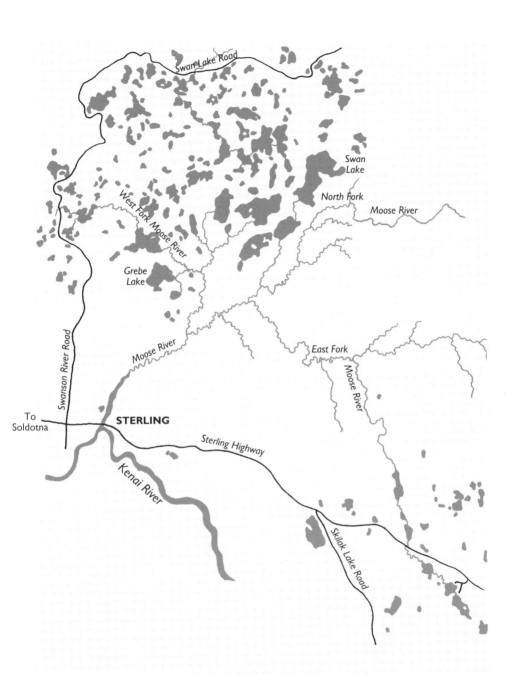

Chapter Contents

The following are the game fish present, the various sections of the Moose River drainage, and the page number in which more detailed information can be found.

TIMING:

Moose River Drainage - Streams

FISH	JAN	FEB	MAR	APR	MAY	JUN	JUL	AUG	SEP	OCT	NOV	DEC
KS												
RS												
SS												
PS												
CS												
RT												
DV												
RW												

Moose River Drainage - Lakes

FISH	JAN	FEB	MAR	APR	MAY	JUN	JUL	AUG	SEP	OCT	NOV	DEC
RS												
KO												
SS												
PS												
RT												
DV												
AC												

SPECIES INFORMATION

Salmon

There are documented reports of four species of salmon in the Moose River drainage, of which only two – reds and silvers – are present in any numbers to speak of. Of these two, the silver is the only one to provide truly consistent angling opportunity, the reason for this being that the lakes and streams in this system lack the type of habitat most kinds of salmon prefer: fast-flowing creeks of at least moderate depth and width along with ample gravel bottom substrate. Streams here are generally small and shallow, the bottom often covered with vegetation mats with only patches of gravel.

The major salmon fishery in terms of popularity and number of salmon caught is located where the Kenai and Moose rivers come together, also known as the confluence. Due to the slack and somewhat deep channel in mid-river, the mouth of the Moose is ideal habitat for salmon to stop and rest on their migration upstream, a fact that anglers readily embrace. In addition to kings, reds, silvers, and pinks, Moose has reported very rare occurrences of chum salmon.

King Salmon

There are a fair number of kings that school up at the confluence, the vast majority of them headed for tributaries further up the Kenai or mainstem Kenai River. Exceptionally few fish will actually proceed up into the Moose River drainage with the appearance of this salmon in any area of the system (except at the mouth) considered strays only. No documented population of king salmon has been reported.

The confluence pose some limited shore opportunity for kings (no boat fishing is allowed here) and a handful of salmon are landed every season, sometimes incidentally to fishing for the more prolific red salmon. The problem, however, is that this is a fly-fishing area with virtually no current flow (not an ideal combination for effective king fishing), thus action can be expected to be slow. Both early- and late-run fish stage here on the way upstream to more distant waters. Try in late June and again in late July using oversized streamers.

Red Salmon

Like the Russian, Moose River supports two runs of red salmon, an early run from mid-June to early July and a late run from mid-July to early August. The fish in these respective runs are predominantly bound for upper reaches of the mainstem Kenai and clearwater tributaries and for the most part only sweep by the confluence to rest. However, some fish do ascend the Moose and spawn in upper reaches of the drainage, including tributary lakes, but total escapement for each run varies from just a few hundred reds in some years to a couple of thousand or more in others. Thus, poor fishing often prevails. Look for these salmon in the more narrow, upstream sections of the Moose where there is some current flow.

Anglers fishing near the headwaters take a few reds, yet the considerable majority of catches reported from this system actually comes from the hundred yards or so within the river mouth. The Moose is a very slow-flowing body of water and not very conducive at all in terms of ideal conditions to catch red salmon consistently. But anglers casting their flies into the sometimes staggering number of fish holding in the slack water at the confluence cannot help but line salmon in the mouth, on purpose or accidentally. The best fishing can be had in the immediate sections of the Kenai River surrounding the mouth of the Moose since the current there is fast and conditions more favorable in hooking reds.

Landlocked reds – or **kokanee** – are also found in the Moose River system, albeit only in one lake (Rock Lake) situated in the West Fork Moose drainage. Present year-round, the best time to target these little salmon is early in the season, preferably soon after ice-out and into the month of June. Tiny spoons, spinners, and flies are favored.

Silver Salmon

Good runs of silvers come through the confluence in late summer and fall, spreading into various forks of the Moose system. The confluence area reflects the general two-run appearance of silvers. The first run consists of fish bound for the entire Moose drainage as well as locations further up the Kenai, while the second run are primarily mainstem Kenai silvers and only available at the mouth of the Moose. Within the Moose River drainage, silvers are the most abundant species of salmon.

Unlike the lock jawed reds, these salmon are often very aggressive as they come up the glacial Kenai and hit the clear waters of the Moose. Although fish can be taken anywhere in the drainage, most anglers find success right at the confluence and in the more concentrated channels of the middle and upper river. Nice catches are also made in the deep hole just upstream and down of the confluence, in the Kenai River.

During the fly fishing only season, relatively few silvers are caught and it is not until after August 15 when all gear becomes legal that anglers can experience the best of what Moose has to offer in the way of silver action. Early morning and evening are the best times on the water, soaking eggs right at the mixing zone of the Kenai and Moose or in likely holes and runs in the middle and upper portions of the drainage being deadly. Casting spinners in silver, bronze, green, and metallic blue are often equally effective. Later in the season, during the late run at the mouth, spoons and spinners in the same colors work but also orange, red, and chartreuse – especially on dark, cloudy, or rainy days. Flash flies stripped in at a fair clip have excellent potential for hookups.

Early-Run Silvers: Just as the late run of reds peak at the mouth in mid-July, the first few silvers of the season appear. Fishing is typically slow until about the second week of August due to small numbers of silvers and the masses of red salmon. The run picks up substantially as the reds finally disappear in mid-month and action stays productive for the next two to three weeks, turning on at the mouth first and then progressively later further up the Moose River drainage.

As the river gradually narrows down in size and establishes some level of current flow, the action improves. The run is at its height in late August and early September but can stay productive even later in the month, particularly at the mouths of tributary spawning streams where the salmon tend to stack up. As September comes to an end, most of the fish have turned color; however, anglers casting for trout or other species occasionally encounter bright silvers into October.

In even-numbered years the mouth may become clogged with pink salmon, rendering most flies and hardware obsolete and bait may be the only effective way of getting to the silvers.

Late-Run Silvers: Anglers start seeing the first few scouts pulling into the mouth around the last week of August or first week of September just as the early run is starting to slow down. The run builds rapidly and by mid-month can yield some very good fishing that lasts right through to the season closure. Fresh silvers will, however, continue to arrive in the area even into December and later.

Pink Salmon

Every even-numbered year, the Moose sees a huge surge of pinks coming into its mouth. Starting in early July and continuing through the month, a small number of salmon will trickle in but it is not until August that the action picks up dramatically. By mid-month, the confluence area runs thick with pinks and anglers often experience fish-on-every-cast action. A few reasonably nice pinks are still present into September with the run ending overall by the third week. Trying to sort out fresher specimens late in the season can be a chore as the river usually teems with hundreds to perhaps a thousand or more aging and dying salmon.

Some of the fish caught are of trophy size. The Moose River currently holds the Alaska State Record at 12 pounds, 9 ounces, a benchmark that has stood since 1974. However, there have been a fair number of pinks taken from this location over the years that weighed in the 10- to 11-pound category.

Pinks in this area are not too finicky went it comes to lure or fly selection. The hordes of fish present at the confluence do seem to have a passion for slowly retrieved spoons, spinners, and flash flies in metallic silver with green, blue, or chartreuse colors.

Sharper colors in orange, red, and pink do well in the mixing zone and in the greenish-blue Kenai.

Abundance of pink salmon beyond the confluence area is very low. According to studies, the number of fish present in upper reaches of the Moose River may be measured in the dozens only.

Trout/Char

The Moose is known as an important producer of predatory species like trout and char. Although Dolly Varden are reasonably abundant in the drainage, it is the rainbow that is truly the main attraction here. Anglers looking to target both these gamesters would be wise to do so in the upper reaches of Moose, where the river narrows down and fish are plentiful and aggressive. They are also found in the great majority of drainage lakes, in addition to arctic char.

An extensive arsenal of lures and flies can be used for both trout and char. These fish are not as focused on salmon spawn as perhaps elsewhere in the Kenai River drainage so casting forage imitation flies and lures work well all season long. In spots where salmon are present and spawning (usually during September and October), egg and flesh imitations are productive. Dry flies are effective in early and mid-summer as well.

Rainbow Trout

The largest population of trout can be found in the upper reaches of the Moose and associated lakes, although fish of Kenai River origin are believed to use the river as a major spawning tributary as well. Many of the area lakes contain overwintering trout, mature adult fish exiting these waters starting in mid-April to reproduce in one of the many small streams connecting the lakes and in the various forks of the Moose River. After the breeding process has been completed, the fish either migrate back to the lakes or stay in the streams to feed until fall.

The mouth of the Moose can be good at times for trout yet the best fishing is without a doubt in one of the lakes or branches of the upper drainage. Although anglers are able to experience some decent action throughout the summer months, it is in September that things really pick up and it stays productive through early October.

Some surprisingly good-sized trout may be located in the predominantly narrow and shallow forks of the Moose, this being especially true in fall when silver salmon spawn. 20- to 24-inch rainbows are common in deeper holes and pools of these streams. But it is in the bigger lakes of the system where one may find the true trophies; specimens up to 28 inches (8 pounds plus) are possible.

Dolly Varden

It is not yet completely understood the extent of distribution of Dolly Varden within the Moose River drainage considering that there also appears to be an overlap in range with arctic char (described below), a very close relative. Dolly Varden seem prevalent in area streams in late summer and fall as there is some level of reproduction taking place and these opportunistic fish also follow the run of silver salmon onto the spawning beds, primarily during September and October.

Although not as widely distributed as rainbow trout, they are nonetheless quite abundant wherever found. Some fish are undoubtedly of Kenai River origin yet a few lakes of the system also contain overwintering populations of char.

Arctic Char

These fish are exclusively located in a few of the larger, deeper lakes of the Moose drainage. Present year-round, they are usually caught early and late in season as arctic char have a tendency to hold in deep water throughout the summer, coming in shallow during the cooler months. Char in the 20-inch category are common and fish weighing several pounds to be expected during the peak season in September and October. Jigs, spoons, and attractor flies all work.

Other Species

Round whitefish are taken incidentally to fishing for trout and char in the lower Moose, mostly at the mouth. **Northern pike** have been caught at the confluence with the Kenai and are occasionally reported in lakes of the upper drainage.

MOOSE RIVER / KENAI RIVER CONFLUENCE

Main Species: Red, silver, and pink salmon, rainbow trout, and Dolly Varden.

Summary: The confluence of Moose and Kenai rivers is a virtually current-free body of water that serves as a staging area for many salmon and other sport fish migrating through. Anglers have learned this is the case and when the fish are in, so are they. This is especially true when the late run of red salmon hits the confluence and fish are jumping everywhere. Like on the Russian, anglers stand elbow-to-elbow in hopes of catching a dime bright red. A little later in summer, big schools of silver and pink salmon gather and provide some outstanding action. Some trout and char are caught here from spring into fall but the far better choice to catch these species is in the middle and upper reaches of Moose and its tributary lakes (see following location descriptions this chapter).

Description: The Moose River at this point in the drainage is a wide and slow-flowing river of moderate depth. The water is clear with a slight brownish tint to it owing to its muskeg and forest lakes. Bottom is of gravel and mud with some boulders. In summer, a fair amount of weeds cover certain areas. A lodge complete with cabins and a popular campground is situated right at the river mouth.

General Access: By road. The Sterling Highway has short and easy access to the confluence.
Access Point: Izaak Walton Campground – MP 82.3 Sterling Highway. South on access road on east side of bridge 0.1 mile to campground and the Moose River. Developed parking, camping, restrooms, and boat launch. Trail leads from campground to river mouth.

Fishing Opportunities

Restrictions: Fly-fishing only area May 15 – August 15. Additional restrictions in effect (consult ADF&G regulations).

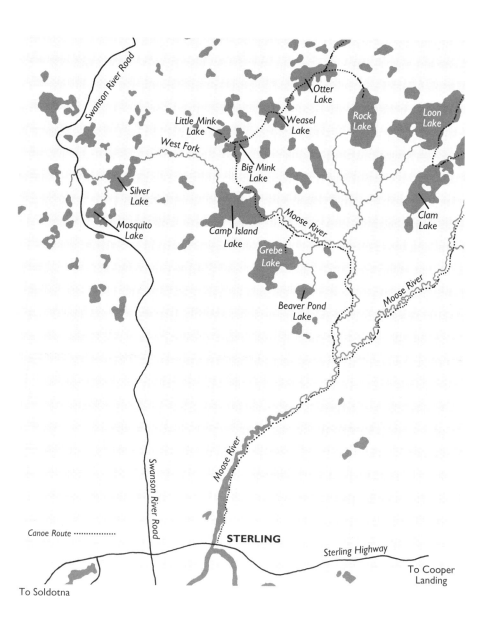

King Salmon
Rating: Poor to fair.
Regulatory Season: January 1 through July 31.
Timing: May 10 – July 31, peak June 15 – 30 (early run) and July 20 – 31 (late run).
Size: Average 20 to 40 pounds (early run) and 30 to 50 pounds (late run), up to 80 pounds or more possible.
Tip: Large, gaudy flies seem to draw a few strikes. Early morning, evening best bet.

Red Salmon
Rating: Fair to good (early run); good to excellent (late run).
Timing: May 15 – September 30, peak June 10 – 20 (early run), July 20 – August 5 (late run).
Size: Average 6 to 7 pounds, up to 11 pounds (early run); 5 to 8 pounds, up to 14 pounds or more (late run).
Tip: One of the very few ways to be successful on these early fish is to try just above or below the river mouth. Watch for jumpers in the slack water. If none are seen, move on.

Silver Salmon
Rating: Good (early run); good to excellent (late run).
Regulatory Season: July 1 – October 31.
Timing: July 15 – October 31, peak August 15 – September 5 (early run), September 20 – 30 (late run).
Size: Average 6 to 10 pounds, up to 18 pounds (early run); 8 to 14 pounds, up to 22 pounds or more (late run).
Tip: Silvers are available throughout the confluence area, from the bridge on down to the mouth and beyond. Early morning and evening best time.

Pink Salmon
Rating: Excellent.
Timing: July 1 – September 15, peak August 10 – 20.
Size: Average 3 to 6 pounds, up to 8 pounds. Trophy/record-sized fish to 10-12 pounds possible.
Tip: The fresher fish are usually found right at the mixing zone of the glacial Kenai and clear Moose. Also, try early in the run for quality. Odd-numbered years only see a few pinks returning to Moose.

Rainbow Trout
Rating: Good.
Regulatory Season: June 11 – May 1.
Timing: June 11 – late December, peak early July – mid-September.
Size: Average 10 to 20 inches, some larger fish to 28 inches and 8-10 pounds. Trophy trout up to 12-15 pounds or more are a possibility in summer.
Tip: Try the clear waters of the Moose between salmon runs. The confluence waters of the Kenai River produce fish during the whole season. Smaller trout feed throughout the confluence all summer and fall, yet larger fish are often caught during August and September by anglers soaking bait for silver salmon. For very good

trout action, consider the upper reaches of the Moose as described elsewhere in this chapter.

Dolly Varden
Rating: Good.
Timing: Mid-March – late December, peak mid-July – early September.
Size: Average 10 to 20 inches, some larger fish to 25 inches and 5-6 pounds. Trophy char up to 10-12 pounds or more a possibility in late summer.
Tip: Try the clear waters of the Moose between salmon runs. As with rainbows, the confluence is mainly a feeding area for char in mid- to late summer. Size of fish is generally not very large but some big Kenai fish occasionally do pull in here. Apart from the late season peak, there is a smaller abundance of Dolly Varden in spring, primarily May, as Kenai and Moose fish are moving downstream from overwintering areas heading to the sea.

Other Species: RW,NP,(CS).

MOOSE RIVER

Main Species: Silver salmon, rainbow trout, and Dolly Varden.

Summary: This section of the Moose River has some good opportunity for both salmon and trout. The "hot spot" areas on the river are a ways upstream from the highway crossing and require a watercraft to access. As the Moose begins to narrow down about four miles up, anglers begin to encounter stream characteristics that are necessary in finding structure and fish concentrations. Silver salmon and rainbow trout action is often very good.

Description: In its lower reaches the river is wide with very little current. The Moose looses its big water appearance in the middle reaches, increasingly looking more like a typical stream than a river the further upstream one goes. Above West Fork Moose, the mainstem river no longer has any resemblance to the lower sections; dense brush along the banks as the stream meanders considerably through a landscape of bogs and forest, vegetation mats covering much of the bottom. Water is clear with a distinct brownish hue, tinted by the numerous marshland lakes of the area.

General Access: By road and watercraft. The far lower end of the Moose is accessible from the Sterling Highway; however, to reach the middle and upper portions of the river a canoe or some other form of watercraft is necessary. There are a few ways to approach this river. One is to launch at the highway bridge in Sterling and move on up the river to the middle river and its tributaries. A second possibility is to launch from Swan Lake Road and portage through to the upper river.

Access Point A: *Izaak Walton Campground* – MP 82.3 Sterling Highway. South on access road on east side of bridge 0.1 mile to campground and Moose River. Developed parking, camping, restrooms, and boat launch available. Travel north up Moose River by canoe about 5.5 miles to confluence with West Fork Moose, or continue another 5 miles up main Moose to confluence of East Fork Moose and the beginning of North Fork Moose.

Access Point B: *Swan Lake Canoe Route (East Entrance)* – MP 83.4 Sterling Highway. North on Swanson River Road 17.2 miles, right on Swan Lake Road 9.7 miles to entrance on right. Parking. See map on page 183 for approximate route of access and distance. Sequence of waters to be traveled: Portage Lake, No Name Pond, Birch Lake, Teal Lake, Mallard Lake, Raven Lake, and Swan Lake to North Fork Moose River. Paddle downstream 3 miles to confluence with East Fork Moose River and the beginning of main Moose. From here it is 10.5 miles to the Sterling Highway Bridge in Sterling.

Fishing Opportunities
Restrictions: King salmon fishing prohibited. Closed to all fishing May 2 – June 10 (consult ADF&G regulations).

Silver Salmon
Rating: Good.
Regulatory Season: July 1 – October 31.
Timing: July 15 – September 30, peak August 20 – September 10.
Size: Average 5 to 10 pounds, some larger fish to 12 pounds. Silvers up to 15 pounds or more are caught every now and then.
Tip: Look for concentrations of silvers in deep holes and runs and at the mouth of tributary streams. The confluence of Moose and West Fork Moose is a local hot spot, as well as near the mouth of East Fork Moose.

Rainbow Trout
Rating: Good.
Timing: June 11 – late November, peak mid-July – early October.
Size: Average 8 to 16 inches, a few larger fish up to 25 inches and 5 pounds.
Tip: Good action possible through summer but better in fall as both aggressiveness and fish size increases.

Dolly Varden
Rating: Good.
Timing: June 11 – late November, peak mid-August – early October.
Size: Average 8 to 16 inches, a few larger fish up to 23 inches and 4 pounds.
Tip: Smaller char available in early summer with larger specimens available in late summer and fall.

Other Species: RS,PS,RW,NP,(KS).

WEST FORK MOOSE RIVER DRAINAGE
Includes Grebe, Camp Island, Silver, Mosquito, Little Mink, Rock, and Loon lakes.
Note: Access to Rock and Loon lakes is through the North Fork Moose River.

Summary: Anglers able to reach these waters can experience some exceptional action for rainbow trout and arctic char with added potential to catch landlocked salmon. Camp Island Lake is recognized as being one of the richer fisheries along the Swan Lake Canoe Route but good opportunities await in all waters, particularly in late summer and fall.

Although anglers can do well from shore, a canoe or some other type of watercraft

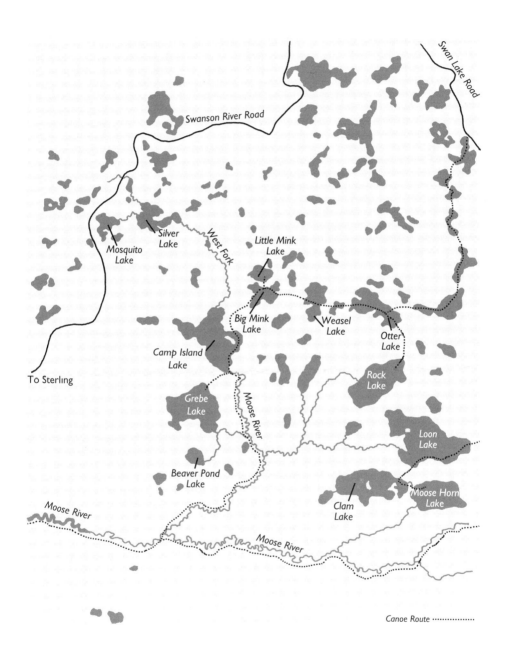

Swan Lake Road

Swanson River Road

Silver
Lake

Little Mink
Lake

West Fork

Mosquito
Lake

Big Mink
Lake

Weasel
Lake

Otter
Lake

Camp Island
Lake

Rock
Lake

To Sterling

Grebe
Lake

Moose River

Loon
Lake

Beaver Pond
Lake

Moose Horn
Lake

Moose River

Clam
Lake

Moose River

Canoe Route · · · · · · · · · · · · · ·

is recommended. It should be noted that Big Mink Lake to the south of Little Mink is barren of fish, and Rock Lake is one of a very few lakes on the Kenai Peninsula that has a population of kokanee. Mosquito, Silver, and Grebe lakes also make for good ice fishing waters since they are readily accessible from Swanson River Road.

Description: The West Fork Moose drainage lakes are clearwater lakes with a slight tannic tint, usually less than two miles long, with a depth varying from 30 to 75 feet. They typically receive only a fair amount of fishing pressure during the year owed to the fact that they are for the most part situated off the road system, very few or no developed trails exists, with the only practical mode of access being by canoe.

General Access: By trail and canoe. The majority of area lakes are reached via the Moose River and West Fork Moose River from the Sterling Highway Bridge in Sterling, a few also reached from Swanson River Road. Portaging is necessary to access some of these waters. Signs are usually posted along lake shorelines marking point of entry/exit for trails. A detailed area map is highly recommended.

South Access: Sterling Highway
Waters: Grebe, Camp Island, Little Mink, Rock, and Loon lakes.
Access Point: Izaak Walton Campground – MP 82.3 Sterling Highway. South on access road on east side of bridge 0.1 mile to campground and Moose River. Developed parking, camping, restrooms, and boat launch available. See map on page 178 for approximate access, sequence of waters to be traveled, and distance. *Note:* Travel on West Fork Moose can be very difficult due to heavy weed and brush.
    Route A: Moose, West Fork Moose, Camp Island, and Grebe.
    Route B: Moose, West Fork Moose, Camp Island, Big Mink, and Little Mink.
    Route C: Moose, North Fork Moose, Swan, Loon, and Rock.

West Access: Swanson River Road
Waters: Grebe, Mosquito, and Silver lakes.
Access Point: MP 83.4 Sterling Highway. North on Swanson River Road.
    Grebe Lake: MP 3.6; pullout on right. Limited parking. Undeveloped trail leads approximately 3 miles northeast to lake.
    Mosquito Lake: MP 7.8; Mosquito Lake Trailhead on right. Parking. Trail leads 200 yards east to lake
    Silver Lake: MP 9.1; Silver Lake Trailhead on right. Parking. Trail leads 1 mile east to lake.

North Access: Swan Lake Road
Waters: Rock, Loon, Little Mink, Camp Island, and Grebe lakes.
Access Point: Swan Lake Canoe Route (West Entrance) – MP 83.4 Sterling Highway. North on Swanson River Road 17.2 miles, right on Swan Lake Road 3.9 miles to entrance on right. Parking. See map on page 183 for approximate access, sequence of waters to be traveled, and distance.
    Route A: Canoe, Canoe #2, Canoe #3, Contact, Marten, Spruce, Otter, Rock and Loon.
    Route B: Canoe, Canoe #2, Canoe #3, Contact, Marten, Spruce, Otter, Duckbill, Weasel, Big Mink, and Little Mink / Big Mink, Camp Island, and Grebe.

Fishing Opportunities

Main Species: Rainbow trout, arctic char, and kokanee.
Other Species: RS,SS,DV,NP.
Area Restrictions: Silver salmon fishing prohibited November 1 – June 30. The Moose and West Fork Moose rivers are closed to all fishing May 2 – June 10 (consult ADF&G regulations).

GREBE LAKE

Access: By trail from Swanson River Road and canoe from Sterling Highway (see access information above).
Fishing:
Rainbow Trout
Rating: Good.
Timing: Year-round, peak mid-May – early June and early September – mid-October.
Size: Average 8 to 16 inches, a few larger fish up to 25 inches and 5 pounds.
Tip: Try lake outlet (east end) in spring and fall.

CAMP ISLAND LAKE

Access: By canoe from Sterling Highway (see access information above).
Fishing:
Rainbow Trout
Rating: Good to excellent.
Timing: Year-round, peak mid-May – early June and early September – mid-October.
Size: Average 10 to 16 inches, a few larger fish up to 26 inches and 6 pounds.
Tip: Try lake outlet (east end) and inlet (northwest end) in spring and fall.

Arctic Char
Rating: Good.
Timing: Year-round, peak mid-May – early June and early September – late January.
Size: Average 10 to 20 inches, a few larger fish up to 23 inches and 4 pounds.
Tip: Try lake outlet (east end) and inlet (northwest end) in spring and fall.

SILVER LAKE

Access: By trail from Swanson River Road (see access information above).
Fishing:
Rainbow Trout
Rating: Good.
Timing: Year-round, peak mid-May – early June and early September – late December.
Size: Average 10 to 16 inches, a few larger fish up to 25 inches and 5 pounds.
Tip: Try lake outlet (east end) and inlet (northwest end) in spring and fall.

Arctic Char
Rating: Fair.

Timing: Year-round, peak mid-May – early June and early September – late January.

Size: Average 10 to 20 inches, a few larger fish up to 23 inches and 4 pounds.

Tip: Try lake outlet (east end) and inlet (northwest end) in spring and fall, the edges of steep drop-offs in winter. Fish are deep in summer.

MOSQUITO LAKE
Access: By trail from Swanson River Road (see access information above).
Fishing:
Rainbow Trout
Rating: Good.

Timing: Year-round, peak mid-May – early June and early September – late December.

Size: Average 8 to 16 inches, a few larger fish up to 25 inches and 5 pounds.

Tip: Try lake outlet (east end) and inlet (northwest end) in spring and fall.

LITTLE MINK LAKE
Access: By canoe from Sterling Highway or Swan Lake Road (see access information above).
Fishing:
Rainbow Trout
Rating: Good.

Timing: Year-round, peak mid-May – early June and early September – mid-October.

Size: Average 10 to 16 inches, a few larger fish up to 24 inches and 4-5 pounds.

Tip: Try edges of steep drop-offs and around weed beds in spring and fall.

ROCK LAKE
Access: By canoe from Sterling Highway or Swan Lake Road (see access information above).
Fishing:
Kokanee
Rating: Fair to good.

Timing: Year-round, peak mid-May to mid-June.

Size: Average 8 to 12 inches, a few larger fish up to 15 inches.

Tip: Move around lake until a fish is hooked. Kokanee travel in schools so try to stay with them.

LOON LAKE
Access: By canoe from Sterling Highway or Swan Lake Road (see access information above).
Fishing:
Rainbow Trout
Rating: Good to excellent.

Timing: Year-round, peak mid-May – early June and early September – mid-October.

Size: Average 10 to 16 inches, a few larger fish up to 24 inches and 4-5 pounds.

Tip: Try the edges of steep drop-offs and around weed beds in spring and fall.

NORTH FORK MOOSE RIVER DRAINAGE

Includes North Fork Moose River, Swan Lake, Clam Lake, and Moosehorn Lake.

Summary: North Fork Moose (also known as just Moose River) offers some great fishing opportunities along with at least a moderate amount of solitude, solely due to the fact that miles of canoeing is required to reach this area. A solid run of silver salmon hits here in late summer accompanied with some fabulous trout and char action lasting into fall.

Swan Lake is one of the best fisheries on the Swan Lake Canoe Route and in the Moose River drainage with exceptional action for trout and char. Near-trophy rainbows are a possibility as well. Clam and Moosehorn lakes also provide top-notch opportunities. Only a small number of other anglers come through here because the lakes are somewhat remote and requires several portages from any which direction one approaches. Spring and fall is the best time to be here.

Description: At this point in the drainage, the Moose is still just a large stream, slow flowing and fairly deep in places. The area lakes are fairly good-sized, some of the largest in the Moose system. Water is clear with a slight tannic stain.

General Access: By canoe. The lakes and streams of this area can be accessed from two opposite sides; one from the Sterling Highway and the other from Swan Lake Road via Swanson River Road. A detailed area map is highly recommended.

Access Point A: *Izaak Walton Campground* – MP 82.3 Sterling Highway. South on access road on east side of bridge 0.1 mile to campground and Moose River. Developed parking, camping, restrooms, and boat launch available. See map on page 183 for approximate route of access and distance. Sequence of waters to be traveled: Moose, North Fork Moose, Swan, Loon, Clam, and Moosehorn.

Access Point B: *Swan Lake Canoe Route (East Entrance)* – MP 83.4 Sterling Highway. North on Swanson River Road 17.2 miles, right on Swan Lake Road 9.7 miles to entrance on right. Parking. See map on page 183 for approximate route of access and distance. Sequence of waters to be traveled: Portage, No Name Pond, Birch, Teal, Mallard, Raven, Swan, Loon, Clam, and Moosehorn.

Fishing Opportunities

Main Species: Rainbow trout, Dolly Varden, and arctic char.
Other Species: RS,PS.
Restrictions: Closed to all fishing May 2 – June 10. Silver salmon fishing prohibited November 1 – June 30 (consult ADF&G regulations).

NORTH FORK MOOSE RIVER

Access: By canoe from Sterling Highway (see access information above).

Fishing:
Silver Salmon
Rating: Fair to good.
Regulatory Season: July 1 – October 31.
Timing: August 1 – October 5, peak August 25 –September 15.

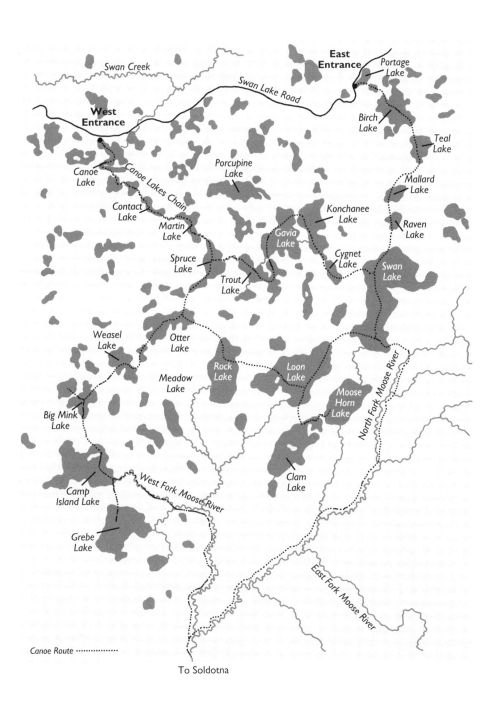

Size: Average 5 – 10 pounds, a few larger fish up to 15 pounds.
Tip: Search out deep holes and runs with minimal vegetation. This fork of Moose River experiences a good return of silvers in fall; however, due to the distance traveled and the small size of the waterway, many of the salmon will have blushed upon arriving here. But there are some nice bright and semi-bright fish to be caught; such as early in the season while the run is still building towards a peak.

Rainbow Trout
Rating: Good.
Timing: June 11 – mid-November, peak mid-July – early October.
Size: Average 8 to 16 inches, a few larger fish up to 25 inches and 5 pounds.
Tip: Productive angling most of summer but gets good and consistent as salmon show in fall.

Dolly Varden
Rating: Good.
Timing: June 11 – mid-November, peak mid-August – early October.
Size: Average 8 to 16 inches, a few larger fish up to 23 inches and 4 pounds.
Tip: A few smaller char available in early summer with larger specimens showing in late summer and fall.

SWAN LAKE
Access: By canoe from Sterling Highway or Swan Lake Road (see access information above).

Fishing:
Rainbow Trout
Rating: Excellent.
Timing: Year-round, peak mid-May – early June and early September – mid-October.
Size: Average 10 to 22 inches, a few larger fish up to 28 inches and 8 pounds.
Tip: Try the lake outlet and the edges of steep drop-offs and around weed beds in spring and fall.

Arctic Char
Rating: Good.
Timing: Year-round, peak mid-May – early June and early September – mid-October.
Size: Average 10 to 20 inches, a few larger fish up to 24 inches and 4-5 pounds.
Tip: Try edges of steep drop-offs and around weed beds in spring and fall. Fish are situated in deep water during summer.

CLAM LAKE
Access: By canoe from Sterling Highway or Swan Lake Road (see access information above).

Fishing:

Rainbow Trout
Rating: Good to excellent.
Timing: Year-round, peak mid-May – early June and early September – mid-October.
Size: Average 10 to 20 inches, a few larger fish up to 25 inches and 5 pounds.
Tip: Try near the lake outlet, edges of steep drop-offs, and around weed beds in spring and fall.

MOOSEHORN LAKE
Access: By canoe from Sterling Highway or Swan Lake Road (see access information above).
Fishing:

Rainbow Trout
Rating: Good to excellent.
Timing: Year-round, peak mid-May – early June and early September – mid-October.
Size: Average 10 to 20 inches, a few larger fish up to 25 inches and 5 pounds or more.
Tip: Try near the lake inlet and outlet, edges of steep drop-offs, and around weed beds in spring and fall.

EAST FORK MOOSE RIVER DRAINAGE
Includes East Fork Moose River, Afonasi Lake, Imeri Lake, Watson Lake, Peterson Lake, and Kelly Lake.

WATSON LAKE

Main Species: Rainbow trout.

Summary: Watson Lake, despite its close proximity to the road system, has some worthwhile trout action in spring and fall. A watercraft of some sort is highly recommended to reach the most productive areas of the lake. There are some big rainbows in here and they are especially susceptible late in the season when salmon run.

Watson also provides limited access to two adjoining lakes, Imeri and Afonasi, both of which has decent trout fishing available. East Fork Moose River connects all of the waters (except Hikers Lake) in the Seven Lakes chain.

Description: Watson is fairly small clearwater lake, perhaps three quarter of a mile long and a quarter of a mile wide.

General Access: By road. The Sterling Highway provides convenient access to lake.
Access Point: Watson Lake Campground – MP 71.3 Sterling Highway. North on gravel road 0.7 mile to campground and lake. Parking, camping, restrooms, and boat launch available.

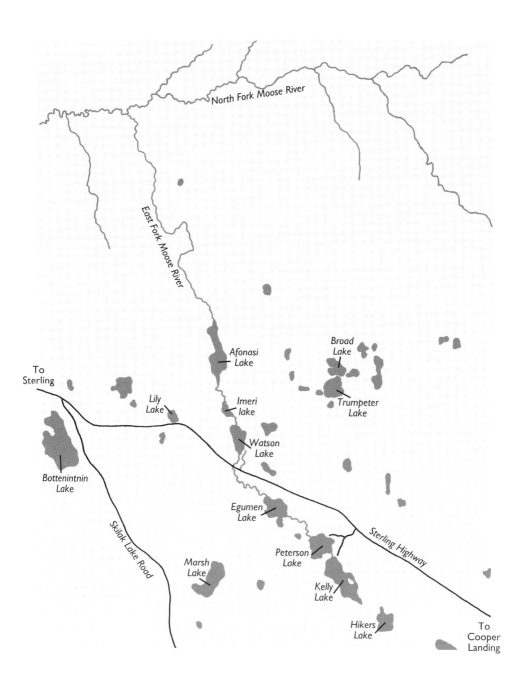

To
Sterling

Bottenintnin
Lake

Lily
Lake

Afonasi
Lake

Imeri
lake

Watson
Lake

Egumen
Lake

Marsh
Lake

Peterson
Lake

Kelly
Lake

Hikers
Lake

Broad
Lake

Trumpeter
Lake

East Fork Moose River

North Fork Moose River

Skilak Lake Road

Sterling Highway

To
Cooper
Landing

Fishing Opportunities

Restrictions: Silver salmon fishing prohibited November 1 – June 30. East Fork Moose River is closed to all fishing May 2 – June 10 (consult ADF&G regulations).

Rainbow Trout
Rating: Good.
Timing: Year-round, peak mid-May – early June and early September – mid-October.
Size: Average 10 to 16 inches, a few larger fish up to 25 inches and 5 pounds or more.
Tip: Try the lake inlet and outlet, edges of steep drop-offs, and around weed beds in spring and fall.

Other Species: SS,DV,NP.

Imeri Lake: The smallest lake of the Seven Lakes chain, offering fair to good rainbow action. Best fishing in fall. Portage canoe via East Fork Moose River or hike through rough terrain to lake.

Afonasi Lake: Situated northwest of Imeri Lake, Afonasi is over a mile long and probably has some of the better rainbow trout fishing of the Seven Lakes due to its relative remoteness. Try in spring and fall. Portage canoe via East Fork Moose River and Imeri Lake or hike through rough terrain to lake.

East Fork Moose River: A small and for the most part shallow stream presenting fair to good opportunities, mainly for rainbow trout, in late summer and fall. Look for bigger fish in September. Dolly Varden are present in the lower reaches during autumn as well. Access is via Moose River from Sterling or from any one of the area lakes. The Sterling Highway crosses the stream at MP 71.4.

The stream is closed to all fishing from May 2 through June 10 (consult ADF&G regulations).

EGUMEN LAKE

Main Species: Rainbow trout.

Summary: A short hike in from the Sterling Highway can put anglers onto some very good trout fishing. Egumen Lake has a good population of rainbows that are highly active in spring and fall. Although fishing off the bank is possible during the peak of the season, the most consistent and best action comes from having a canoe or other type of watercraft to access the most productive locations.

Description: Of moderate depth, Egumen is quite small at no more than approximately half a mile long and wide. The water is clear with a slight brownish tint.

General Access: By trail. The Sterling Highway provides trailhead to lake.
Access Point: MP 70.8 Sterling Highway. South at pullout and small parking area. Trail leads 0.25 mile to lake. No facilities.

Fishing Opportunities

Restrictions: Silver salmon fishing prohibited November 1 – June 30. East Fork Moose River is closed to all fishing May 2 – June 10 (consult ADF&G regulations).

Rainbow Trout

Rating: Good.

Timing: Year-round, peak mid-May – early June and early September – mid-October.

Size: Average 10 to 16 inches, a few larger fish up to 25 inches and 5 pounds or more.

Tip: Try the lake inlet and outlet, edges of steep drop-offs, and around weed beds in spring and fall.

Other Species: SS,DV,NP.

PETERSON & KELLY LAKES

Main Species: Rainbow trout.

Summary: Peterson and Kelly lakes are road accessible and sees a fair amount of angling pressure during the season, but they sustain a healthy rainbow population and fishers can still do quite well in spring and fall. As usual, a canoe or other type of watercraft is recommended in reaching the best spots.

Description: Peterson and Kelly are the headwaters of East Fork Moose River, which at this point is merely a trickle of a stream. Like other lakes within this system, the clarity of both waters is influenced by the marshland surroundings, giving them a brownish tint.

General Access: By road. Sterling Highway provides access to lakes via side road.

Peterson Lake

Access Point: Peterson Lake Campground – MP 68.4 Sterling Highway. South on gravel road 0.3 mile to a "Y," right fork 0.2 mile to campground and lake. Parking, camping, boat launch.

Kelly Lake

Access Point: Kelly Lake Campground – MP 68.4 Sterling Highway. South on gravel road 0.3 mile to a "Y," left fork 0.3 mile to campground and lake. Parking, camping, boat launch.

Fishing Opportunities

Restrictions: Silver salmon fishing prohibited November 1 – June 30. East Fork Moose River is closed to all fishing May 2 – June 10 (consult ADF&G regulations).

Rainbow Trout

Rating: Fair to Good.

Timing: Year-round, peak mid-May – early June and early September – mid-October.

Size: Average 10 to 16 inches, a few larger fish up to 25 inches and 5 pounds or more.

Tip: Try the lake inlet and outlet, edges of steep drop-offs, and around weed beds in spring and fall.

Other Species: SS,DV,NP.

UPPER KENAI RIVER

Description

The upper Kenai is essentially the stretch of river from the outlet of Kenai Lake and the Sterling Highway Bridge at Cooper Landing downstream to the Skilak Lake inlet, a distance of 17.3 miles. As the Kenai pours out of Kenai Lake, the current is very slow and steady, the river wide and fairly deep in places. This continues until the "chute" at *Fisherman's Bend* (river mile 80.5), where the current finally picks up speed, the river narrows, and a true float experience can be achieved. Class I water dominates most of the river (which makes it easy to navigate for a novice rafter/boater) until Kenai Canyon below Jim's Landing, where Class II and III water takes hold for the next two miles before the river slows down again the next three miles prior to dumping into Skilak Lake. The average stream gradient between the lakes is 13.9 feet per mile.

Much of the Kenai is concealed by thick vegetation and trees, making any excursion by trail into the river or a float downstream a sense of semi-wilderness. The Chugach Mountains lining the river valley add considerably to the scenic beauty.

Wildlife such as moose, bears, waterfowl, and other animal species are a common sight along this stretch of river. Eagles are a common sight anytime but perhaps particularly so during the winter and early spring months as several dozen birds congregate in the area to feed on late-spawning silver salmon.

Access

Since the Sterling Highway parallels almost the entire upper section of Kenai River, access is not a problem. There are a multitude of turnouts and several campgrounds present, all with trails in varying conditions leading to and along the river. A cable ferry (at MP 54.9) provides, for a fee, additional access to the southern shore of the river with trails upstream and down.

Fishing

Angling on the Upper Kenai River can be described as legendary. Already in the early 1900s did people report on the outstanding sport fishing opportunities at hand in the Kenai and main tributary Russian River. But it was not until the 60s that word really got out about the excellent salmon and trout fishery and interest boomed through the 70s and 80s until today.

Salmon runs are still prolific and healthy as ever and the trout and char populations are in great shape. Although the upper river is closed year-round to king salmon fishing and the appearance of pink and chum salmon is considered negligible, the massive numbers of red and silver salmon and the outstanding action in which they offer is nothing short of incredible. The throng of anglers at the confluence of Kenai and Russian rivers is a testament to the popularity and quality of salmon fishing available. As a matter of fact, the upper Kenai drainage is responsible for catches measuring in the tens of thousands of salmon per season. But despite anglers standing elbow-to-elbow in a few locations in what is the second largest sport fishery in the state, much of the upper Kenai remains remarkably unspoiled. It is entirely possible still, with a little scouting, to have a stretch of river to oneself, even during the height of the salmon runs.

And the trout and char of upper Kenai attracts its own culture of anglers as fly-fishers from around the world gather here in summer and fall in pursuit of a trophy. Besides fish reaching dimensions of 30 to 35 inches, skilled anglers have the realistic potential of hooking rainbows and Dolly Varden by the dozens per day during the peak of the season in August and September.

As a means of getting away from the more popular fishing spots, a trip by raft or drift boat on the upper Kenai is a great idea and an experience in itself. Guided trips are available out of Cooper Landing. For anglers wishing to go by foot, there exist a lot of possibilities (see access information above). Even though there are developed trails in the area, the surrounding vegetation is not as dense as to prevent a fisher from exploring new and seemingly untouched territory along the river away from the beaten path. However, this is bear country and appropriate measures should be taken to avoid a potentially dangerous confrontation.

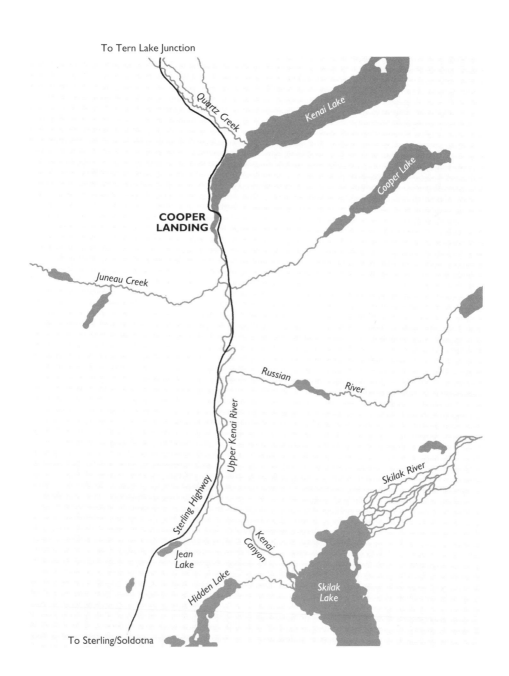

To Tern Lake Junction

Quartz Creek

Kenai Lake

Cooper Lake

COOPER LANDING

Juneau Creek

Russian River

Upper Kenai River

Skilak River

Sterling Highway

Kenai Canyon

Jean Lake

Hidden Lake

Skilak Lake

To Sterling/Soldotna

Chapter Contents

The following are the game fish present, the various sections of the Upper Kenai River drainage, and the page number in which more detailed information can be found.

TIMING:

Upper Kenai River

FISH	JAN	FEB	MAR	APR	MAY	JUN	JUL	AUG	SEP	OCT	NOV	DEC
RS												
SS												
PS												
CS												
RT												
DV												
AG												
RW												

Species Information

Salmon

Several runs of salmon occur, giving anglers a generous season lasting from mid-June until November, with exceptional opportunities for red and silver salmon. There are several intense bursts of fish that come through here starting with the reds in June and July and carrying on into August, September, and even October for silver salmon. Pink and king salmon are present as well along with a trickle of chum salmon.

Red Salmon

Reds are present continuously from May to October counting both early and late runs, with anglers focusing on the peak of the respective runs in June and July yielding superb action. The late run can be almost overwhelming as it stages in the lower portion of the upper Kenai between the canyon and Skilak Lake, soon after flooding the entire river in a matter of days.

The prime area for reds has long been regarded as the stretch of water between the Canyon and the mouth of Russian River and experiences a relatively prolonged peak compared to that section of the Kenai between the lake and the Russian, which tends to be very brief. Success can be had most anywhere during the height of the runs, however.

From June into August, anglers find masses of fish swimming upstream close to shore, making them easy targets for properly presented flies. The best areas to try are along gravel beaches with fast to moderately fast moving water just upstream of slow-flowing current associated with deep holes, pools, and runs. In years when the river has relatively good visibility, bright reds may be easily spotted, making sight fishing an excellent option; however, if visibility is somewhat low, fish are difficult to see. In the latter case, many anglers learn to observe and time schools of salmon moving through by the presence of fish that have started turning red, which tend to stand out in the turquoise Kenai. Where there are red or dark shapes indicating fish, there are usually also fresh reds to be found.

When water visibility is good and/or the skies clear and sunny, try darker colored streamer flies or very sparsely tied yarn flies in green, blue, and purple, as well as black from time to time. Chartreuse can be hot. Smaller egg imitations created for trout and char can work very well. Oftentimes under such conditions, the reds migrate a few feet further away from the shoreline to take cover in deeper water. When visibility is down, reds migrate very close to shore in shallow water and anglers score better on bulkier flies in sharp chartreuse, orange, red, and pink. Orange or pink are good colors at dawn and dusk or on dark and rainy days. Yarn flies are often as good as anything else but the majority of anglers use traditional streamers in a combination of colors.

Early Run Reds: These fish represent the beginning of the salmon season on the upper Kenai River. Already in mid-May are they speeding through the canyon area destined for Russian River and beyond. Anglers, however, have to wait until the season opener on June 11 to get to them, at which time the peak of the run is very near. In some years, the bulk of the run has gone through this river section by the third week of June, giving anglers less than ten days to thoroughly enjoy the early fish.

Unlike late-run reds, the pace of early fish is faster and they are usually not found in large concentrations as consistently as the mainstem Kenai reds. Move around until fish can be located. Successful anglers focus their efforts in the stretch of river from the confluence area of Russian River downstream about a mile or two where the reds have a tendency to slow down somewhat and stack up in greater numbers. Additionally, the closer in distance the fish get to the mouth of the Russian, the more they will hug the southern shoreline.

As July comes around, the run is down to a trickle. Early-run reds will be coming through for another couple of weeks still, or about the same time that the bulk of late-run fish hits the river.

The vast majority of these early fish are bound for Russian River so the action tends to be most reliable within the vicinity of this drainage. However, schools of salmon heading to tributaries of Kenai Lake can be intercepted at times in the section of water between the lake and the Russian.

Late Run Reds: The second wave of salmon consists of fish bound for tributaries of Kenai River and Lake as well as the mainstem river. There is a trickle of reds that shoots through during the first two weeks of July but the run will not hit actual stride until the third week of the month. Although the tributary fish will arrive and swim quickly through this section, the mainstem Kenai reds display a slower, steadier pace of infiltration into the upper river. The river can appear completely jammed with salmon in years when the runs are big, seemingly occupying every run, hole, and slough.

The braided water from the mouth of Russian River downstream to Jim's Landing and on into the Canyon to the inlet of Skilak Lake is best to find chrome late-run salmon. The least productive section is the one immediately downstream of Kenai Lake. Albeit a major spawning area for late-run reds, the slow current does not lend for very productive fishing for the species yet some fish may be caught using the right method in the right place.

There are still a reasonably good number of fresh reds left during the first week of August but anglers have to work just a little bit harder to get them since many salmon will be in the process of attaining sexual maturity and finding a fresh specimen beyond mid-month can prove exceedingly difficult. In some years, it is common for a good portion of these late-run fish to start blushing even prior to entering the upper river. Because of this rapid maturation process, many anglers will hit the Kenai hard in July and move on to Russian River in August where the possibility of hooking bright reds is much greater. Yet there are a few stragglers that are available in the Kenai through September and even later. With few exceptions, the only anglers that catch fresh reds in the fall are the ones that sight fish in shallows along gravel beaches or sandbars.

Late-run Kenai reds, apart from their fame of abundance, are also bigger in physical size than fish of most populations around the state. A typical red may weigh seven or eight pounds with 10-pounders not being unusual. It must be noted that the state record red salmon came from the Kenai River, a male of 16 pounds. One specimen reported to have weighed approximately 18 pounds was landed on the upper Kenai near Russian River years ago but was never certified.

Silver Salmon

Of all the salmon species in the Kenai River, none has such widespread timing base as the silvers. From July into February and even later, silver salmon are present in varying degrees of abundance. Two main populations – or runs – represent silver salmon in this area. The first run consists of tributary-bound fish, mainly heading to Russian River and streams draining into Kenai Lake. The second run is made up of mainstem Kenai River salmon.

The fish have a tendency to school up in slow water areas such as sloughs and the mouth of tributaries and side channels, moving upstream through shallows near shore, particularly in the morning and late afternoon and evening. Anglers are commonly able to sight fish for silvers as they migrate between holes or holding areas. This upstream movement generally does not consist of large numbers of fish but rather interspersed individual specimens or small groups of three to four silvers at a time.

Silver salmon are in general not as finicky as reds tend to be and will mouth or attack artificial lures and flies with more vigor. Although anglers will use a wide range of color and pattern flies and lures for silvers, the darker or neutral hues usually do better, such as black, brown, purple, green, and blue. Brighter colors in orange and red and so forth are best on dark days or at dawn and dusk, especially patterns modeled to resemble eggs or roe. When pursuing silver salmon in calm or current free water, a silver or bronze spinner with a touch of blue, green, or chartreuse is best, but a Flash Fly in the same color patterns stripped through a quiet hole can be equally deadly. Bulk yarn flies or egg and roe imitations fished deep in runs with moderate current work exceptionally well at times.

Some anglers prefer to "hunt" for small schools of salmon or individual fish in the more shallow channels using darker-colored fly patterns, this being an especially rewarding method during the early run.

Silvers are much more reliable than reds in this area considering the number of salmon present and holes and runs ideally suited for holding and catching fish. The vast majority of effort on silvers here comes from drift boats but there exists several good roadside access points for anglers to hike in and experience some awesome action.

Early Run Silvers: All of the early-run fish are headed for tributaries of Kenai Lake and usually only makes a casual appearance in this river section before moving on. Appearing already in July with some specimens present as late as October, anglers will find the most productive time to try being around the end of August and the first part of September. It is also common for these fish to appear ever so slightly blushed, especially after Labor Day, so the best quality fish are early in the run. Very few bright or semi-bright tributary silvers remain after the third week of the month.

There are some opportunities to sight fish for silvers between the mouth of Russian River and Jim's Landing (as well as before the river empties into Skilak Lake). It can be a challenge at times considering the abundance of spawning late-run reds present in the same locations, yet success is often very good in early morning and evening.

Late Run Silvers: As the last of the red salmon battalion dies off and the first silver run comes to an end, it is time to look for the heavyweight mainstem silvers to arrive. Scouts move into the upper Kenai starting in mid-September, numbers building into October with a mid-month peak. The run continues strong until the last of the month (and the end of the regulatory silver season) but fair numbers of bright salmon will keep arriving through November on into December. By January the run is down to a trickle.

Silvers have a habit of lingering around in holding spots, sometimes for several weeks, and are very susceptible to lures and flies. Unlike early-run fish, these late silvers are best pursued in deep water of quiet stretches on the Kenai and at the mouths of sloughs and channels instead of shallow stream flows near shore. In other words, sight fishing is generally not a very effective method on late fall salmon.

Successful anglers will either float or hike in to likely holding areas such as deep holes and pools and quiet runs where late-run silvers tend to stack up. Cast spinners and attractor flies in various color combinations.

King Salmon

Early-run kings appear here in June and July heading to streams draining into Kenai Lake. Come August and September, late-run king salmon occupy this stretch of river for spawning purposes. A few of these kings may weigh as much as 80 or 90 pounds or more. Since this area is closed to king fishing, anglers are encouraged to break off any fish hooked as soon as possible.

Pink Salmon

An occasional decent specimen may be caught here in July and August but the majority of pinks anglers may encounter are near or in spawning condition, thus action is poor. The fish passing through here early in the season are fairly small and likely salmon destined for Kenai Lake tributaries, while the late summer pinks are physically larger and probably mainstem Kenai spawners.

Chum Salmon

Very rare catch, may be encountered in July and August. These salmon spawn in tributaries of Kenai Lake.

Trout/Char

The abundance of rainbow trout and Dolly Varden in this river section is, as in the rest of the upper Kenai, based on two main factors: reproduction and food. While the two species largely function the same way in approval of artificial lures and flies based on their common fondness of insect life and salmon by-products, the reproductive cycle are completely opposite in timing as trout spawn in the spring, char in the fall.

The usual pattern of seasonal offerings should be applied in this section of Kenai as elsewhere in the drainage. During the month of June, anglers do well using small spoons and spinners in chrome and smolt pattern flies to imitate the flood of juvenile salmon that pour out of Kenai Lake. As the late run of reds and the first run of silvers arrive, things change gear quickly and egg imitation flies, beads, and attractors are what works. August is the best time but September can be very productive too. As the salmon start to die off, flesh flies are the way to go, especially for rainbows, although char will hit egg offerings quite readily into October and later.

Another bonus opportunity anglers are handed in this area is the fairly decent opportunity for trout and char at the inlet of Skilak Lake where Kenai River dumps in. The fishery begins early in the season and lasts well into winter. (See Skilak Lake description in chapter 8, page 165.)

Rainbow Trout

In late winter (March), the first few rainbow trout of the season begin their migration from Kenai and Skilak lakes into the upper river. By late April and early May, the run is at its peak. There are several spawning streams along the upper Kenai River, the Russian being one of the top producers in terms of both big trout and population size, but parts of the mainstem river act as spawning beds as well. The smaller, immature trout or older fish that are not in the reproductive cycle this time around usually appear in June. All of the upper Kenai River and its tributaries are closed to fishing in spring and early summer to protect these fish. After the process of procreation has been completed (by early June), the trout either drifts spent down back into the mainstem

Kenai or remain in or near the spawning area to feed for the summer and fall.

By the season opener on June 11, there are good numbers of rainbow trout spread throughout this river section and more arriving by the day. Anglers casting smolt and forage imitation flies and small silvery spoons and spinners in side channels and at the mouths of tributary streams and sloughs are usually rewarded with fast and consistent action.

The overall trout population hits a peak starting in late July with the onslaught of late-run red salmon and stays intense through August and into September. As the bulk of the run begins to reach maturity, the rainbow trout season begins in earnest. This is the zenith of trout fishing on the upper Kenai, with successful anglers using beads and egg imitation flies. However, the action may slow down in the first part of September, as the water is full of drifting eggs and the fish gorged and appetite satisfied. Anglers see a spike in activity again about mid-month as the salmon begin to die off, the rainbows now hitting flesh flies. Yet some success may be experienced using forage patterns. This last cycle of feeding lasts into October, at which time anglers will notice a swift drop in action.

With late fall rainbows feel the urge to vacate the upper waters of the Kenai and thus begins a slow migration back to the lakes for the winter. Productive fishing can last until mid-October on the far lower end of the river, in the area of braided channels just above Skilak Lake. By November there are relatively few fish left in the Kenai but anglers may still get into one or two if trying near concentrations of spawning silver salmon; however, these trout will more than likely be gone by December.

Some rainbows will, however, remain in the section of river near Kenai Lake throughout the winter into spring to feed on a run of late-spawning silver salmon. From February until the season closure on May 2, egg and flesh imitations are it.

Lake Trout

Although angling for this species of char is usually associated with a lake environment, a small number of these fish can be found from the highway bridge at the Kenai Lake outlet downstream to approximately river mile 81. The very slow to almost still current and moderately deep water in this section of Kenai River allows lake trout to partake in the feeding opportunities associated with the area salmon runs. Since anglers do not target lake trout in the river, all char are caught incidentally to fishing for other species.

Already in spring do these char move out of the lake to hunt for juvenile salmon and anglers continue to encounter lake trout through summer and fall into winter. Smolt and forage imitation flies and lures work.

Dolly Varden

The Upper Kenai requires a different perspective of sorts regarding char. Not many Dolly Varden are believed to move from Skilak Lake through the rapids into the far upper reaches of the river. Therefore, the fish located above the canyon are speculated to be mainly Kenai Lake char while the fish below the canyon are Skilak char, or, simply put, possibly two distinct populations of Dolly Varden.

The section of water above the canyon has some fish available on the June 11 opener but generally there is not an abundance of char until late July when the second run of red salmon appears. August and September is the season peak. Excellent fishing is the norm using egg imitation flies, corkies, and beads. Spinners in chrome and metallic blue or green fished slowly and deep in likely holes and runs can be deadly for larger than average char.

In mid- to late October, things slow down as the fish begin a slow retreat to the wintering grounds. Dolly Varden in full nuptial coloration are often caught this time of year. Like rainbow trout, some char elect to stay in the river throughout the dark months into spring, taking advantage of the steady flow of protein from late-spawning silver salmon. From the outlet of Kenai Lake and the next two miles of river harbor a small winter population of char. Again, try egg and flesh imitations.

The same time frame can be applied to the river below the Canyon except that fishing may pick up earlier in the summer and stay productive slightly later in the fall. Some decent fishing can be had in the latter part of April in some years before the spring closure takes effect, primarily where the Kenai drains into Skilak. Smolt imitation lures and flies work. Since there is quite a bit of salmon spawning activity in this portion of the Kenai, char tend to linger in the area through most of October. By December, most Dolly Varden will have backed out into Skilak Lake for the winter.

Other

Anglers fishing for trout and char encounter **arctic grayling** every so often, usually in backwater channels and clearwater sloughs in the braided section of the river starting about a mile downstream of Russian River. Round whitefish are more numerous and generally found in late summer and fall. **Northern pike** are believed to be present.

Round Whitefish

The fish begin entering the drainage in June, becoming quite abundant by July and are at their peak from August through October. In November things slow down but catches can be made into December and beyond. Their proliferation in the drainage is largely unknown to most anglers since the fish are only encountered on rare occasion while casting for trout and char.

Early in the season, small insect imitation flies (including nymphs) do get some strikes, as do tiny spoons. Later on when the salmon run, egg imitations, beads, and corkies all produce fish. The trick in many instances to get these fish to bite is to fish the offering very slowly along the bottom, sometimes just letting it sit and dangle in the current. Focus on holes and pools with some depth, very similar structures as when fishing for trout and char.

KENAI RIVER (RM 65 – 69.5)
Area: Skilak Lake Inlet to Jim's Landing.

Main Species: Red and silver salmon, rainbow trout, Dolly Varden, and whitefish.

Summary: There is some phenomenal fishing to be experienced for salmon and trout in this stretch of river. The hot spots include where the upper Kenai flows into Skilak Lake and approximately 2.5 miles upstream, and again downstream of Jim's Landing just above of the canyon. However, there are pockets of water in the canyon itself that sees heavy concentrations of all kinds of fish in season and responsible for some of the biggest rainbow trout caught in the Kenai River.

Upper Kenai River

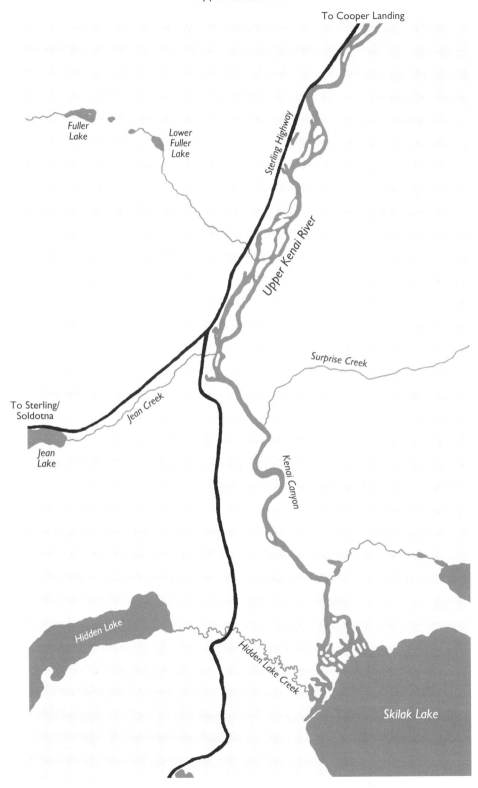

Salmon, rainbow trout, and char all congregate at the braided river mouth and the first couple of miles upstream to the bottom of the canyon. Because of the fairly remote access into this area, there are relatively few other anglers present and the fishing some of the best on the whole river in terms of scenery and abundance of game fish.

Description: The upper river drops into the Kenai River Canyon, a set of Class III rapids stretching for some two miles, just downstream of Jim's Landing. The rapids are not for beginners but can easily be negotiated by individuals having at least some level of floating experience. Scouting the rapids is not necessary. The canyon walls are fairly steep but not that high in most places.

Above and below the canyon, the river flattens out with the traditional deep holes and runs and gravel bars that the upper river is characterized by.

General Access: By boat, trail, and road. Skilak Lake Road from the Sterling Highway (West Entrance, MP 75.2/East Entrance MP 58.0) provides direct as well as trail access to virtually the whole length of the river section. Drift boats are popular to reach south riverbank and stretches of the canyon to river mouth at Skilak Lake.

Roadside/Trail Access

Access Point A: *Jim's Landing* – MP 0.1 Skilak Lake Road. South on access road to campground. Parking, camping, restrooms, and boat launch.

Access Point B: *Upper Kenai River Trailhead* – MP 0.7 Skilak Lake Road. South at turnout to trailhead. Parking and restrooms. Trail leads 0.25 mile to river. Main trail continues south along river canyon to junction with trail coming from the Lower Kenai River Trailhead and provides further access to Skilak Lake Inlet. Little actual river access along most of trail length.

Access Point C: *Lower Kenai River Trailhead*   MP 2.1 Skilak Lake Road. South at turnout to trailhead. Parking and restrooms. Trail leads 0.3 mile to a "Y," take right fork 0.5 mile to river area. Trail parallels river next two miles with some undeveloped/improvised trails leading to riverbank.

Access Point D: *Hidden Creek Trailhead* – MP 4.7 Skilak Lake Road. South at turnout to trailhead. Parking. Trail leads 1.5 mile to "Y," take left fork 0.5 mile to second juncture, keep left 0.75 mile to river. Trail parallels river for the next two miles with some undeveloped/improvised trails leading to riverbank.

Boat Access

Access Point E: *Jim's Landing* – MP 0.1 Skilak Lake Road. South on access road to campground. Parking, camping, restrooms, and boat launch. Float from here 4.5 miles through Kenai Canyon to inlet of Skilak Lake. Takeout is at Upper Skilak Lake Campground, another six miles of flat-water crossing. An outboard engine is highly recommended.

Access Point F: *Upper Skilak Lake Campground* – MP 8.5 Skilak Lake Road. South on access road by sign 1.9 mile to campground and Skilak Lake. Developed parking, campground, restrooms, and boat launch. Motor from here east six miles across lake to inlet and mouth of Upper Kenai River. Locate trail leading upstream along river. *Note:* Motorized boats not allowed on upper Kenai.

Fishing Opportunities

Restrictions: King salmon fishing prohibited. Closed to all fishing May 2 – June 10. Additional restrictions are in effect (consult ADF&G regulations).

Red Salmon

Rating: Good (early run) and excellent (late run).

Timing: June 11 – October 15, peak June 15 – 25 (early run) and July 20 – August 5 (late run).

Size: Average 6 to 7 pounds, up to 11 pounds (early run); 5 to 9 pounds, up to 12 pounds (late run). Catches of reds up to 14 pounds or more possible, especially in late July.

Tip: Search the braided section of the river near its mouth for schools of reds moving through or the area immediately above the canyon for resting fish. The lower river from the canyon to Skilak Lake is often hot.

Silver Salmon

Rating: Good to excellent.

Regulatory Season: July 1 – October 31.

Timing: July 15 – October 31, peak August 20 – September 5 (early run) and October 1 – 20 (late run).

Size: Average 6 to 10 pounds, up to 14 pounds (early run); 8 to 14 pounds, up to 18 pounds (late run). A very few trophy specimens up to 22 pounds or more may be present the first half of October.

Tip: Look for silvers at the edges of fast current and slow water, such as in sloughs, backwater channels, or the head of holes and pools. Fish often travel close to shore. Any deep hole or run with some slack water usually holds fish, including the outer edges of sloughs and backwater channels.

Rainbow Trout

Rating: Good to excellent.

Timing: June 11 – late December, peak late July – early October.

Size: Average 10 to 20 inches, some larger fish to 25 inches and 5-6 pounds. Trophy rainbows up to 30 inches and 12 pounds or more possible. Exceptional specimens weighing as much as 20 pounds are known to be in this river.

Tip: Side and back channels, deep holes, and areas behind spawning salmon are hot spots. The canyon area is famed for yielding trophy trout.

Dolly Varden

Rating: Good.

Timing: June 11 – late December, peak late July – mid-October.

Size: Average 10 to 20 inches, some larger fish to 30 inches and 10-12 pounds. Trophy char up to 18 pounds or more possible.

Tip: Besides promising spots along the main river, anglers also catch many char in deeper side and back channels and the rear end of holes and pools containing spawning salmon.

Round Whitefish

Rating: Poor to fair.

Timing: June 11 – mid-January, peak late July – late October.

Size: Average 10 to 16 inches, a few larger fish up to 20 inches and 3 pounds.
Tip: Try areas just downstream of spawning salmon.

KENAI RIVER (RM 69.5 – 74)
Area: Jim's Landing to Russian River.

Main Species: Red and silver salmon, rainbow trout, Dolly Varden, and whitefish.

Summary: Without a doubt this is the top stretch of water on the upper Kenai River for all game fish present. Salmon runs, aided by strong pulses of fish bound for Russian River, are heavy and consistent. There are a multitude of structure that lends to experiencing superb red and silver salmon action, and rainbow trout and Dolly Varden are at their peak here in both sheer numbers as well as size. Also, the fishing season is extended – lasting from mid-June until May – so anglers virtually have close to a full year to hone their skill. This river section is perfectly suited for both boat and shore fishing.

Description: Unlike the upper section of Kenai River above the Russian River confluence, this stretch of the Kenai has an abundance of islands, side channels, sloughs, and gravel beaches, perfect habitat for both fish and fishers. There is little settlement in the area, except for around Russian River, with much of the land situated within the Kenai National Wildlife Refuge. Wildlife is common here; moose, eagles, and both brown and black bears are all spotted frequently along the river.

General Access: By road. The Sterling Highway parallels the river more or less for three miles with a multitude of access points along the way. Some of the more popular points are described below.

Roadside Access

Access Point A: *Kenai-Russian River Campground* – MP 55.0 Sterling Highway. South on paved road short distance to recreation area including and river. Developed parking, camping, restrooms, and boat launch. Trail leads downstream along river from campground. Additionally, anglers can take cable ferry across river and hike both upstream and down for two to three miles or more. This is also the access site for the Russian River.

Access Point B: MP 55.5 Sterling Highway. South on turnout. Parking. Trails lead upstream and down along the river.

Access Point C: MP 56.4 Sterling Highway. South on turnout. Parking. Trails lead along slough and through forest 200 yards to river and continue downstream along Kenai approximately a quarter of a mile.

Access Point D: MP 56.9 Sterling Highway. South on turnout. Parking. Trails lead short distance to river and continue upstream and down along river.

Access Point E: *Jim's Landing* – MP 58.0 Sterling Highway. Southwest on Skilak Lake Road short distance to access road on left, continue short distance to campground. Parking, camping, restrooms, and boat launch. Trails lead upstream and down from camping/parking areas.

Boat Access

Anglers wanting to float this portion of the river have two main put-in locations; one at Kenai Lake outlet and the Sterling Highway Bridge (see description on page 207 this chapter), the other at Sportman's Landing near the Russian River confluence (see Point A description above). Take-out is usually at Jim's Landing (see Point E description above), unless one wants to continue down through Kenai Canyon to Skilak Lake and Upper Skilak Lake Campground. *Note:* There are no other roadside take-out points for boats between Jim's Landing and Upper Skilak Lake Campground. Motorized boats not allowed on upper Kenai.

Fishing Opportunities

Restrictions: King salmon fishing prohibited. Closed to all fishing May 2 – June 10. Additional restrictions are in effect (consult ADF&G regulations).

Red Salmon

Rating: Good to excellent (early run) and excellent (late run).

Regulatory Season: June 11 – August 20 in the stretch of water from the confluence with Russian downstream to the Powerlines.

Timing: June 11 – October 15, peak June 15 – 25 (early run) and July 20 – August 5 (late run).

Size: Average 6 to 7 pounds, up to 11 pounds (early run); 5 to 9 pounds, up to 12 pounds (late run). Catches of reds up to 14 pounds or more possible, especially in late July.

Tip: Scout quiet water of the river for signs of fish rolling at the surface, indicating that a school has been located, and then work the faster current just upstream. The area of river near the Powerlines below Russian River is a hot spot. For the biggest and brightest fish, the last week of July is best. Fish caught from mid-August on into the fall are usually small, around four to six pounds.

Silver Salmon

Rating: Good to excellent.

Regulatory Season: July 1 – October 31.

Timing: July 15 – October 31, peak August 20 – September 5 (early run) and October 1 – 20 (late run).

Size: Average 6 to 10 pounds, up to 14 pounds (early run); 8 to 14 pounds, up to 18 pounds (late run). A very few trophy specimens up to 22 pounds or more may be present the first half of October.

Tip: Look for small schools or individual fish traveling close to shore. Try on the edge of still water and swift current, such as the mouths of channels and sloughs, and along deep holes and runs of mainstem Kenai.

Rainbow Trout

Rating: Excellent.

Timing: June 11 – late December, peak late July – late September.

Size: Average 10 to 20 inches, some larger fish to 25 inches and 5-6 pounds. Trophy rainbows up to 30 inches and 12 pounds or more possible. Exceptional specimens weighing as much as 20 pounds are known to be in this river.

Tip: Side and back channels, deep holes with overhanging brush and log jams, areas behind spawning salmon, and the mouths of clearwater tributaries are all worth checking out. There are a multitude of such habitat and locations between Russian River and Jim's Landing.

Dolly Varden
Rating: Excellent.
Timing: June 11 – late December, peak late July – early October.
Size: Average 10 to 20 inches, some larger fish to 30 inches and 10-12 pounds. Trophy char up to 18 pounds or more possible.
Tip: Besides promising spots along the main river, anglers also catch many char in deeper side and back channels and the rear end of holes and pools containing spawning salmon.

Round Whitefish
Rating: Poor to fair.
Timing: June 11 – mid-January, peak late July – late October.
Size: Average 10 to 16 inches, a few larger fish up to 20 inches and 3 pounds.
Tip: Try areas just downstream of spawning salmon.

KENAI RIVER (RM 74 – 80.5)
Area: Russian River to Fisherman's Bend.

Main Species: Red and silver salmon, rainbow trout, Dolly Varden, and whitefish.

Summary: The Kenai River changes hue considerably from just a mile or two upstream, with more surrounding forest, stronger river current, and better fishing opportunities. Boaters and rafters will find an abundance of gravel beaches to pull up on as well as deep holes and runs teeming with salmon, trout, and char. Shore-bound anglers have several points of access available to them with plenty of room to scout the river through a network of faint trails. This part of the river sees the most action from mid-summer on into fall when all game fish species are at their peak in both numbers and aggression.

Concentrations of bald eagle are a common sight during the winter and early spring months.

Description: This portion of the Kenai flows quite fast but still there are plenty of holes and runs with slower water. The river stays ice-free through the winter. Unlike the immediate Cooper Landing area, much of the surrounding land here is located within the Chugach National Forest and thus public access is easier.

General Access: By road. The Sterling Highway parallels the river between MP 49.5 and 54.7, crossing the river at MP 53.0. There are numerous access points; the main ones are described below.
Access Point A: Cooper Creek Campground – MP 50.7 Sterling Highway. North on road to campground. Developed parking, camping, restrooms. Trails lead upstream and down along river.
Access Point B: MP 53.1 Sterling Highway. North on turnout. Parking. Anglers can choose either to fish at road crossing by bridge or hike upstream about a quarter mile to a slough. The east bank of the river provides beach fishing and, a few hundred feet upstream, a good hole can be located.
Access Point C: MP 54.7 Sterling Highway. South on turnout by sign and the river. Parking. This access point is just upstream of the Russian River / Kenai River confluence (see chapter 12, page 232 for description). Main fishing is in channel at turnout.

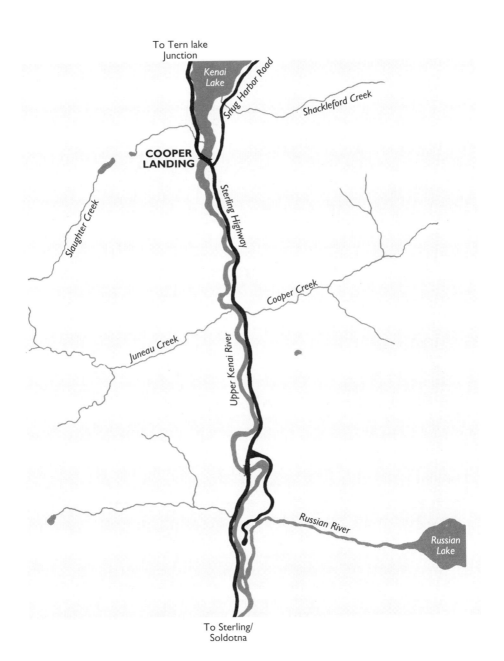

To Tern lake Junction

Kenai Lake

Snug Harbor Road

Shackleford Creek

COOPER LANDING

Slaughter Creek

Sterling Highway

Cooper Creek

Juneau Creek

Upper Kenai River

Russian River

Russian Lake

To Sterling/ Soldotna

Fishing Opportunities

Restrictions: King salmon fishing prohibited. Closed to all fishing May 2 – June 10. Additional restrictions are in effect (consult ADF&G regulations).

Red Salmon
Rating: Poor to fair (early run) and good to excellent (late run).
Timing: June 11 – October 15, peak June 15 – 25 (early run) and July 20 – August 5 (late run).
Size: Average 6 to 7 pounds, up to 11 pounds (early run); 5 to 9 pounds, up to 12 pounds (late run). Catches of reds up to 14 pounds or more possible, especially in late July.
Tip: Locate reds surfacing in a hole and try immediately upstream where there is some level of current. Try early in the run for the brightest fish.

Silver Salmon
Rating: Good to excellent.
Regulatory Season: July 1 – October 31.
Timing: July 15 – October 31, peak August 20 – September 5 (early run) and October 1 – 20 (late run).
Size: Average 6 to 10 pounds, up to 14 pounds (early run); 8 to 14 pounds, up to 18 pounds (late run). A very few trophy specimens up to 22 pounds or more may be present the first half of October.
Tip: Fish often travel close to shore and will mingle with crimson reds in holes and runs. Unlike early-run silvers, late-run fish are more likely to be found in deeper water of mainstem Kenai.

Rainbow Trout
Rating: Good to excellent.
Timing: June 11 – May 1, peak late July – late September.
Size: Average 10 to 20 inches, some larger fish to 25 inches and 5-6 pounds. Trophy rainbows up to 30 inches and 12 pounds or more possible. Exceptional specimens weighing as much as 20 pounds are known to be in this river.
Tip: Look for areas that have a concentration of salmon and fish just below. The mouth of Juneau Creek can be good.

Dolly Varden
Rating: Good to excellent.
Timing: June 11 – May 1, peak late July – early October.
Size: Average 10 to 20 inches, some larger fish to 30 inches and 10-12 pounds. Trophy char up to 18 pounds or more possible.
Tip: Search mouths of clearwater streams early in the season, shifting attention to riffles and the lower end of deep holes and runs in late summer and fall.

Round Whitefish
Rating: Poor to fair.
Timing: June 11 – mid-January, peak late July – late October.
Size: Average 10 to 16 inches, a few larger fish up to 20 inches and 3 pounds.
Tip: Try areas just downstream of spawning salmon.

KENAI RIVER (RM 80.5 – 82)
Area: Fisherman's Bend to Sterling Highway Bridge at Kenai Lake outlet.

Main Species: Red and silver salmon, rainbow trout, Dolly Varden, and whitefish.

Summary: The highway crossing at the outlet of Kenai Lake is a starting point for the vast majority of float excursions down the river. But it is, as well as the next mile-and-a-half, also a good stretch of water to fish for salmon, trout, and char. From mid-summer into fall, most fishing in this area is done from drift boat or raft. As the water retreats in late fall, fishing becomes productive off the bank.

There are very large spawning populations of both red and silver salmon present and trophy king salmon use parts of the area too, but it is the silvers that draw the most attention from anglers. Expect outstanding action at times during the peak of the runs.

A unique fact about this river section and the entire upper Kenai is that it does not freeze over, giving anglers an open-water opportunity to fish for trout and char straight through the winter into spring. Additionally, eagles concentrate in trees along the river in winter and early spring, feeding off an unusually late run of silver salmon.

Description: This section of the upper Kenai is quite different than most parts of the drainage. The Kenai flows wide and very calm, moderately deep, with little current to speak of until approximately river mile 80.5 (Fisherman's Bend), where the velocity picks up.

A fair amount of private land is present along the south side of the river, at Cooper Landing, with limited bank access.

General Access: By road. The Sterling Highway provides two main points of access as the road parallels the river for nearly two miles. Additionally, there are private campgrounds and lodges situated along the highway that allow clients shore access to the river.

Access Point A: *Kenai River Campground* – MP 47.7 Sterling Highway. Road crosses river at outlet of Kenai Lake. North on access road short distance to entrance to campground on right. Parking, camping, restrooms, and boat launch available. Boardwalk leads to river. *Note:* This is a closed riverbank area July 1 – August 15.

Access Point B: MP 49.5 Sterling Highway. North on pullout. Parking. River is adjacent to road and anglers can hike upstream or down for quite some distance. *Note:* High water, such as during the summer months, may prevent access much beyond the immediate road access point.

Fishing Opportunities
Restrictions: King salmon fishing prohibited. Closed to all fishing May 2 – June 10. Additional restrictions are in effect (consult ADF&G regulations).

Red Salmon
Rating: Poor (early run) and fair (late run).
Timing: June 11 – October 15, peak June 15 – 25 (early run) and July 20 – August 5 (late run).
Size: Average 6 to 7 pounds, up to 11 pounds (early run); 5 to 9 pounds, up to 12

pounds (late run). Catches of reds up to 14 pounds or more possible, especially in late July.

Tip: Drift egg imitation pattern and yarn flies through the channel immediately below the bridge. The bend at river mile 81 might be a spot to try as well.

Silver Salmon

Rating: Good to excellent.

Regulatory Season: July 1 – October 31.

Timing: July 15 – October 31, peak August 20 – September 5 (early run) and October 1 – 20 (late run).

Size: Average 6 to 10 pounds, up to 14 pounds (early run); 8 to 14 pounds, up to 18 pounds (late run). A very few trophy specimens up to 22 pounds or more may be present the first half of October.

Tip: Small spoons and plugs work in the main channel, flies and spinners closer to shore. Try neutral colors in blue, green, and silver on sunny days, red, orange, pink, and chartreuse on cloudy days. One of the top spots is the small section of river right next to the road at MP 80.5.

Rainbow Trout

Rating: Good.

Timing: June 11 – May 1, peak late July – late September.

Size: Average 10 to 20 inches, some larger fish to 25 inches and 5-6 pounds. Trophy rainbows up to 30 inches and 12 pounds possible. Exceptional specimens weighing as much as 20 pounds are known to be in this river.

Tip: Try from a couple hundred yards up into the lake outlet (see chapter 13, page 250 for description) to downstream of the bridge a few hundred yards. Also, the bend at river mile 81 is a good spot.

Dolly Varden

Rating: Good.

Timing: June 11 – May 1, peak late July – early October.

Size: Average 10 to 20 inches, some larger fish to 30 inches and 10-12 pounds. Trophy char up to 18 pounds or more possible.

Tip: Top spots for late summer and fall char is the area from the highway bridge downstream a hundred yards or so and the bend at river mile 81.

UPPER KENAI RIVER
Tributaries

Description

What constitutes as tributaries of the upper Kenai are smaller streams and lakes, most of which drain into the river from the north. The main tributary, Russian River, is discussed as a separate chapter (page 223) because of its size and abundance of angling opportunities.

All of the lakes and creeks in the area are clearwater drainages situated within the Chugach National Wildlife Refuge or Chugach National Forest. Some of the locations are high in the Chugach Mountains where sub-alpine terrain and short summer seasons dominate, others in the lush river valley surrounded by a plethora of trees, brush, and other vegetation.

Wildlife is a common sight, with both brown and black bears a present. Dall sheep are abundant on the various mountaintops in the region and moose may be spotted just about anywhere. Anglers visiting some of the more remote lakes report occurrences of wolves and wolverines.

Access

The Sterling Highway is the main artery of access to all of the tributaries of the upper Kenai, complete with pullouts, trailheads, and developed trails. Some waters are next to the highway while a few are quite remote and require a hike of several miles to reach. Secondary paved and gravel/dirt roads are present as well.

Fishing

The more accessible lakes do yield decent angling opportunities during the height of the season in spring and fall, but for more excitement and faster action, fishers should look to the waters of the Juneau Creek drainage. Less angling pressure and great fishing in a relatively unspoiled natural setting is what awaits hikers willing to put in some time and effort.

Trout and Juneau lakes have some superb rainbow trout to offer in addition to lake trout – even burbot, the only place to catch them on the entire Kenai Peninsula. Lower Fuller Lake is a great place to challenge arctic grayling.

Chapter Contents

The following are the game fish present, the various sections of the Upper Kenai River drainage, and the page number in which more detailed information can be found.

TIMING:

Upper Kenai River Tributaries - Lakes

FISH	JAN	FEB	MAR	APR	MAY	JUN	JUL	AUG	SEP	OCT	NOV	DEC
RT												
LT												
DV												
AG												
RW												

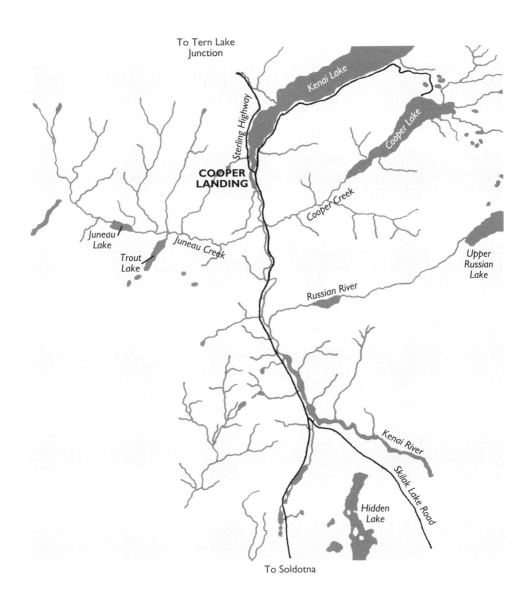

Species Information

Salmon

With the exception of Russian River, the drainages of upper Kenai River do not harbor any significant runs of salmon. Small runs of **red** and **silver salmon** return to Jean Lake and Creek and some fish are present in the lower section of Juneau Creek as well. The latter location also sees a few **king salmon**. Cooper Creek is home to a very small contingent of silver salmon.

Trout/Char

There exists some healthy populations of both trout and char in lakes of the upper Kenai drainage and these fish are available on a year-round basis. Smaller populations also thrive in area streams yet for the most part these flowing waters are only used as spawning sites or for temporary migration corridors between Kenai River and the lakes. All streams of the upper Kenai drainage are closed to fishing from May 2 through June 10 to protect spawning trout.

Best fishing is after breakup and before freezeup, the lakes in higher elevations experiencing a later thaw and earlier ice conditions than lowland waters.

Rainbow trout are reasonably abundant in several area lakes with Trout and Juneau also containing decent stocks of **lake trout**. The ADF&G also plants Rainbow Lake with rainbows on a regular basis. Migratory **Dolly Varden** can be found in Jean Lake while resident species of these char are both present in Cooper and Devils Pass lakes.

Small spoons and spinners and flies representing juvenile salmon and other forage items are all effective. Bait is good too.

Other

Arctic grayling provide opportunity at Lower Fuller Lake (the result of past stocking efforts by ADF&G) while the only **burbot** population on the Kenai Peninsula can be located in Juneau Lake. **Round whitefish** are fairly abundant at both Trout and Juneau lakes.

UPPER KENAI RIVER TRIBUTARIES

Includes Jean, Lower Fuller, Cleaver, Rainbow, Cooper, Trout, Juneau, and Devils Pass lakes.

JEAN LAKES

Main Species: Rainbow trout and Dolly Varden.

Summary: Jean and Upper Jean lakes provide anglers with a good opportunity to tangle with native trout and char. Fishing pressure is for the most part light, despite being situated next to Sterling Highway, as nearby Kenai and Russian rivers draw the majority of attention away from these two serene lakes. Action at breakup is decent but the late summer and fall fishing is better. Both Jean and Upper Jean can easily be fished from the bank with success but a canoe or some other type of watercraft is

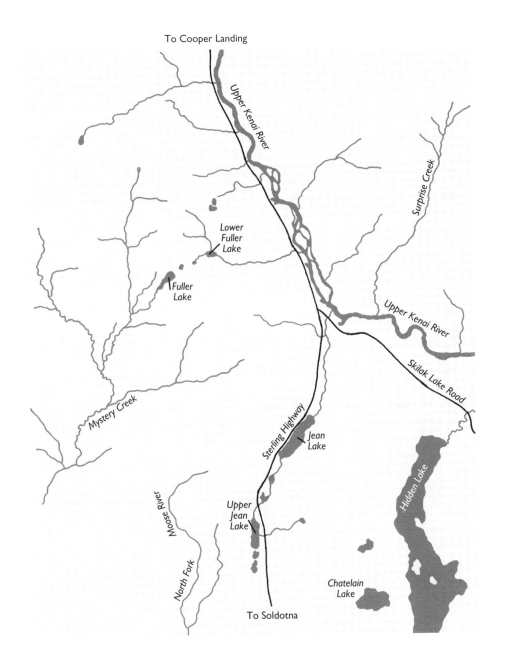

recommended to access the more brush-covered shoreline areas as well as deeper water.

Description: Both Jean and Upper Jean are clearwater lakes connected by a tiny trickle of a creek. Jean is about twice the size of Upper Jean yet both display similar appearances in habitat and surroundings.

General Access: By road. The Sterling Highway parallels the shoreline of Jean Lake for about a mile with trail access to nearby Upper Jean. Faint trails lead from access points to other parts of the lakes.

Jean Lake
Access Point: MP 59.5 – 60.5 Sterling Highway. Road parallels lake with access road at MP 60.0 heading west to Jean Lake Campground and the lake. Parking and camping facilities. Trail leads along shoreline.

Upper Jean Lake
Access Point A: MP 61.5 Sterling Highway. North on turnoff to small parking area. Trail leads 0.3 mile to lake. No facilities.
Access Point B: MP 62.0 Sterling Highway. North on dirt road to small parking area. Faint trail leads 200 yards to lake. No facilities.

Fishing Opportunities
Restrictions: None. Jean Lake Creek: Salmon fishing prohibited. Seasonal closure in effect (consult ADF&G regulations).

Rainbow Trout
Rating: Good.
Timing: Year-round, peak early May – early June and late July – mid-October.
Size: Average 8 to 16 inches, some larger fish up to 22 inches and 3 pounds or more.
Tip: The inlet and outlet of Jean Lake is productive as is many locations providing brush cover and weed beds along the shoreline on both lakes. Ice fishing can be productive on Upper Jean in November and December.

Dolly Varden
Rating: Fair.
Timing: Year-round, peak early May – early June and late August – mid-October.
Size: Average 8 to 15 inches, a few larger fish up to 22 inches and 3 pounds.
Tip: Best fishing is at Jean Lake; try the inlet and outlet in spring and fall. Upper Jean only has a few char present.

LOWER FULLER LAKE

Main Species: Arctic grayling.

Summary: Lower Fuller Lake was stocked with grayling years ago and today has a healthy self-sustaining population that produces very good fishing for anglers willing to negotiate the steep trail leading to the lake. Another lake that is on the trail system is Fuller Lake (technically not part of the Kenai River drainage), which offers good action for char. It is located another mile beyond Lower Fuller Lake.

Description: Small clearwater lake, situated in a narrow mountain valley.

General Access: By trail. The Sterling Highway provides access to trailhead. Once at the lake, a watercraft of some sort comes in useful in accessing deeper, more productive waters away from the often-weedy shoreline.
Access Point: Fuller Lakes Trailhead – MP 57.1 Sterling Highway. North to large parking area and trailhead. No facilities. Trail leads approximately 2 miles north to lake. This trail is rated as strenuous as the ascent is steep. Continuing on the trail another mile will lead to Fuller Lake.

Fishing Opportunities
Restrictions: None (consult ADF&G regulations).

Arctic Grayling
Rating: Good to excellent.
Timing: Year-round, peak early June – late September.
Size: Average 8 to 14 inches, some larger fish up to 18 inches.
Tip: Best fishing for larger grayling occurs near weed beds on northern portion of lake.

RAINBOW LAKE

Main Species: Rainbow trout.

Summary: Rainbow Lake is a small body of water not far from Cooper Lake. It is stocked with trout by the ADF&G yet the lake does not receive much fishing pressure. Anglers do well both from the bank and an assortment of watercraft, success rates being very good in early summer and fall. Ice fishing is productive in November and December.
Because of the altitude where the lake is located, breakup occurs a little later and freezeup a little earlier than some other lakes in the area.

Description: Small clearwater lake less than a mile in length with a maximum depth of some 26 feet, situated at an elevation of 1,300 feet.

General Access: By road. The Snug Harbor Road provides direct roadside access heading east from MP 47.9 of the Sterling Highway.
Access Point: MP 8.7 Snug Harbor Road. Follow sign to the right at "Y" 2.3 miles to parking area on left. Trail leads 0.25 mile to lake. No facilities.

Fishing Opportunities
Restrictions: None (consult ADF&G regulations).

Rainbow Trout
Rating: Good.
Timing: Year-round, peak late May – mid-June and late August – late December.
Size: Average 8 to 18 inches, a few larger fish up to 24 inches and 5 pounds.
Tip: Look for schools of fish in spring and fall.

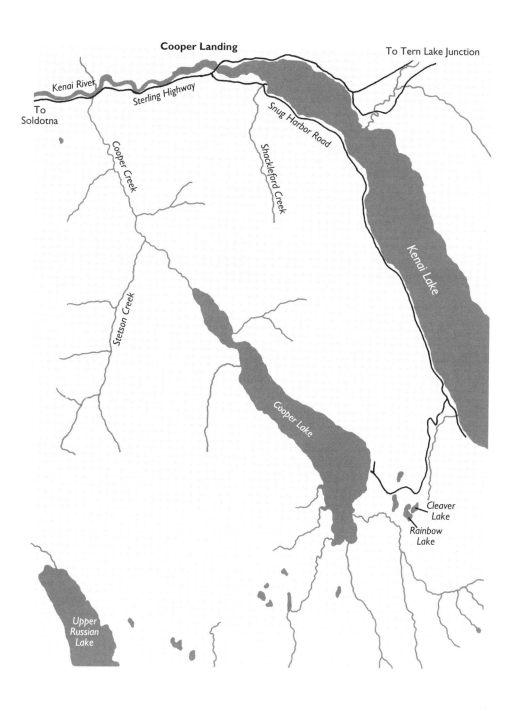

COOPER LAKE

Main Species: Dolly Varden.

Summary: Cooper Lake is not known as an angling destination. Like some other large lakes on the peninsula, finding structure can be an obstacle in locating concentrations of fish. The most efficient way is to search out inlet streams that carry nutrients into the lake but some success can also be experienced in spots with heavy vegetation growth.

Description: Located in a steep and narrow valley, Cooper Lake tends to run very deep. Hiking along the lake shoreline can be very strenuous due to dense vegetation. Strong winds can make the lake inhospitable, especially in fall and winter.

Access: By road and floatplane. The Snug Harbor Road provides direct roadside access heading east from MP 47.9 of the Sterling Highway. A boat is useful in reaching the remote parts of the lake, such as the outlet on the north end and the numerous small inlet streams on the south end.

Access Point: MP 8.7 Snug Harbor Road. Follow sign to the right at "Y" 3.5 miles, left on dirt road short distance to lake. No facilities.

Fishing Opportunities

Restrictions: None (consult ADF&G regulations).

Dolly Varden
Rating: Fair to good.
Timing: Year-round, peak late May – mid-June and mid-August – early October.
Size: Average 8 to 16 inches, a few larger fish up to 22 inches and 3 pounds.
Tip: Search for confluences of clearwater tributaries and nearby structure.

Other Species: RT,(RW).

JUNEAU CREEK DRAINAGE
Includes Trout, Juneau, and Devils Pass lakes.

TROUT LAKE

Main Species: Rainbow trout and lake trout.

Summary: Trout Lake receives little angling pressure due to its remoteness. Fishing is typically very good in early summer and fall for both trout and char although rainbows can be caught in decent numbers all summer long. A watercraft is recommended to access deeper portions of lake. A small rowboat is provided with the Forest Service cabin on the lake.

Description: This is a deep, clearwater lake, down to 100 feet or more in places, and almost two miles long, situated in a narrow mountain valley with tremendous views.

General Access: By trail and floatplane. The Sterling Highway represents the starting point in reaching this lake and others along the Resurrection Pass Trail.

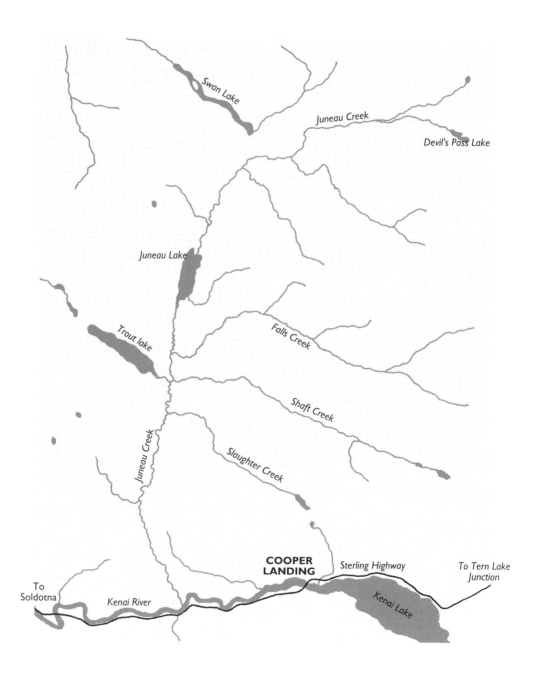

Access Point: Resurrection Pass Trailhead – MP 53.2 Sterling Highway. North on small gravel road near Kenai River bridge short distance to parking area and trailhead. No facilities. Trail leads 6.8 miles north to break, follow left fork an additional half mile to east end of lake and Forest Service cabin.

Fishing Opportunities

Restrictions: None (consult ADF&G regulations).

Rainbow Trout

Rating: Good.
Timing: Year-round, peak late May – mid-June and late August – early October.
Size: Average 10 to 16 inches, some larger fish up to 23 inches and 4 pounds.
Tip: Productive fishery all season but best in spring and fall. The western and eastern portions of the lake have concentration of fish.

Lake Trout

Rating: Good.
Timing: Year-round, peak late May – mid-June and late August – early October.
Size: Average 2 to 5 pounds, a few larger fish up to 12 pounds or more.
Tip: The west and east ends of lake are good early and late in the season while structure at the steep drop-offs along the north and south shoreline are productive throughout the year.

Other Species: RW.

JUNEAU LAKE

Main Species: Rainbow trout, lake trout, arctic grayling, and burbot.

Summary: Along with Trout Lake, Juneau Lake does not see a lot of angling pressure but action can be very good for several species. Late spring/early summer and fall is the best time to be here to catch fish. A watercraft of some sort is recommended in reaching deeper water away from shore, especially when targeting lake trout and big rainbows. Small rowboats are provided with the two Forest Service cabins. Juneau Lake is also the only lake on the peninsula documented to contain a population of burbot.

Description: Fairly deep, clearwater lake located in a valley in the Chugach mountain range. The panoramic views are outstanding.

General Access: By trail and floatplane. The Sterling Highway represents the starting point in reaching this lake and others along the Resurrection Pass Trail.

Access Point: Resurrection Pass Trailhead – MP 53.2 Sterling Highway. North on small gravel road near Kenai River bridge short distance to parking area and trailhead. No facilities. Trail leads approximately 9 miles north to southern part of lake and Romig Forest Service Cabin. The trail continues along eastern shoreline another half a mile to Juneau Forest Service Cabin on the left. From here the trail runs to the far northern section of the lake where a tentsite is located. The trail goes on from here to other destinations, such as Swan Lake and Devils Pass Lake (see description on page 220), ending at the small community of Hope on Turnagain Arm.

Fishing Opportunities
Restrictions: None (consult ADF&G regulations).

Rainbow Trout
Rating: Good.
Timing: Year-round, peak late May – mid-June and late August – early October.
Size: Average 10 to 16 inches, some larger fish up to 23 inches and 4 pounds.
Tip: Best bet is lake inlet and outlet, especially early and late in season.

Lake Trout
Rating: Good.
Timing: Year-round, peak late May – mid-June and late August – early October.
Size: Average 2 to 5 pounds, a few larger fish up to 12 pounds or more.
Tip: Inlet and outlet may see fish in spring and fall but the deeper sections around the northern half of the lake is better.

Arctic Grayling
Rating: Good.
Timing: Year-round, peak late May – late September.
Size: Average 8 to 15 inches, some larger fish up to 18 inches.
Tip: Lake inlet and outlet may have an abundance of fish early and late in season. The larger specimens, however, are found in deeper water on the edges of drop-offs.

Burbot
Rating: Fair to good.
Timing: Year-round, peak March – April and September – December.
Size: Average 15 to 22 inches, a few larger fish up to 5-6 pounds.
Tip: Fish are found deep during the summer months. At night or in early spring/late fall, the cod move into shallow water to feed.

Other Species: RW.

DEVILS PASS LAKE

Main Species: Dolly Varden.

Summary: This is probably one of the least-fished lakes in the Kenai River drainage due to its remote location and population of below average-sized char. The action for these recluse fish, however, can be quite good and usually stays productive throughout the summer and fall season. A watercraft of some sort is not required but recommended in reaching the best "holes."

Description: Formerly known as Upper Juneau Lake, half-mile-long Devils Pass Lake is situated in an alpine environment at the 2,400-foot level.

General Access: By trail. The shortest, yet by far the most strenuous, route to the lake is from the Seward Highway trailhead. The Sterling Highway trailhead route is easier but almost twice as long.
Access Point A: Devils Pass Trailhead – MP 39.5 Seward Highway. West on turnout to

trailhead. Developed parking, restrooms. Trail leads approximately 9.5 miles through rough terrain to lake on right. The climb is quite steep. No facilities.

Access Point B: *Resurrection Pass Trailhead* – MP 53.2 Sterling Highway. North on small gravel road near Kenai River bridge short distance to parking area and trailhead. No facilities. Trail leads 17.6 miles to junction with Devils Pass Trail, passing Juneau Lake at mile 9 and Swan Lake at mile 13. Take right at forks and continue about 1.5 mile to lake on left. No facilities at Devils Pass Lake but Forest Service cabins are available at Juneau and Swan lakes along with seven dispersed tentsites.

Fishing Opportunities

Restrictions: None (consult ADF&G regulations).

Dolly Varden

Rating: Fair to good.
Timing: Year-round, peak mid-June – late September.
Size: Average 8 to 12 inches, a few larger fish up to 18 inches.
Tip: Try the outlet of the lake anytime during the open-water season, as well as structures along the shoreline.

Other Species: (AG).

highwayangler.com

The Source for Information on Fishing Alaska's Roadside Waters

Featuring:

Guide Books
Publications specifically catered to fishing Alaska's road system and beyond

Fishing Reports
Read weekly state reports, daily private submissions, or post your own

Forum & Discussion Boards
Question and Answer format and discuss topics of interest

Photo Galleries
View pictures of catches from roadside fisheries around the state

Highwayangler.com provides anglers of all skill levels and disciplines with accurate and timely information regarding fishing opportunities along Alaska's continuous road system.

RUSSIAN RIVER
Drainage

Description

The crystal clear waters of the Russian River and Lakes are situated in a fairly narrow valley in a central part of the Chugach Mountains. The river also serves as a border between the Kenai National Wildlife Refuge and the Chugach National Forest.

The drainage begins in a small lake just north of the Harding Ice Field, some 20 miles northwest of the town of Seward. From there Russian Creek spills out into Upper Russian Lake, the largest body of water within the system. Upper Russian River begins here and connects the lake with Lower Russian Lake. A set of falls is located near the outlet of Lower Russian as the river continues its journey towards the upper Kenai River.

Tall cottonwoods and birch along with dense old growth spruce and poplar are the primary vegetation surrounding the lower Russian River. The upper river and lakes are located in a slightly more open terrain with spruce and brush being dominant.

Wildlife is commonplace. Both black and brown bears inhabit the river on a daily basis during the salmon runs and can be observed fishing in summer into fall. Moose and beaver are plentiful, especially in the upper river sections and the lakes. Eagles often sit perched in trees along the river in fall and winter.

The Russian River Falls is a popular salmon-viewing destination from mid-June into early July and again during the month of August into September. Thousands of salmon are commonly seen here during the peak of the runs. A trail leads to the viewing platform overlooking the falls from Russian Lakes Trailhead near the entrance to Russian River Campground.

Access

Most visitors to the area arrive by road via the Sterling Highway. The lower Russian River receives the most traffic as only a short walk from the Russian River Campground leads right to the water. Lower Russian Lake and Upper Russian River requires a hike of at least two miles plus but the trail is extremely well maintained and is even wheelchair accessible a good portion of the way. Upper Russian Lake can be accessed both by trail from the highway as well as by floatplane.

It should be noted that the US Forest Service maintains a few cabins on the Upper and Lower Russian lakes and reservations are recommended during the peak of the angling season in summer and fall.

Fishing

The Russian River (lower section) is one of the most famed stretches of water in Alaska, known for its superb sport fishing for red salmon. Huge runs of this species ascend the river annually in two separate pulses, one in June and another in July-August. The first run has an average escapement of 55,000 fish and the second run 86,000 (not counting fish harvested by anglers). In good years the river sees more than 100,000 reds come through in any one run during the course of a few short weeks. Sight fishing can be extremely exciting and rewarding. Silver salmon is another species of growing popularity.

The lakes and upper river are best known for its excellent opportunities for trout and char, primarily during the late summer and fall months. Salmon proliferate the lakes and tributary streams with their presence, fueling the appetite of forage species, although fishing for them is prohibited.

Russian River Drainage

CHAPTER CONTENTS

The following are the game fish present, the various sections of the Russian River drainage, and the page number in which more detailed information can be found.

TIMING:

Russian River

FISH	JAN	FEB	MAR	APR	MAY	JUN	JUL	AUG	SEP	OCT	NOV	DEC
RS												
SS												
PS												
RT												
DV												
AG												
RW												

Russian Lakes

FISH	JAN	FEB	MAR	APR	MAY	JUN	JUL	AUG	SEP	OCT	NOV	DEC
RT												
DV												

SPECIES INFORMATION

Salmon

All five species of salmon inhabit the Russian drainage to one degree or another. Red salmon are by far the most numerous but relatively good runs of silver salmon occur as well. King and pink salmon also breed in the Russian but in much more conservative numbers compared to reds and silvers. Chum salmon are extremely rare with no existing spawning population present.

The vast majority of anglers come to the Russian River to participate in the world-class salmon fishery that takes place here every summer and fall. Red salmon is the top species in terms of both numbers of fish and popularity although silver salmon are gaining notoriety as well. Of the 40-45,000 reds harvested in the Russian River area every season, a great many of these come from the confluence with the Kenai River. In years of low water in the Russian proper, reds and silvers will often hold in the deeper mixing zone of the confluence waiting for rains to raise the water level. It is during these times that anglers take advantage of the heavy concentration of salmon for some superb action. Sight fishing can be hugely rewarding in the main Russian when schools proceed upstream.

The salmon in the early part of their respective runs do not waste time getting here, some of them even carrying sealice upon arrival. It is estimated that reds and silvers are capable of making the journey from Cook Inlet to the mouth of the Russian in a matter of just three to four days, a distance of some 74 river miles.

Red Salmon

There are two distinct runs of red salmon that migrate up the Russian to spawn from the end of May into October, with some overlapping of the two. The first run peaks in June, escapement averaging approximately 55,000 reds, while the stronger second run peaks in July/August, with escapement averaging 86,000 fish. In some years the runs will exceed 75-100,000 fish. Anglers will harvest some 20,000 or more reds out of each run, so without a doubt action can be expected to be excellent.

Anglers use a wide assortment of colored flies and most do work as fish density allows. Smaller, sparsely tied flies in fluorescent orange or green are good on a dead drift in the ferry area while more neutral colors are better in the channel area of the Sanctuary or on sunny days. Brighter colors seem to work best on dark or rainy days. Flies in subtle hues of green, blue, purple, and black work very well most of the time in Russian River proper or wherever clear water can be found

Schools of salmon move from hole to hole through the shallows and are easily targeted by sight fishing. These schools can be observed coming through all day long if water levels permit or if the runs are very strong. Low water levels and bright sunlight have a way of stopping the migration temporarily into the clear waters of the Russian. Anglers are usually most successful at dawn as the fish have been moving into the river in cover of darkness and are stacked in abundance in holes and runs throughout the lower river.

Early Run Reds: As soon as mid-May there will be a few reds pulling into the Kenai-Russian confluence area with scouts infiltrating the river by Memorial Day weekend. As the season progresses, schools of fish begin heading upstream yet numbers will typically be small into second week of June when the vanguard of salmon begin to stack up at the mouth. The majority of the run will hold at the confluence waiting for ideal water conditions or until the area becomes so congested with salmon that the run is forced into the Russian.

In years when the run is early or if water conditions are ideal, the bulk of the run will hit by June 15 with action remaining hot through the month. If the run is somewhat late or exceptionally strong, anglers may find very good fishing even into the first week of July, but generally the best is over by the Fourth of July weekend in any given year. A few stragglers are still around as the second run arrives in force, in late July.

The early run is made up of, on average, fish that are slightly larger than the late-run Russian reds as they have spent an additional year of growth at sea, and they are consistently brighter too because they are relatively nowhere near their spawning beds yet. All of these fish are bound for tributaries of Upper Russian Lake, primarily Russian Creek, with spawning peaking during the month of August.

Late Run Reds: Some late-run reds will begin to trickle in the first week of July, overlapping the first run, but are generally not present in any numbers until mid-month. The bulk hits the confluence with some predictability, usually about July 22 give or take a few days. It is typical of this run to come in fast and heavy when it arrives, fish usually storming the river in waves of thousands of salmon per day by the last week of July and lasting into early August.

Unlike the early reds, which peak in a short time frame and then quickly disappear, the late run has a tendency to linger for a while, partially because many of these fish will eventually spawn in the immediate area and not at the headwaters far upstream. The intensity of movement noticeably starts to decrease after the first week of August but if water levels are very low (slowing the migration), the run – and the great fishing – will last into mid-month.

Toward the latter part of the run, in mid-August, the average size of fish suddenly drops, with most reds caught being in the 3- to 5-pound category. Yet action often remains good until the season closure. Bright salmon will, however, continue to trickle into the confluence area and river until late September (and thus sometimes mistaken for silvers).

Late-run reds predominately utilize the Upper Russian River between Upper and Lower Russian lakes, Lower Russian Lake shoreline, and the Lower Russian River for reproductive purposes. The water seems to boil with red-hued fish in September as the spawning ritual peaks and makes for a very picturesque setting.

Silver Salmon

There are two components to the presence of silvers at or near the confluence – early and late runs. The early run is composed of fish heading up the Russian proper as well as to tributaries further upstream on the Kenai, while the late run are exclusively mainstem Kenai River fish. Early-run silvers are best targeted in the Sanctuary section of the confluence and the Russian River, unlike late-run fish that prefer the lower section around the ferry crossing in the Kenai.

Due to the fact that the run is not very large and the presences of spawning reds far outnumber the silvers, sight fishing is without a doubt the most productive way of catching fish on the Russian. The confluence typically yields some outstanding silver action. Because water conditions in the Russian are generally very low and clear when the silvers run, it is imperative that anglers wanting success be out on the water at dawn. The upstream migration from the river mouth halts to a large extent as the sun comes up.

Flies are what work best, preferably something in a dark-colored pattern of purple or black. Orange and red are good colors in very early morning and late evening or on rainy days. Hardware (when regulations allow), such as spinners, can be good. Metallic silver, bronze, green, and blue are colors that produce.

Early-Run Silvers: A few silvers will begin showing up at the confluence area by the third week of July, heading into the clear Russian soon after, their presence usually obscured by the masses of red salmon in the area at that time. The run will remain a trickle until about mid-August when fishable numbers appear just as the reds are thinning out. The run builds slowly, most arriving silvers deciding to hold in the deeper water at the mouth of the river, shooting upstream at night or waiting for the typical low water levels this time of year to rise with season rains. By the last week of August, the run has reached critical mass in the confluence area and fish begin entering the Russian in small schools alongside crimson-colored red salmon.

Expect good to excellent action through Labor Day weekend and into the second week of September. By mid-month the best is over, with the majority of silvers starting to blush. Some bright and semi-bright specimens ascend the river until mid-October.

In some years, the actual peak migration of silvers into the Russian proper does not commence until late September or early October. These late-arriving fish are almost entirely in spawn or pre-spawn condition after holding at the mouth of the river for several weeks. Silver salmon in the Russian drainage primarily breed in the Upper and Lower Russian rivers during October and November.

Late Run Silvers: A trickle of late-run silvers start appearing near the confluence in about mid-September with numbers slowly building to a peak in October, with salmon remaining in the area through December and later. Generally, late-run fish will not enter the clear waters of Russian River, staying instead in deep holes and pools of the green-blue Kenai.

Chrome or silver tinseled lures and flies in combination with chartreuse, metallic blue, and green are proven effective most anytime. Sharper colors such as red, orange, and pink may work better on darker days.

Pink Salmon

The Russian River drainage supports a very modest run of pinks numbering probably no more than a few hundred fish in any given year. Fishing for them, however, is poor and not recommended since the majority of the pinks will have attained full nuptial condition upon arriving here. Catch-and-release is the order of the day for these 3- to 5-pound salmon. They are present during August and early September in the lower portion of Russian.

Chum Salmon

Very rare species in this area. A few fish move though the confluence in July and August heading to spawning tributaries of Kenai Lake. Stray specimens in the lower Russian River are reported every few years.

King Salmon

Both Russian- and Kenai-bound king salmon stage at the confluence and are often seen or accidentally hooked by anglers casting for reds and silvers. The Russian River drainage is closed to king fishing year-round, including catch-and-release, and anglers are advised to break off any fish hooked as soon as possible. Some late-run Kenai fish use the channel between the Island and the mainland as a breeding ground and are present primarily during August and early September.

A few of these giant salmon do ascend the Russian every year to reproduce. Usually they will hold at the confluence area until ripe, moving upstream into the clear and shallow river and spawning soon thereafter, in August. The total run numbers no more than 250 to 300 fish. A few kings may spawn as far upstream as Upper Russian River and the outlet of Upper Russian Lake yet most utilize the lower river between the falls and the mouth.

Trout/Char

The Russian River area, including the lower and upper river and the confluence with Kenai, has always been a reputed hot spot for rainbow trout and Dolly Varden on the Kenai Peninsula and certainly a top contender in this region of Alaska. Clear water and well-defined holes and runs along with a healthy population of both trout and char of above average size easily support this notion. Along with the masses of salmon in summer and fall comes an abundance of food that will sustain the local population of rainbows and Dollies for several months. Not only that but the Russian River also is an important breeding ground for these two species.

The peak of the salmon runs as they move into and through the confluence is not the best time to pursue trout and char since angling pressure will be extreme, with the better prospects definitely being higher up in system above the campground. The best opportunity drainage-wide comes in late summer and early fall, as the throng of people are gone, the salmon are in the midst of spawning, and rainbows and Dolly Varden in the process of gorging themselves on salmon eggs and flesh. Where the Russian hits the Kenai and the channel downstream to the ferry crossing can be exceptional fishing, and anglers are often able to sight fish to individual trout and char.

In the upper drainage, some good fishing takes place just after the season opener on June 11 and stays reasonably productive until salmon begin arriving in July when the action spikes with more and bigger trout and char (including some specimens that can weigh several pounds) moving out of the depths of Russian lakes into shallower near-shore areas and tributary streams. Key in on areas where concentrations of salmon can be found.

It is believed that the trout and char of the lower Russian below the falls and those in the upper drainage above the falls are in reality two distinct populations of fish that do not mingle, hence the quite obvious physical size differences between them. Specimens in the upper sections do not even remotely attain the length and weight of those of Kenai River origin.

Early in the season (June into July), insect and smolt imitation flies work best as there are no ripe salmon present, although some success can also be achieved using egg and even flesh patterns near fish cleaning stations on the lower river. As salmon establish a presence in late July and August, egg patterns, including beads, will become more effective and should be applied as long as spawning salmon are in the area. Later in the season, from about late August in the upper drainage and mid-September on in areas below Upper Russian Lake, anglers switch to flesh and forage pattern flies as salmon begin to die off and decay.

Small- and medium-sized spinners in silver and metallic blue can be deadly early and late in the season.

Rainbow Trout

Spring spawners begin to appear at the confluence sometime in March, increasing in numbers through April, with anglers usually landing a few big trout before the season closes on May 2. Rainbow trout begin moving up into the Russian from the mouth in mid-April, with the peak in-migration taking place in early to mid-May. These fish are often very large since they represent a good segment of Upper Kenai River's brood stock of trophy trout. A few of the larger specimens may weigh 15 to 20 pounds, averaging 3 to 5 pounds.

Spawning peaks the second half of May, with the subsequent out-migration to Kenai River occurring in early June. However, a good number of large rainbows elect to remain in the Russian to feed during the summer and these fish will be available to anglers on the season opener on June 11. Fishing can be quite good, yet improves in late July with the most consistent action taking place from mid-August into September in the lower Russian and at the mouth along the Island.

After about mid-September, as salmon spawning activity has peaked, the action slows down on the Russian as the trout begin a steady downstream movement toward Kenai River. By October and later, the majority of trout will be hanging in the mainstem Kenai below the ferry crossing with only a few specimens remaining in the Russian. As fall progresses into winter, numbers of trout dwindle with most fish having vacated the area by December. A very few smaller trout will be overwintering in deeper holes and runs of the Kenai, however.

Rainbows in the upper drainage have a similar migratory pattern of behavior as fish in the lower river. Mature adults move out of the lakes in spring, usually in May, into the Upper Russian River and Russian Creeks to reproduce. Some fish remain in the upper river through summer into fall feeding on salmon byproducts before backing down into the lakes again for the winter, while other trout only utilize streams for spawning purposes and thus feed in Upper and Lower Russian lakes during the remainder of the open water season.

Dolly Varden

There is little activity before the May 2 closure and anglers will really not have any opportunity until the lower Russian opens again to fishing on June 11, and even then action will only be fair at best. Some smaller char move up the river starting in June but typically the species do not appear in any solid numbers until the late run of red salmon shows up in July. Size-wise the fish are still not that large, perhaps 10-15 inches on average, yet as late summer rolls around this will change as mature adult Dolly Varden arrive from the mainstem Kenai River. Fishing improves steadily to good and remains so through August, which is prime time for char in the Russian River area.

Fall is a great time to land large, colorful Dolly Varden and since Russian River is a spawning ground for these fish, expect to catch some beautiful char. In late August and September, near-trophy fish can be found sulking in the deeper holes and runs on the river as the salmon begin their cycle of reproduction. Action picks up to excellent and stays hot until mid-September on the Russian and its mouth, at which time the char begin their exodus downstream to the Kenai River. Angling stays productive even into early October in the lower section of the confluence.

By October, most char have left the Russian (some large Dolly Varden will remain to complete their reproductive cycle) and fishing tapers off fast at the confluence as well as numbers of fish present in the area decreases rapidly with the approach of winter. The vast majority of Dolly Varden leave the area by December.

Dolly Varden above the falls are year-round residents of the lakes, mature adults breeding in fall in various tributaries, including upper Russian River and Russian Creek. As soon as the salmon runs begin to infiltrate the area in mid-summer, char of all sizes leave the lakes and ascend streams to feed on salmon eggs and flesh for the duration of the season.

Other Species

Arctic grayling and **round whitefish** are taken in small numbers in the Russian and its mouth during the summer and fall months, the former being available throughout the lower river up to the falls below Lower Russian Lake. Anglers casting flies and small spinners may encounter one or two fish. Whitefish, although present in large schools from July into October near the confluence in the Kenai, rarely venture into the Russian proper. One **northern pike** has been documented from the mouth of the Russian River.

RUSSIAN RIVER / KENAI RIVER CONFLUENCE

Main Species: Red and silver salmon, rainbow trout, and Dolly Varden.

Summary: The confluence of the Kenai and Russian rivers is one of the most heavily fished spots in all of Alaska. Several hundred anglers – even up to a thousand during height of salmon runs – can routinely be seen lining up elbow-to-elbow within an area no greater than a mile. However, there is a reason for this voluntary congestion and that being the heavy return of red salmon that flood this part of the drainage through the summer. Action is generally excellent at the peak of the two respective runs in June and July-August.

As reds decline in numbers, silver salmon begin to fill the void. Although not as numerous as the former reds, the silvers can provide very good fishing as well and much less density in terms of other anglers. For many local fishers, this is the best time of the year to be here as the summer crowds are gone, there are still enough reds around to make things interesting, and the silvers are becoming more abundant

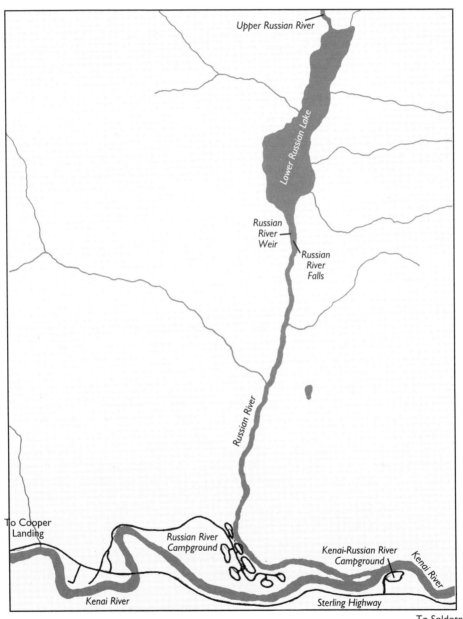

Upper Russian River

Lower Russian Lake

Russian River Weir

Russian River Falls

Russian River

To Cooper Landing

Russian River Campground

Kenai-Russian River Campground

Kenai River

Kenai River

Sterling Highway

To Soldotna

by the day as Labor Day closes in.

For those having had their fill of salmon, this area offers prime trout and char fishing, especially in August and September after the masses of salmon anglers disappear. Action is good – sometimes even excellent – with always the potential to hook into a trophy rainbow or Dolly Varden.

Description: The Russian River runs clear in summer and fall, mixing with the turquoise waters of the mainstem Kenai. In years of heavy snowmelt, it may be difficult for anglers to cross the Russian River to access the downstream side of the confluence where fishing is typically best due to the strong current. By July the runoff is done with the Russian settling down to normal summer levels and can easily be forded.

Anglers can also cross the narrow Kenai River channel at the mouth of the Russian to reach the "Island," which provides further access to the confluence area. The channel separating the Island and the mainland is two to three feet deep or more during summer and early fall, dropping to only a few inches to a foot in late fall and winter.

General Access: By road. The Sterling Highway provides two main points of access to the confluence area, one requiring a short ferry ride across the Kenai River, the other a 20-minute hike.

Access Point A: Russian River Campground – MP 52.7 Sterling Highway. South on paved road by sign 1.4 mile to entrance of campground. Several parking and camping areas available, all of which have trails that lead to Russian River proper. Main trail along river leads 0.5 mile to confluence.

Access Point B: Kenai-Russian River Campground – MP 54.9 Sterling Highway. South on paved road by sign 0.1 mile to campground. Developed parking and camping, boat launch, restrooms. Cable ferry crosses Kenai River to the Russian River confluence. Trails lead up- and downstream.

Fishing Opportunities

Restrictions: King salmon fishing prohibited. Fly-fishing only Season Opener – August 20. Seasonal closures and additional restrictions are in effect (consult ADF&G regulations).

Note: There are two sections to what is considered the "confluence." The upper section, known as the "Sanctuary," extends from the far lower portion of the Russian River proper downstream to the ferry crossing (just below the Island). This section is, by regulation, closed to all fishing from May 2 through July 14 to protect spawning rainbow trout and staging salmon. However, when the first run of red salmon is large and the escapement goal projected to be met, the Sanctuary is opened to fishing early (which is the case in many years).

The lower confluence section runs from the ferry crossing downstream about a mile along the mainstem Kenai to the "Powerline." This area is closed to fishing from May 2 through June 10 to protect staging and spawning rainbow trout.

Red Salmon
Rating: Excellent.
Regulatory Season: June 11 – August 20.

Timing: June 11 – August 20, peak June 15 – 30 (early run) and July 20 – August 10 (late run).

Size: Average 6 to 7 pounds, some larger fish up to 11 pounds (early run); 4 to 8 pounds, up to 12 pounds (late run). Catches of reds to 14 pounds or more are reported almost every year and are usually mainstem Kenai fish just passing through.

Tip: In years with low water in the Russian and if regulations allow, masses of reds can be intercepted in the channel just downstream of the mouth. For bigger and, later in the season, brighter reds, cast into the milky green waters of the Kenai just beyond the mixing zone.

Silver Salmon

Rating: Good to excellent.

Regulatory Season: July 1 – October 31.

Timing: July 20 – October 31, peak August 25 – September 10 (early run) and October 10 – 20 (late run).

Size: Average 6 to 10 pounds, some larger fish to 14 pounds (early run), 8 to 14 pounds, up to 18 pounds (late run). A very few trophy specimens up to 22 pounds or more may be present in October.

Tip: Focus efforts in the channel between the mainland and the Island. Sight fishing can be excellent in the clear water, especially in early morning and evening. Look for late-run silvers starting at the ferry crossing downstream to the Powerline.

Rainbow Trout

Rating: Good to excellent.

Regulatory Season: June 11 – May 2.

Timing: June 11 – mid-January, peak late July – early October.

Size: Average 10 to 20 inches, some larger fish to 32 inches and 12 pounds. Trophy specimens up to 15 to 20 pounds or more possible in this area in fall.

Tip: Avoid crowds of other anglers. Try more undisturbed waters just upstream of Russian River mouth, along the shoreline of the Island, and the faster water along the bluffs between the ferry crossing and the Powerline. Early mornings and evenings are good.

Dolly Varden

Rating: Good to excellent.

Regulatory Season: June 11 – May 2.

Timing: June 11 – mid-January, peak late July – mid-October.

Size: Average 10 to 20 inches, some larger fish to 30 inches and 10-12 pounds. Trophy specimens up to 15 pounds possible in this area in fall.

Tip: Avoid crowds of other anglers. Try just upstream of Russian River mouth and along the shoreline of the Island when salmon runs peak, and the confluence itself starting in August. Early mornings and evenings are best.

Other Species: PS,AG,(KS,CS,RW,NP).

LOWER RUSSIAN RIVER

Main Species: Red and silver salmon, rainbow trout, and Dolly Varden.

Summary: Next to the Kenai River, the Russian is the largest fishery in the state of Alaska. Hordes of anglers gather here through the summer in search of the valuable red salmon of which two distinct runs enter the river every year. The early run in June and the late run in July/August are legendary for producing some phenomenal action where an angler actually has a reasonable chance of hooking 20-50 salmon a day.

Even though the river may seem crowded everywhere, it is actually possible to find some form of solitude on the Russian since most anglers only focus on the far lower end and the mouth of Russian, leaving about two miles of fishable water upstream by those willing to hike to get their salmon.

Another aspect of the river's popularity is the surrounding scenery and the often crystal clear waters that anglers are easily able to spot big schools of salmon and cast to individual fish. Sight fishing is popular on reds as well as silvers and wading the river searching for big schools of fish easily accomplished. Silver salmon storm the river in August and September and are distinguishable by their husky silvery-gray bodies and black tails among a sea of crimson reds. Although the silver run cannot compare in size to that of red salmon, somewhere between 2,000 and 9,000 of these fish escape to spawn in the river system every season.

Rainbow trout and Dolly Varden are plentiful and offer good to excellent action in summer and fall. Salmon anglers, often after having satisfied their lust for salmon, resort to catch-and-release enjoyment for these species. Opportunities abound throughout the lower river, from its confluence with the Kenai River upstream to the falls below Lower Russian Lake. In the process, a few arctic grayling may also be hooked.

Anglers and others visiting the Russian River between late August and mid-September will witness an astounding spectacle as thousands upon thousands of red-bodied salmon can be observed spawning throughout the shallow river, some holes and runs being completely scarlet in color. And, of course, Russian River is also known for its population of both brown and black bears that come here to fish.

Description: Russian is a fast flowing, clearwater river, with rock and gravel bottom structure. The Russian River Campground is one of the most popular in Alaska because of the splendid mountain scenery and great fishing. Wildlife is common with both bear and moose sighted almost daily during the summer season. The Russian is for the most part easy to fish as walking in the river poses no problems and anglers can ford the stream in many places.

Water levels are low in spring and do not begin to rise from snowmelt until mid-May. Most of the runoff is done by mid-June but may persist through the month in years following a heavy snow winter. The water levels remain stable through July into August but may drop very low by late month barring periods of prolonged rainfall. Later on in fall and winter, water conditions in the Russian may become extremely low, only a foot or two in most places except for the deeper holes and runs.

General Access: By road. The Sterling Highway provides two main access points, one requiring a ferry to cross the Kenai River in order to reach the Russian River proper, the other a short hike by trail from a major roadside campground.

Access Point A: *Russian River Campground* – MP 52.7 Sterling Highway. South on paved road by sign 1.4 mile to campground. Developed parking, camping, restrooms. A series of established walkways and trails lead from parking and camping areas a short distance to river. These paths then lead both up- and downstream along the river. The river mouth is located by a 1.5-mile hike downstream. In the opposite direction, it is a 2.5-mile hike to reach the falls and Lower Russian Lake.

Access Point B: *Kenai-Russian River Campground* – MP 54.9 Sterling Highway. South on paved road by sign 0.1 mile to Kenai-Russian River Campground. Developed parking and camping, boat launch, restrooms. Cable ferry crosses Kenai River to the Russian River confluence. Trails lead upstream along the Russian River.

Fishing Opportunities

Restrictions: King salmon fishing prohibited. Closed to all fishing May 2 – June 10. Fly-fishing only June 11 – August 20. Additional restrictions are in effect (consult ADF&G regulations).

Red Salmon
Rating: Excellent.
Regulatory Season: June 11 – August 20.
Timing: June 11 – August 20, peak June 15 – 30 (early run) and July 25 – August 10 (late run).
Size: Average 6 to 7 pounds, some larger fish up to 11 pounds (early run); 4 to 8 pounds, up to 12 pounds (late run). Catches of reds to 14 pounds or more possible.
Tips: In years of low water, search deep holes and runs early in the morning or late in the evening as darkness usually sends pulses of fish upstream from the mouth. If water levels are normal, salmon may be caught in good numbers throughout the day along the whole river. Sight fishing is superb.

Silver Salmon
Rating: Good to excellent.
Regulatory Season: July 1 – September 30.
Timing: July 20 – September 30, peak August 25 – September 15.
Size: Average 6 to 10 pounds, some larger fish to 14 pounds. Silvers up to 16 pounds or more possible.
Tips: Often, schools of fish will move out of the Russian/Kenai confluence at night in cover of darkness, speeding through the low and clear Russian toward Lower Russian Lake. Anglers are advised to intercept these fish in deep holes and runs in the very early morning.

Rainbow Trout
Rating: Good to excellent.
Regulatory Season: June 11 – May 1.
Timing: June 11 – mid-November, peak mid-June – mid-September.

Size: Average 10 to 20 inches, fair number of larger fish to 25 inches and 5-6 pounds. Trophy trout up to 15 to 20 pounds inhabit river in spring and early summer but usually exit the drainage by the June 15 season opener. A few rainbows to 30 inches and 12 pounds will be present through summer and fall.

Tip: Cast near or just downstream of the fish-cleaning stations located up and down the river, especially early in the season. Trout are guaranteed to sit in waiting for scraps of salmon and are particularly susceptible to egg imitation and flesh flies.

Dolly Varden
Rating: Good to excellent.
Regulatory Season: June 11 – May 1.
Timing: June 11 – late November, peak early August – mid-September.
Size: Average 10 to 20 inches, a few larger fish up to 25 inches and 5-6 pounds. Look for biggest char in late summer and early fall.
Tip: As with rainbows, try near fish-cleaning stations using egg pattern and flesh flies.

Other Species: PS,AG,(KS,CS,RW).

LOWER RUSSIAN LAKE

Main Species: Rainbow trout and Dolly Varden.

Summary: Anglers spending some time on this beautiful lake are treated to some nice fishing for rainbow trout and Dolly Varden. Casting from the bank is possible, particularly at the lake inlet and outlet, but a small watercraft is undoubtedly the way to proceed in accessing the better locations – or at least to fish them more effectively.

Description: This is a fairly deep clearwater lake situated in a mountain valley. At just over a mile in length it is the smallest of the Russian lakes.

General Access: By trail or floatplane. The Sterling Highway provides access to trailhead near the Russian River Campground. The trail to Lower Russian Lake is wheelchair-accessible. Access beyond the developed trail is minimal due to thick vegetation.

Access Point: *Russian Lakes Trailhead* – MP 52.7 Sterling Highway. South on paved access road by sign (Russian River Campground) 1 mile to trailhead on left. Developed parking, restrooms. Trail leads 2 miles to a "Y," right fork proceeds 0.6 mile to Russian River and the lake outlet, left fork continues 1 mile to Lower Russian Lake Forest Service Cabin and the lake. Trail continues on to Upper Russian River and Lake (see description on page 239/241).

Fishing Opportunities
Restrictions: Salmon fishing prohibited. Additional restrictions in effect (consult ADF&G regulations).

Rainbow Trout
Rating: Good.
Regulatory Season: June 11 – May 1.
Timing: June 11 – May 1, peak mid-August – early October.
Size: Average 10 to 18 inches, some larger fish up to 22 inches and 4 pounds or more.
Tip: Focus on lake inlet and outlet late in season but also anytime spawning salmon are present. In lake proper, search out weed beds and steep drop-offs.

Dolly Varden
Rating: Good.
Timing: Year-round, peak mid-August – mid-October.
Size: Average 10 to 18 inches, some larger fish up to 20 inches and 3 pounds or more.
Tip: In late summer and fall, the lake inlet and outlet yield the best action, especially when salmon are running.

Other Species: (KS,RS,SS).

UPPER RUSSIAN RIVER

Main Species: Rainbow trout and Dolly Varden.

Summary: Anglers searching for a remote stream complete with great opportunities for good-sized trout and few other people, the Upper Russian River has what it takes. It is a long river with plenty of space to search out productive holes and runs. When salmon run here in summer and fall, the trout action can be exceptional. However, this is prime bear habitat so caution is advised.

Description: The Upper Russian River originates at the outlet of Upper Russian Lake, flows through a dense forest of brush and spruce about 8.5 miles to the inlet of Lower Russian Lake. The Russian Lakes Trail parallels the river for much of its length, lending opportunity for anglers to access much of its waters. The river runs clear and cool, the current slow and smooth. There are a multitude of deep holes and runs with overhanging vegetation.

General Access: By trail. The Sterling Highway provides main access to two trailheads, one from the Russian River Campground, the other from Russian Lakes Trailhead by Cooper Lake.
Northern Route
Access Point A: Russian Lakes Trailhead – MP 52.7 Sterling Highway. South on paved access road by sign (Russian River Campground) 1 mile to trailhead on left. Developed parking, restrooms. Trail leads 2 miles to a "Y," left fork proceeds 1 mile to Lower Russian Lake Forest Service Cabin and Lower Russian Lake (see description on page 238). Trail continues on from here approximately 1.25 mile to the lower portion of Upper Russian River. From this point on to the outlet of Upper Russian Lake, the trail will parallel the river more or less for the next 7.5 miles. Aspen Flat Forest Service Cabin available at mile 9 of the trail, and the Upper Russian Lake Forest Service Cabin at mile 12.

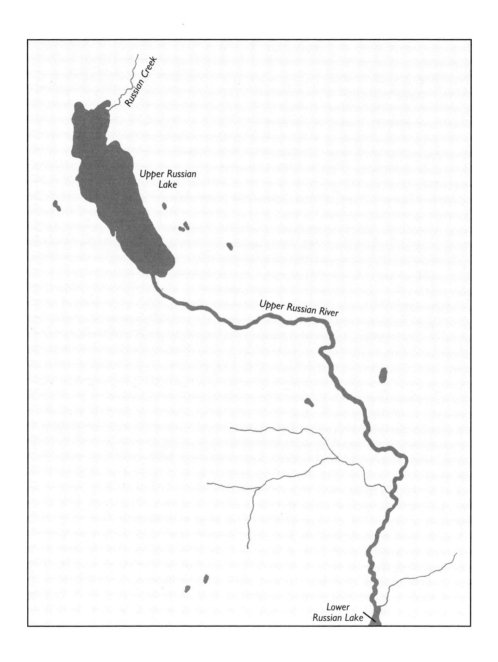

Southern Route

Access Point B: *Russian Lakes Trailhead* – MP 47.9 Sterling Highway. Southeast on Snug Harbor Road 8.7 miles, follow sign to the right at "Y" 2.8 miles to pullout on left and trailhead. Parking and restrooms. Trail leads 5 miles to junction with Resurrection River Trail, take right fork and proceed approximately 2 miles to shores of Upper Russian Lake. Continue 1.5 mile, passing the Upper Russian Lake Forest Service Cabin, to outlet of lake and Upper Russian River. From here on the trail parallels river more or less for the next 7.5 miles.

Fishing Opportunities

Restrictions: Salmon fishing prohibited. Closed to all fishing May 2 – June 10. Additional restrictions in effect (consult ADF&G regulations).

Rainbow Trout

Rating: Good to excellent.
Regulatory Season: June 11 – May 1.
Timing: June 11 – early November, peak mid-August – late September.
Size: Average 10 to 18 inches, some larger fish to 20 inches. In fall, a few big trout to 24 inches and 5 pounds are present.
Tip: Trout are available all summer but are most active when salmon spawn in late summer and fall.

Dolly Varden

Rating: Good.
Regulatory Season: June 11 – May 1.
Timing: June 11 – mid-November, peak mid-August – late September.
Size: Average 10 to 18 inches, some larger fish up to 22 inches and 3 pounds.
Tip: Scout deep holes and runs for large char in late summer and fall.

Other Species: (KS,RS,SS).

UPPER RUSSIAN LAKE

Main Species: Rainbow trout and Dolly Varden.

Summary:
Of the two Russian lakes, the Upper Russian yields the best rainbow action. The lake is more remote, hence less angling pressure and more aggressive fish. The lake is also quite a bit larger in surface area and thus supports a larger population of trout. Dolly Varden fishing is good as well. Anglers willing to make the trip this far can expect excellent success and reasonable solitude.

Early-run reds and silvers utilize inlet streams for spawning purposes in August and October, respectively, and the most productive rainbow and Dolly fishing coincides with these runs.

Description: Upper Russian Lake is approximately 2.5 miles long and not quite a mile wide. The water is crystal clear and cold.

General Access: By trail and floatplane. The Sterling Highway provides two points of access, one from the Russian River Campground, the other from the Russian Lakes Trailhead near Cooper Lake. The southern access route is by far the shortest course.

Northern Route

Access Point A: Russian Lakes Trailhead – MP 52.7 Sterling Highway. South on paved access road by sign (Russian River Campground) 1 mile to trailhead on left. Developed parking, restrooms. Trail leads 2 miles to a "Y," left fork proceeds 1 mile to Lower Russian Lake Forest Service Cabin and Lower Russian Lake (see description on page 238). Trail continues on from here approximately 1.25 mile to the lower portion of Upper Russian River (see description on page 239). From this point on the trail will parallel the river more or less for the next 7.5 miles to the outlet of Upper Russian Lake. Aspen Flats Forest Service Cabin available at mile 9 of the trail, and the Upper Russian Lake Forest Service Cabin at mile 12.

Southern Route

Access Point B: Russian Lakes Trailhead – MP 47.9 Sterling Highway. Southeast on Snug Harbor Road 8.7 miles, follow sign to the right at "Y" 2.8 miles to pullout on left and trailhead. Parking and restrooms. Trail leads 5 miles to junction with Resurrection River Trail, take right fork and proceed approximately 2 miles to shores of Upper Russian Lake. Continue 1.5 mile, passing the Upper Russian Lake Forest Service Cabin, to outlet of lake and Upper Russian River (see description on page 239).

Fishing Opportunities

Restrictions: Salmon fishing prohibited. Additional restrictions in effect (consult ADF&G regulations).

Rainbow Trout

Rating: Good to excellent.
Regulatory Season: June 11 – May 1.
Timing: June 11 – May 1, peak mid-July – early October.
Size: Average 10 to 18 inches, some larger fish up to 24 inches and 5 pounds or more.
Tip: The lake inlet and outlet are focal points of trout.

Dolly Varden

Rating: Good.
Timing: Year-round, peak mid-July – mid-October.
Size: Average 10 to 18 inches, some larger fish up to 22 inches and 4 pounds or more.
Tip: Lake inlet and outlet are hot spots.

Other Species: (KS,RS,SS).

RUSSIAN CREEK

Main Species: Rainbow trout and Dolly Varden.

Summary: Russian Creek is for the most part a major spawning stream for early-run reds but there is some decent trout and char fishing to be had in the lower sections of the creek, as well as at or near the mouth where it empties into Upper Russian Lake. Use extreme caution in this area as bears are common, especially in August.

Description: The Russian at this point is merely a shadow of what it becomes below the lakes. It is narrow and fairly shallow throughout, thick vegetation surrounds stream.

General Access: By trail and floatplane. The Sterling Highway provides trailhead access via Snug harbor Road. Floatplanes land on Upper Russian Lake at the lake inlet where Russian Creek flows in.
Access Point: Russian Lakes Trailhead – MP 47.9 Sterling Highway. Southeast on Snug Harbor Road 8.7 miles, follow sign to the right at "Y" 2.8 miles to pullout on left and trailhead. Parking and restrooms. Trail leads 5 miles to junction with Resurrection River Trail, take right fork and proceed approximately 2 miles to Upper Russian Lake (see description on page 241). Continue south on trail along lakeshore to southern-most end of lake. Russian Creek empties into southwest corner of the lake. No facilities except a Forest Service cabin located at the north end of Upper Russian Lake.

Fishing Opportunities
Restrictions: Salmon fishing prohibited. Closed to all fishing May 2 – June 10. Part of the stream is closed to fishing August 1-31. Additional restrictions in effect (consult ADF&G regulations).

Rainbow Trout
Rating: Fair to good.
Regulatory Season: June 11 – May 1.
Timing: June 11 – mid-October, peak early August – mid-September.
Size: Average 8 to 15 inches, a few larger fish up to 24 inches and 5 pounds.
Tip: Try deeper holes and runs in late summer and fall using egg imitations and flesh flies. A good number of fairly large rainbow trout spawn in this stream in spring (hence the spring closure). After the spawn the trout migrate back into the lake until the salmon arrive later in summer. Some smaller trout can be found in late June and July but improves later on in the season. Most anglers focus on the far lower section of the creek that is open to fishing during the salmon run in August.

Dolly Varden
Rating: Fair to good.
Regulatory Season: June 11 – May 1.
Timing: June 11 – mid-October, peak early August – mid-September.
Size: Average 8 to 16 inches, a few larger fish up to 22 inches and 4 pounds.
Tip: Search out deeper holes and runs in late summer.

Other Species: (RS,SS).

KENAI LAKE
& *Tributaries*

CHAPTER 13

Description

The area surrounding Kenai Lake and its drainage streams and lakes is perhaps one of – if not the most – scenic part of the entire Kenai River system. Confined within the Chugach National Forest, there is very sparse human influence to be found and an abundance of trees and shrubs in numerous valleys lined by rolling hills and jagged mountain ranges.

The community of Cooper Landing adores the northwest end of Kenai Lake while the smaller settlements of Lawing and Lakeview are situated on the southeast end. Moose Pass is another small community that sits on the shores of Upper Trail Lake.

Kenai Lake and Upper and Lower Trail Lakes are all glacial waters as are Trail and Snow rivers. Pristine clearwater lakes and creeks pour into these silty drainages, creating very picturesque settings of contrast along with the dense northern rainforest.

Wildlife is commonplace as the area teems with habitat perfect for browsing moose and beaver. Salmon spawn by the thousands in the multitude of streams and both brown and black bear, along with eagles, roam the banks looking for an easy meal in late summer and fall.

Access

An ample number of area waters are accessible by car via the Seward and Sterling highways. Other locations are more remote with at least a fair amount of hiking required to reach them. A few lakes are only accessible by floatplane.

Note: Several of the area trails are closed to motorized vehicles from May 1 through November 30. Extreme caution advised if traveling on these trails in winter as parts of them are high-risk avalanche areas.

Fishing

With the possible exception of the Russian River, the streams and lakes of Kenai Lake are the most popular sport fishing destinations for anglers visiting the Kenai system. Quartz Creek is without a doubt the area hot spot with its superb Dolly Varden and rainbow trout action in August and September. Ptarmigan Creek is another waterway with similar productivity. These two and other drainages are not just angling favorites in terms of numbers of fish available but also because of ease of access.

To enjoy more solitude, anglers have several options to choose from. One is to hike in by trail to one of several lakes; another is to use roadside lakes as gateways to explore more distant waters by canoe. A third option is to fly in to spots such as Paradise and Crescent lakes with their phenomenal grayling fishery and equally astounding scenic qualities.

For the more patient angler, hungry lake trout await offerings in the glacial Kenai and Trail lakes. While the action may not be hot, it is a worthwhile shot and good reason to be on the water.

Chapter Contents

The following are the game fish present, various waters of the Kenai Lake drainage, and the page number in which more detailed information can be found.

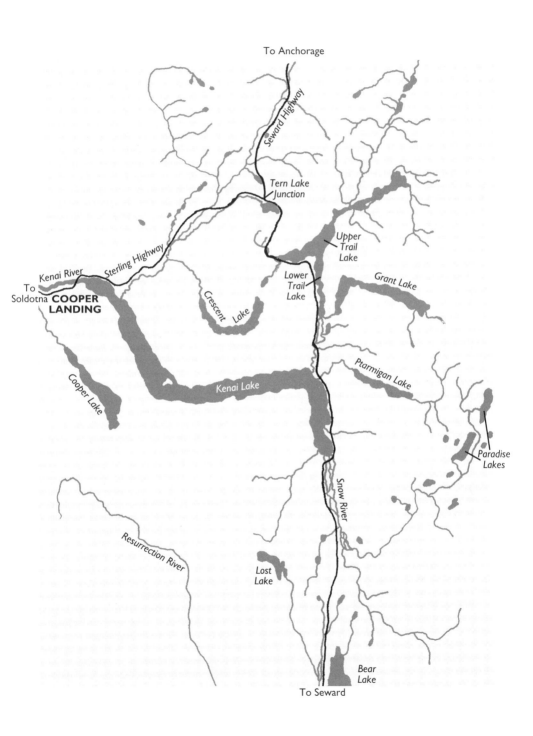

East Kenai Lake Drainages

Ptarmigan Creek	RT,DV	264
Ptarmigan Lake	DV	265
Paradise Lakes	AG	265
Meridian Lake	RT	266
Grayling Lake	AG	266

TIMING:

Kenai Lake & Tributaries - Streams

FISH	JAN	FEB	MAR	APR	MAY	JUN	JUL	AUG	SEP	OCT	NOV	DEC
RT												
LT												
DV												
AG												
RW												

Kenai Lake & Tributaries - Lakes

FISH	JAN	FEB	MAR	APR	MAY	JUN	JUL	AUG	SEP	OCT	NOV	DEC
RT												
LT												
DV												
AG												
RW												

Species Information

Salmon

All five species of salmon inhabit Kenai Lake at one time or another during the year, using it as a migration corridor to reach tributary lakes and streams. Currently, all waters in this area are closed to salmon fishing year-round, as these drainages are major or important spawning grounds for these species.

King salmon are not particularly abundant in streams draining into Kenai Lake, with populations probably consisting of no more than a few hundred fish at most. Quartz, Ptarmigan, and Trail are among the waters where kings may be observed. Present during July and August.

Red salmon are particularly abundant and can be found spawning in both glacial and clearwater creeks and lakes. Some populations use lake shorelines for reproductive purposes. Quartz and Ptarmigan creeks and the Trail Lakes receive runs that may number anywhere from a few thousand to 10,000 or more fish. Most stocks are of the late-run variety (from late July to late September) although the Quartz Creek drainage also has an earlier return lasting from early July to late August.

Silver salmon are present in good numbers in many area waters from mid-August to late November. The Quartz Creek and Trail Lakes drainages both are important producers. A very unique late run of silver salmon enters Kenai Lake in late fall and winter, moving into the outlet and the immediate upper reaches of Kenai River in late winter and early spring to spawn.

Pink and **chum salmon** are not represented in any numbers to speak of in the tributaries of Kenai Lake with runs typically being no more than a few hundred specimens. Quartz and Ptarmigan creeks along with Trail River has some fish, the two former locations containing the only documented populations of chum within the Kenai River drainage. Present from late July into September.

Trout/Char

Rainbow trout and **Dolly Varden** are considered abundant, or at least moderately so, in most waters draining into Kenai Lake, including several area lakes. They are present in rivers and streams starting in spring (April-May) but do not appear prolific until June or July when insect activity increases and the first salmon runs commence. Please note, however, that many flowing waters of the Kenai Lake drainage are closed to fishing from May 2 through June 10 to protect spawning trout. The late summer and fall months are best for anglers as this is when salmon are spawning and fish aggressive.

Lake fishing for rainbows and Dollies is best after breakup in spring (May-June) and as the weather cools before freezeup in fall (late August-October).

A variety of lures and flies work but anglers should remember that the fish in this area are largely tied into what the salmon are doing. As with most anywhere else within the Kenai River system, try smolt and forage patterns early on in the season mimicking juvenile salmon migrations and insect hatches, switching to egg and flesh imitations later on as mature salmon spawn and die. Forage imitations also work very well late in the season as salmon disappear and from spring through fall in lakes.

Lake trout are also relatively common and inhabit deeper glacial lakes. They are present year-round but tend to be more prevalent in late winter/early spring and during the cooler fall months. Smolt and forage imitations are always good and best presented at the mouths of clearwater streams. Bait can be very effective in these glacial waters.

Other Species

Arctic grayling are not native to this area but available as a result of past stocking efforts by the Alaska Department of Fish & Game and the original stocking locations still produce some very productive fishing. Some grayling are straying into adjoining waters within the area and a few specimens are picked up every so often by anglers targeting other species. Smolt and insect/forage imitations are a favorite anytime between June and October.

Round whitefish may be encountered in good numbers in several of the larger rivers and streams of Kenai Lake. Not targeted exclusively by anglers, whitefish are considered a by-catch when trying for trout and char. They are generally present from July into November and respond best to very small lures and flies.

Northern pike, although present in the Kenai River drainage, have not been reported from waters flowing into Kenai Lake.

KENAI LAKE

Main Species: Rainbow trout, lake trout, and Dolly Varden.

Summary: Kenai Lake is not known for its fishing opportunities as the water is turbid and very deep with few points of reference in terms of underwater structure and the alike which so many anglers rely on to find concentrations of fish. Yet the lake does harbor very large populations of game fish, such as trout, char, and whitefish, especially during the dark months, as a great many of the fish that spend the open water season in Kenai River and its tributaries overwinter in the lake.

Some success, however, can be had at the mouth of several clearwater tributaries draining into the lake at various times of the year for certain species. Also, the lake outlet at Kenai River in Cooper Landing is a favorite with some boat and shore anglers seeking trout and char. The use of strong-scented bait and visibility-enhanced lures are recommended wherever and whenever regulations allow.

Description: Water is turquoise or greenish blue in color from glacial silt sediment, at times appearing greenish gray. In winter and early spring, water visibility improves slightly. The lake is also the deepest lake on the peninsula, measured to 600 feet or more in places. Due to its temperate environment, the lake seldom freezes more than a few inches and, in some mild winters, does not freeze up at all.

General Access: By road and floatplane. Both Sterling and Seward highways provide main access to the west and east ends of lake, respectively, with numerous secondary road and trail access points. A boat comes useful in reaching the mouth of some tributary streams and several remote picnic areas along the lake's shoreline.

West Kenai Lake

Access Point A: *Quartz Creek Campground* – MP 45.0 Sterling Highway. South on Quartz Creek Road 0.6 mile to campground on right. Several trails lead 0.25 mile from campground and parking area to and along lower section of stream to mouth of creek and Kenai Lake. Additional access from south portion of parking area that includes boat launch. Paved parking and camping, restrooms.

Access Point B: *Kenai River Campground* – MP 47.7 Sterling Highway. Road crosses lake outlet at Kenai River. North on access road at MP 47.8 to campground with access to outlet. Paved parking and camping, restrooms, boat launch.

East Kenai Lake

Access Point C: *Trail River Campground* – MP 24.1 Seward Highway. West on access road 1.2 mile to campground with developed parking and campsites. Several trails lead from campground to lake and also the mouth of Trail River.

Access Point D: MP 23.5 Seward Highway. West on #2497 road 0.2 mile to lake. Developed parking and boat launch.

Access Point E: MP 23.4 Seward Highway. Southwest on gravel road along railroad tracks 0.3 mile to Ptarmigan Creek. Parking. Trail leads downstream along creek to Kenai Lake.

Access Point F: *Primrose Creek Campground* – MP 17.0 Seward Highway. Northwest on access road 1.2 mile to campground, mouth of Primrose Creek, and lake. Developed parking, some campsites, and boat launch.

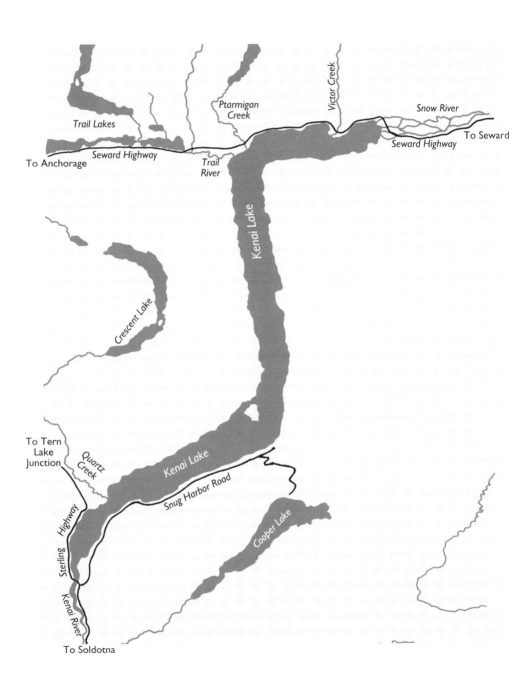

Fishing Opportunities

Restrictions: Salmon fishing prohibited. Seasonal closure in effect for the mouths of some tributaries and the lake outlet (consult ADF&G regulations).

Rainbow Trout

Rating: Fair to good,

Timing: Year-round, peak mid-July – mid-October.

Size: Average 10 to 20 inches, some larger fish to 25 inches and 5-6 pounds. Trophy specimens are a possibility, with catches up to 30 inches (10-12 pounds plus) or more known. Biggest trout are generally caught in early spring and late fall at lake outlet as fish move to and from upper Kenai River.

Tip: The mouths of Quartz and Ptarmigan creeks and Trail River are good from July into September. The lake outlet at Kenai River is fairly productive in March and the first half of April and again from July into October.

Lake Trout

Rating: Fair.

Timing: Year-round, peak late October – early December.

Size: Average 2 to 5 pounds (18-25 inches), some larger fish to 10-12 pounds. Trophy-size char up to 25 pounds and more have been reported.

Tip: The mouths of Quartz and Ptarmigan creeks and Trail River hold some smaller fish in summer and fall when salmon migrate through. The lake outlet at Kenai River is worth a try in late fall and early winter.

Dolly Varden

Rating: Fair to good.

Timing: Year-round, peak late July – mid-October.

Size: Average 10 to 20 inches, some larger fish to 25 inches and 5-6 pounds. Catches of trophy char up to 30 inches and 10-12 pounds or more not unheard of.

Tip: The mouths of Quartz and Ptarmigan creeks and Trail River are productive. Fish are often on the smaller side during early summer with larger char appearing in August and September. The lake outlet at Kenai River can be worthwhile at times when salmon are present.

Other Species: AG,RW,(KS,RS,SS,PS,CS).

QUARTZ CREEK

Main Species: Rainbow trout and Dolly Varden.

Summary: Quartz Creek has grown into one of the premier streams for Dolly Varden on the peninsula, known for a healthy population of char containing specimens that may reach trophy proportions. Most anglers fish the stream in August and September when salmon are spawning and trout and char aggressively feeding. Sight fishing may be good in the shallower middle and upper reaches of the creek. In the far upper reaches, around the Seward Highway crossing, fishing is poor.

Description: Medium-sized clearwater stream, tinted slightly green in summer and fall.

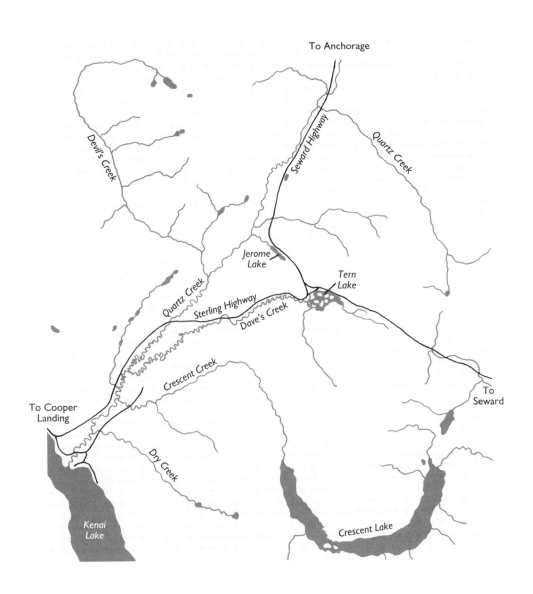

General Access: By road. Sterling Highway provides multiple access points to the lower and middle stream sections, while Seward Highway offers two access points to the upper stream. Undeveloped or improvised trails are common at most access points, particularly along the middle and lower creek.

Lower Quartz Creek

Access Point A: Quartz Creek Campground – MP 45.0 Sterling Highway. South on Quartz Creek Road 0.6 mile to campground on right. Paved parking and camping, restrooms, and boat launch on Kenai Lake. Several trails lead from campground and parking area to and along lower section of stream. Mouth of creek at Kenai Lake is 0.25 mile from recreation area.

Access Point B: MP 45.0 Sterling Highway. South on Quartz Creek Road 0.7 mile to stream crossing. Turnout with faint trails lead up- and downstream along creek. Primitive parking.

Middle Quartz Creek

Access Point C: MP 40.9 Sterling Highway; road crosses stream. Paved turnout. Faint trails lead up- and downstream along creek. Wading in creek and hiking along gravel bars is also possible.

Access Point D: MP 42.0 – 44.0 Sterling Highway; road parallels stream. Several turnouts available, some with trails leading up- and downstream along creek. Paved turnout.

Access Point E: Crescent Creek Campground – MP 45.0 Sterling Highway. South on Quartz Creek Road 2.7 miles to campground on left. Primitive parking. Trail leads short distance to and along creek.

Upper Quartz Creek

Access Point F: MP 42.2 – 41.0 Seward Highway; road parallels stream, crossing it at MP 42.2. Park on road shoulder. Very faint or no trails present. No facilities.

Access Point G: Devils Pass Trailhead – MP 39.5 Seward Highway. West on access road to parking area and trailhead. Trail leads about 0.5 mile to stream crossing. Paved parking.

Fishing Opportunities

Restrictions: Salmon fishing prohibited. Seasonal closure in effect (consult ADF&G regulations).

Rainbow Trout

Rating: Good in lower and middle stream, poor to fair in upper reaches.

Timing: June 11 – late November, peak mid-July – mid-September.

Size: Average 10 to 15 inches, some larger fish to 20 inches. During salmon spawn, a very few specimens up to 25 inches and 5-6 pounds may be present.

Tip: The middle stream section is best in July and August, the upper reaches being productive from late July into September.

Dolly Varden

Rating: Excellent, especially in the middle reaches. Expect fair success in upper stream.

Timing: June 11 – early December, peak mid-July – mid-September.

Size: Average 10 to 20 inches, some larger fish to 22 inches or more. In late summer and fall, look for trophy fish up to 25-30 inches and 5-10 pounds. Char to 15 pounds have been caught.

Tip: Early in the season (July), fish are concentrated in the lower stream section. As salmon move through the char will follow into the middle and upper reaches (July-September).

Note: Upper Quartz above the highway is an important spawning area for large char and currently closed to fishing in fall (consult ADF&G regulations).

Other Species: AG,RW,(KS,RS,SS,PS,CS).

Daves Creek: A narrow but fairly deep tributary of Quartz Creek, this stream is easily accessed from the Sterling Highway. The road parallels the stream more or less from the outlet of Tern Lake near MP 37.3 to 40.1, crossing it and MP 39.5 and 39.7. Daves Creek does offer some limited opportunities for smaller trout and char – even grayling – during the summer and fall months, especially when salmon spawn here in August. Come fall, look for char up to 24 inches and several pounds.

The stream is closed to all fishing from May 2 through June 10 (consult ADF&G regulations).

CRESCENT LAKE

Main Species: Arctic grayling.

Summary: Crescent Lake is arguably the most productive grayling water on the Kenai Peninsula in terms of numbers and size of fish, hence its popularity. As a matter of fact, catching 20-inch-plus grayling is not a lofty goal here. The lake was stocked with grayling many years ago by ADF&G but today the population is self-sustaining and very healthy. Fish are present year-round with best angling in summer and fall.

Description: Beautiful crescent-shaped, clearwater mountain lake. Fairly deep.

General Access: By trail and floatplane. Both Sterling and Seward highways provide developed trail access to the northwest end and northeast end of lake, respectively. The Seward Highway access point is the shortest route. Be prepared to ford small streams, especially after heavy rainfall. Aircraft land on the lake fairly often.

Northwestern Lake

Access Point A: Crescent Creek Trailhead – MP 45.0 Sterling Highway. South on Quartz Creek Road 3.4 miles to trailhead on right and end of main road. Developed trail leads 6.5 miles east along Crescent Creek to lake outlet and the Crescent Lake Forest Service Cabin. There is also a campsite situated across from cabin on other side of creek. A rough, undeveloped trail leads from the campsite an additional 4 miles along southern shore of lake to Saddle Forest Service Cabin.

Northeastern Lake

Access Point B: Carter Lake Trailhead – MP 33.1 Seward Highway. West at turnout to trailhead. Developed trail leads 3 miles south to lake inlet and campsite. It is a fairly steep ascent. Hikers will pass Carter Lake on the way (described separately on page 257). A rough, undeveloped trail leads from the campsite an additional 4 miles along southern shore of lake to Saddle Forest Service Cabin.

Fishing Opportunities

Restrictions: Closed to all fishing May 2 – June 30 (consult ADF&G regulations).

Arctic Grayling

Rating: Good to excellent, lake inlet and outlet are hot spots.

Timing: Early July – late October, peak early July – mid-September.

Size: Average 10 to 17 inches, larger fish to 20 inches. A few trophy specimens up to 21-22 inches and 3 pounds are in this lake.

Tip: The main inlet at northeast end of lake and outlet at Crescent Creek at northwest end of lake are the two best locations. Use a canoe or inflatable craft to reach the mouth of smaller streams for good action as well. However, productive fishing can be had almost anywhere at times.

Note: Lake is closed to fishing in spring and early summer to protect spawning grayling.

Other Species: DV.

Crescent Creek: Fishing for grayling may be good from mid-summer into early fall with some quite large fish available immediately after the season opener on July 1. Anglers do best focusing on the stretch of water near the outlet of Crescent Lake but a few fish are present throughout the stream. Dolly Varden, which may be of good proportions, are sometimes caught in the far lower stream portion near its confluence with Quartz Creek in August and September.

The stream is closed to all fishing from May 2 through June 30 to protect spawning grayling.

JEROME LAKE

Main Species: Rainbow trout and Dolly Varden.

Summary: Jerome Lake, adjacent to the Seward Highway, is stocked with trout by the ADF&G and also contains a small natural population of char. Since it is right next to the highway, the lake is a popular spot with anglers wanting to take a break and make a few casts on their way to other angling destinations. The action is quite good at times both from shore and watercraft. The weeds at the southern end of the lake and the brush-covered western shoreline hold concentrations of fish.

Description: Small clearwater lake, about half a mile long and very narrow with moderate depth (15 feet).

General Access: By road. The Seward Highway runs adjacent to the entire length of the lake. Access is at south end. A canoe or other watercraft is necessary to reach the vegetated west side. No developed trails in area.

Access Point: MP 38.6 – 38.3 Seward Highway. East on turnoff at MP 38.3 to paved parking area next to lake. No facilities.

Fishing Opportunities
Restrictions: None (consult ADF&G regulations).

Rainbow Trout
Rating: Fair to good.
Timing: Year-round, peak mid-May – early June and early September – mid-October.
Size: Average 8 to 15 inches, some larger fish to 22 inches and 3 pounds.
Tip: The weeds on the southern end of the lake hold trout, as does the entire western shoreline and near the outlet on the northern end.

Dolly Varden
Rating: Fair.
Timing: Year-round, peak mid-May – early June and early September – mid-October.
Size: Average 10 to 15 inches, a few larger fish to 22 inches and 3 pounds.
Tip: Same areas as the trout but may hold in deeper water.

TRAIL LAKES DRAINAGE
Includes Carter Lake, Trail Lakes, Johnson Lake, Vagt Lake, and Trail River.

CARTER LAKE

Main Species: Rainbow trout.

Summary: Carter Lake, like so many other peninsula lakes, is stocked with trout by the ADF&G. Because of its strenuous trail and somewhat remoteness, angling pressure is light with the possibility of experiencing good fishing and a chance of landing some bigger than average rainbows than in most stocked lakes. A canoe or other type of watercraft is recommended.

Description: Small alpine lake situated less than a mile from Crescent Lake. Water is clear and moderately deep (60 feet); east portion of the lake has steeper bottom gradient.

General Access: By trail. A developed trail begins at Seward Highway and leads to west shore of lake, continuing on to the eastern section of Crescent Lake.
Access Point: Carter Lake Trailhead – MP 33.1 Seward Highway. South at turnoff to trailhead. Paved parking and restrooms. Trail heads due south 1 mile to lake on left. First portion of trail is steep and can be rough going for some individuals. No facilities at lake.

Fishing Opportunities
Restrictions: Salmon fishing prohibited (consult ADF&G regulations).

Rainbow Trout
Rating: Good.
Timing: Year-round, peak late May – mid-June and late August – early October.

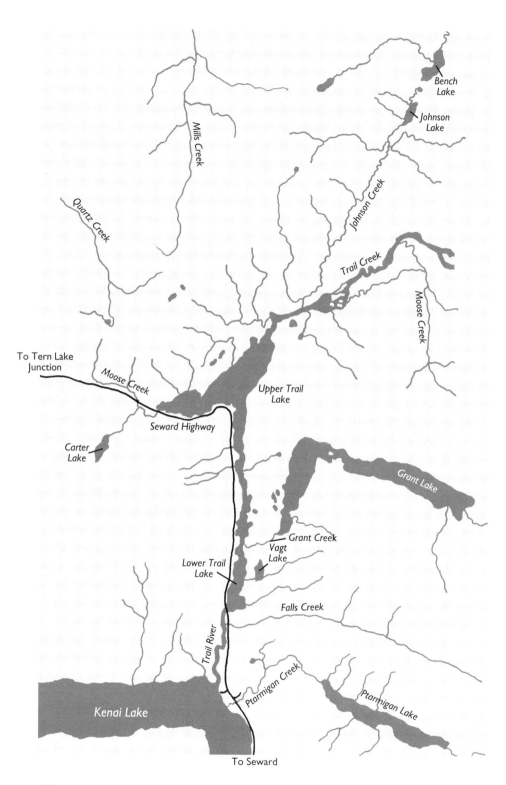

Size: Average 8 to 16 inches, some larger fish to 22 inches and 4 pounds. A few trout approaching 25 inches and 6 pounds are said to be in lake.

Tip: Look for areas with submerged vegetation or spots where the bottom suddenly drops off into deeper water for better success and larger fish.

TRAIL LAKES

Main Species: Rainbow trout, lake trout, and Dolly Varden.

Summary: Upper and Lower Trail Lakes, like most glacial lakes on the peninsula, are not much appreciated by anglers due to the milky coloration of the water and difficulty in getting fish to strike artificial lures and flies. Although fishers may experience some success using strong-scented bait and visibility-enhanced lures in lake proper, the best action can undoubtedly be had zeroing in on main feeding areas such as the mouth of clearwater streams where both trout and char can be found in relatively good numbers.

Description: Glacial lake; water is colored grayish green with silt.

General Access: By road and floatplane. The Seward Highway parallels western shore of lakes for several miles, providing easy roadside access. A canoe or other watercraft is a good way to reach more remote clearwater streams away from the highway.

Upper Trail Lake

Access Point A: MP 32.3 Seward Highway. North on access road short distance to old highway bridge and confluence of Moose Creek and Upper Trail Lake. Parking. No facilities.

Access Point B: *Upper Trail Lake Wayside* – MP 31.9 Seward Highway. North on turnout to wayside. Limited parking, picnic area.

Access Point C: MP 30.3 Seward Highway. Northwest on gravel road 0.1 mile to lake. Undeveloped parking with primitive boat launch.

Lower Trail Lake

Access Point D: MP 25.3 Seward Highway. Road crosses lake outlet and Trail River. East on gravel access road at MP 25.2 leading 0.1 mile to lake. Parking available at Vagt Lake Trailhead. Vagt Lake Trail follows south shore of lake for about half a mile.

Fishing Opportunities

Restrictions: Salmon fishing prohibited (consult ADF&G regulations).

Rainbow Trout

Rating: Fair.

Timing: Year-round, peak late July – late September.

Size: Average 8 to 15 inches, a few larger fish to 20 inches and 3 pounds. Look for bigger trout when salmon run.

Tip: Any sizable inlet of clear water may hold fish but the mouths of Moose, Johnson, and Grant creeks may be the best bets. Lake outlet may be productive.

Lake Trout

Rating: Fair.

Timing: Year-round, peak late July – late October.

Size: Average 2 to 4 pounds (18-22 inches), a few larger fish to 25 inches and 6 pounds. Char tend to run on the small side in summer with heavier specimens taken in fall.

Tip: The mixing zone of clearwater streams and the silty lake is a relative hot spot. Also, smaller lake trout tend to follow spawning salmon into mouths of tributaries. A few lake trout are caught at the outlet of Lower Trail after ice-out in early spring and again in late summer and fall as salmon concentrate in the area.

Dolly Varden
Rating: Fair to good.
Timing: Year-round, peak late July – mid-September.
Size: Average 10 to 16 inches, some larger fish to 20 inches and 3 pounds. A few large specimens may exceed 24 inches and 5 pounds in fall.
Tip: Try the confluences of Moose, Johnson, and Grant creeks in late summer when spawning salmon are present, as well as the outlet of Lower Trail. In fall it is not unusual to spot schools of char moving into these areas.

Other Species: AG,RW,(KS,RS,SS,PS).

Moose Creek: Located at the northwest end of Upper Trail Lake, Moose is easily accessed from the Seward Highway, the road paralleling the stream more or less for less than a mile, crossing it at MP 32.9 and 32.2. This is a major spawning stream for red salmon and may provide some decent fishing for Dolly Varden along with a few rainbow trout between late July and late September. In fall, look for large char up to 25 inches.

The stream is closed to all fishing from May 2 through June 10 (consult ADF&G regulations).

JOHNSON LAKE

Main Species: Rainbow trout.

Summary: Johnson Lake has a good population of trout and since it is so remote the action can be very good. Some large fish are in this lake and may be encountered particularly in early summer and fall. Due to the lake's altitude, ice conditions persist longer in spring and earlier in the fall.
Note: Good to excellent arctic grayling fishing can be had in nearby Bench Lake, about 0.5 mile north of Johnson Lake on Johnson Pass Trail.

Description: Small clearwater lake, less than a mile long, in sub-alpine environment.

General Access: By trail. The Seward Highway provides a starting point (as well as an alternate ending point) for trail leading to lake. Following a portion of the Iditarod National Historic Trail, it continues from Johnson Lake to Upper Trail Lake. If originating at Upper Trail Lake, the trail terminates at Johnson Pass near Silvertip on the Seward Highway. Developed campsites are available at southern end of Johnson Lake.
Northern Route

Access Point A: Johnson Pass Trailhead – MP 63.8 Seward Highway. South at turnoff 0.3 mile to trailhead. Developed parking. Trail leads south along and crossing Bench Creek to Bench Lake and eventually Johnson Lake, about 10.5 miles total.

Southern Route
Access Point B: Johnson Pass Trailhead – MP 32.6 Seward Highway. North at turnoff to trailhead. Developed parking. Trail leads north along Upper Trail Lake, crossing Johnson Creek, to Johnson Lake, about 12 miles total.

Fishing Opportunities
Restrictions: None (consult ADF&G regulations).

Rainbow Trout
Rating: Good, especially after breakup and before freezeup.
Timing: Year-round, peak late May – mid-June and early September – mid-October.
Size: Average 8 to 16 inches, a few larger fish up to 25 inches and 6 pounds.
Tip: The southern end of lake near outlet is productive, as can be the inlet on the northern end.

VAGT LAKE

Main Species: Rainbow trout.

Summary: Lake is stocked regularly with trout by the ADF&G. A good population is present yielding productive and consistent catches, especially in fall. As is sometimes the case with lakes that are stocked and see relatively little angling pressure, the rainbows here may grow quite large.

Description: Small clearwater lake, depth to 50 feet.

General Access: By trail. A developed trail leads from trailhead at Seward Highway to Vagt Lake.
Access Point: Vagt Lake Trailhead – MP 25.2 Seward Highway. East on access road 0.1 mile to trailhead at the outlet of Lower Trail Lake. Parking and restrooms. Trail heads due east 1.5 miles to lake.

Fishing Opportunities
Restrictions: Seasonal closure in effect (consult ADF&G regulations).

Rainbow Trout
Rating: Good to excellent.
Timing: Year-round, peak late August – early October.
Size: Average 8 to 15 inches, several larger fish to 22 inches and 4 pounds. A few specimens up to 25 inches and 5-6 pounds or more reported.
Tip: Hike or paddle around lake finding drop-offs to deep water and submerged vegetation. Larger rainbows often hold in deeper sections of lake (the southern half) and a canoe or other watercraft may be necessary to find them. In September, a few big fish may come in fairly shallow near shore.

TRAIL RIVER

Main Species: Rainbow trout and Dolly Varden.

Summary: Trail River is an important salmon spawning and migratory stream and thus sees a decent population of trout and char in season. Due to the coloration of the water, bright lures and flies work best. Some anglers do quite well around the highway crossing but most interest is in the lower river near Kenai Lake in late summer and fall for char.

Description: Glacial river; water has greenish gray appearance. Current flow is slow to moderate in the upper section near Lower Trail Lake, picking up speed to moderate to fast as it approaches the confluence with Kenai Lake. It is a short river, only two miles long.

General Access: By road. Seward Highway provides several main and secondary access points along entire length of river. Undeveloped trails are present on the lower river at Trail River Campground.

Access Point A: MP 25.3 – 24.1 Seward Highway. Road crosses river at MP 25.3, paralleling it for almost a mile. A few turnouts present west of highway. Limited parking. No facilities.

Access Point B: Trail River Campground – MP 24.1 Seward Highway. West on access road 0.4 mile to river crossing. Limited parking. Continue 0.8 mile to campground with developed parking and campsites. Numerous trails lead from campground to river with access both up- and downstream.

Fishing Opportunities

Restrictions: Salmon fishing prohibited. Closed to all fishing May 2 – June 10 (consult ADF&G regulations).

Rainbow Trout

Rating: Fair to good.

Timing: June 11 – early December, peak mid-July – late September.

Size: Average 8 to 16 inches, some larger fish to 20 inches and 3 pounds. Occasional catches of trout up to 25 inches and 6-7 pounds possible when salmon run.

Tip: Some nice fish are taken in the upper river at or near the confluence with Falls Creek in summer. The lower river and its mouth at Kenai Lake can be good at times in late summer and fall.

Dolly Varden

Rating: Fair to good.

Timing: June 11 – mid-December, peak late July – early October.

Size: Average 8 to 18 inches, some larger fish to 22 inches and 3-4 pounds. Expect a few big char up to 25 inches and 6-7 pounds to be present in the lower river in fall.

Tip: Fish are spread throughout river but appear to be more numerous and easier to catch in the faster portions near Kenai Lake. Good action possible when salmon are spawning.

Other Species: LT,AG,RW,(KS,RS,SS,PS).

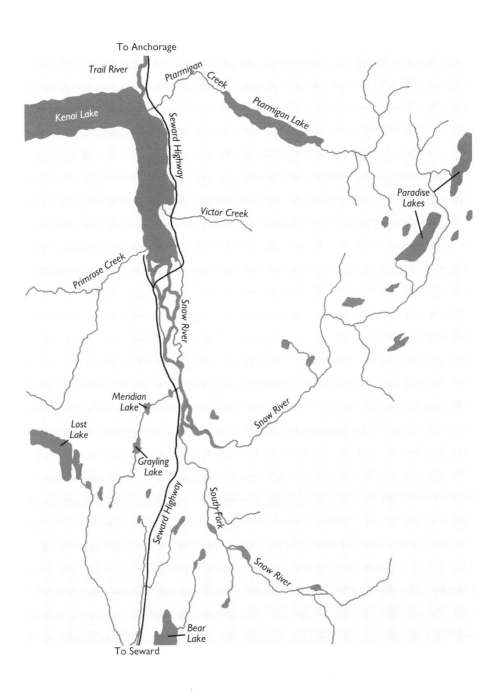

EAST KENAI LAKE DRAINAGES

Includes Ptarmigan Creek and Lake, Snow River, Paradise, Meridian, and Grayling lakes.

PTARMIGAN CREEK

Main Species: Rainbow trout and Dolly Varden.

Summary: Ptarmigan Creek is one of the most popular locations to catch char in the Kenai Lake drainage, next to Quartz Creek. Thanks to large runs of salmon the stream sports a healthy population of Dolly Varden, some specimens of which can get quite large. August and September are good months to find the big fish as well as some decent trout action. Sight fishing is possible in fall.

Description: Semi-glacial stream, running low and clear in spring and fall.

General Access: By road. The Seward Highway provides a couple of points of access. Undeveloped trails lead from road downstream to confluence with Kenai Lake. Developed trail heads upstream from campground along creek to Ptarmigan Lake and beyond.

Access Point A: MP 23.4 Seward Highway. Southwest on gravel road along railroad tracks 0.3 mile to stream. Parking. Trails lead up- and downstream along creek.

Access Point B: Ptarmigan Creek Campground – MP 23.3 Seward Highway. Road crosses stream. At bridge, turn east onto road leading to campground and trailhead. Developed parking and camping with restrooms. Trail leads northeast from campground along creek 3 miles to outlet of Ptarmigan Lake.

Fishing Opportunities

Restrictions: Salmon fishing prohibited. Closed to all fishing May 2 – June 10 (consult ADF&G regulations).

Rainbow Trout

Rating: Fair to good in lower and middle stream, poor to fair in upper reaches.
Timing: June 11 – late November, peak late July – mid-September.
Size: Average 10 to 15 inches, some larger fish to 20 inches. During salmon spawn, a very few specimens up to 25 inches and 5-6 pounds may be present.
Tip: The lower stream section is best in July and August, the middle and upper reaches being productive from late July into September.

Dolly Varden

Rating: Good, especially in the lower and middle reaches, fair in upper portions.
Timing: June 11 – early December, peak late July – mid-September.
Size: Average 10 to 20 inches, some larger fish to 22 inches or more. In late summer and fall, look for trophy fish up to 25-30 inches and 5-10 pounds.
Tip: Fish are concentrated in the lower and middle stream sections as salmon move through. Some productive char action in upper stream at outlet of Ptarmigan Lake.

Other Species: AG,RW,(KS,RS,SS,PS,CS).

PTARMIGAN LAKE

Main Species: Dolly Varden.

Summary: Ptarmigan Lake is often overlooked by anglers due to the fact that the lake is quite large and the fish populations not so. However, at certain times of the year the non-anadromous char can be found in moderate concentration providing decent fishing opportunities in an area several miles from the highway with no crowds of other anglers. The use of strong-scented bait and visibility-enhanced lures are recommended wherever and whenever regulations allow.

Description: Deep, semi-glacial lake, appearing greenish blue in color.

General Access: By road or floatplane. The Seward Highway provides access to trailhead. Trail follows northern shore of lake. A canoe or other watercraft may come in useful in reaching the mouths of small clearwater streams.

Access Point: Ptarmigan Creek Trailhead – MP 23.2 Seward Highway. East on turnout at campground to trailhead. Developed parking and camping, restrooms. Trail leads 3 miles east to lake outlet, continuing along lake shore another 4 miles to eastern end of lake.

Fishing Opportunities
Restrictions: None (consult ADF&G regulations).

Dolly Varden
Rating: Fair to good.
Timing: Year-round, peak late August – early October.
Size: Average 8 to 12 inches, some larger fish to 18 inches.
Tip: Schools of char encountered at lake inlet and outlet in fall as fish prepare to spawn.

PARADISE LAKES

Main Species: Arctic grayling.

Summary: Once stocked years ago by the ADF&G, the grayling populations in Paradise Lakes are very healthy and self-sustaining. Due to difficulties in accessing the area, the fishing here is exceptional and other anglers few and far apart.

Description: Incredible scenic views surround these clearwater lakes.

General Access: By floatplane. Chartered flights can be arranged from one of several Kenai Peninsula towns and communities, Moose Pass and Seward being the closest ports. Flying time is approximately 10-15 minutes. There are two Forest Service cabins available, one on each of the larger lakes.

Fishing Opportunities
Restrictions: Salmon fishing prohibited. Seasonal closure in effect (consult ADF&G regulations).

Arctic Grayling
Rating: Excellent.
Timing: Year-round, peak mid-June – late September.
Size: Average 8 to 14 inches, a few larger fish up to 20 inches.
Tip: Grayling are abundant and very aggressive. Great fishing from both shore and watercraft. At times it helps to look for small inlets and outlets where fish may congregate.

Other Species: RT.

MERIDIAN LAKE

Main Species: Rainbow trout.

Summary: Meridian Lake is stocked with trout by the ADF&G. Action is often good as lake is situated off the road by a mile and other anglers kept to a minimum.

Description: Small clearwater lake of moderate depth.

General Access: By trail. From the trailhead at Seward Highway, it is an easy hike to the lake. A canoe or other watercraft may enhance success.
Access Point: Grayling Lake Trailhead – MP 13.3 Seward Highway. Turn west at turnoff to trailhead. Parking and restrooms available. Developed trail leads 1 mile due west to a "Y," take right fork 0.6 mile to lake (left fork leads to Grayling Lake).

Fishing Opportunities
Restrictions: None (consult ADF&G regulations).

Rainbow Trout
Rating: Good.
Timing: Year-round, peak late May – mid-June and late August – mid-October.
Size: Average 8 to 15 inches, a few larger fish up to 22 inches and 3 pounds.
Tip: Try early and late in the season, after breakup and before freezeup. Look for small schools of trout near shoreline.

GRAYLING LAKE

Main Species: Arctic grayling.

Summary: Grayling Lake has a small but productive self-sustaining population of arctic grayling. It is a fairly popular fishery in summer and early fall due to the relatively good action and easy access from Seward Highway.

Description: Fairly small clearwater lake.

General Access: By trail. From the trailhead at Seward Highway, it is an easy hike to the lake. Although not entirely necessary, a canoe or other watercraft may enhance success.
Access Point: Grayling Lake Trailhead – MP 13.3 Seward Highway. Turn west at turnoff to trailhead. Parking and restrooms available. Developed trail leads 1 mile due west to a "Y," take left fork 0.6 mile to lake (right fork leads to Meridian Lake).

Fishing Opportunities
Restrictions: Seasonal closure in effect (consult ADF&G regulations).

Arctic Grayling
Rating: Fair to good.
Timing: Year-round, peak mid-June – late September.
Size: Average 8 to 12 inches, a few larger fish to 20 inches.
Tip: Although action can be decent all summer, the best is early and late in the season both in terms of catch rate and fish size.

APPENDIX

ALASKA RECORD & TROPHY FISH

The Alaska Department of Fish & Game (ADF&G) documents record catches and has established a trophy fish program to enhance the angling experience. For details on how to participate in the program or submit a potential record fish, consult a current copy of the ADF&G rules and regulations booklet or contact the department directly.

Catch-and-Release Trophy Certificate
Minimum lengths for catch-and-release certificates:
- Arctic Char/Dolly Varden: 30 inches
- Arctic Grayling: 18 inches
- Brook Trout: 20 inches
- Cutthroat Trout: 20 inches
- Lake Trout: 36 inches
- Lingcod: 53 inches
- Northern Pike: 40 inches
- Rainbow/Steelhead Trout: 32 inches
- Sheefish: 45 inches

Alaska Record Fish
& Minimum Weight Required for Trophy Certificate

Species	Weight	Location	Trophy Min.
Arctic Char/Dolly Varden	27-6	Wulik River (NW)	10 Lbs.
Arctic Grayling	4-13	Ugashik Narrows (SW)	3 Lbs.
Brook Trout	0-0	(No Submissions)	3 Lbs.
Burbot	24-12	Lake Louise (SC)	8 Lbs.
Chum Salmon	32-0	Caamano Point (SE)	15 Lbs.
Cutthroat Trout	8-6	Wilson Lake (SE)	3 Lbs.
King Salmon	97-4	Kenai River (SC)	75 Lbs.*
Lake Trout	47-0	Clarence Lake (SC)	20 Lbs.
Ling Cod	81-6	Monty Island (SC)	55 Lbs.
Northern Pike	38-0	Innoko River (SW)	15 Lbs.
Pacific Halibut	459-0	Unalaska Bay (SW)	250 Lbs.
Pink Salmon	12-9	Moose River (SC)	8 Lbs.
Rainbow/Steelhead Trout	42-3	Bell Island (SE)	15 Lbs.
Red Salmon	16-0	Kenai River (SC)	12 Lbs.
Rockfish	38-11	Prince William Sound (SC)	18 Lbs.
Sheefish	53-0	Pah River (NW)	30 Lbs.
Silver Salmon	26-0	Icy Strait (SE)	20 Lbs.
Whitefish	9-0	Tozitna River (IN)	4 Lbs.

* Trophy weight for king salmon in the Kenai River is 75 pounds, and the rest of the state 50 pounds.

SPORT FISHING RULES & REGULATIONS

The Alaska Department of Fish & Game (ADF&G), through laws enacted by the Board of Fisheries, publishes several booklets annually, each according to designated state-wide regions, describing open or closed seasons and areas, gear restrictions, bag and possession limits, and many other points to follow in order to protect fish populations from potential harm or over-exploitation. The Kenai River drainage is covered in the Southcentral Regional Booklet under the Kenai Peninsula section.

Due to the ever changing and near unpredictable nature of fishing rules and regula-tions, they have been practically omitted from this book to prevent the content of becoming outdated too soon. Besides, certain locations have very specific and lengthy restrictions that would almost require a chapter in itself to list and explain, the main-stem Kenai River being one of them. The information contained within all chapters in this book adheres to current laws; however, any set rule and regulation is, of course, subject to change through "emergency orders" posted by the ADF&G and the Board of Fisheries.

Also, it is entirely the responsibility of the individual angler to have knowledge and be in complete compliance of existing rules and regulations for the water he or she intends to fish. In other words, ignorance is not an excuse. Always consult a current and official copy of the sport fishing regulations before making that first cast. Cop-ies are available in many retail outlets in Anchorage and on the Kenai Peninsula. If in doubt or have any questions, contact the nearest ADF&G office. Numbers are listed below.

Soldotna: (907) 262-9368 Anchorage: (907) 267-2218

For a copy of current rules and regulations contact:

ADF&G Division of Sport Fish
P. O. Box 25526
Juneau, AK 99802-5526
(907) 465-4180
www.sf.adfg.state.ak.us/statewide/sf_home.cfm

Enforcement of Rules & Regulations

Troopers of the Fish & Wildlife Service and authorized personnel of ADF&G conduct enforcement of fishing laws and/or issue citations and warnings. They patrol the entire Kenai River system and may be in uniform or civilian clothing and often dressed as an angler. Commonly broken rules include snagging or attempting to snag fish (fish must be hooked in mouth to be legal), harvesting more than the legal bag or possession limit, and fishing without a license.

If observing law being broken, inform angler(s) of wrongful act one time only but do not proceed beyond that in actions or words. Do not take law into own hands. Some violations are blatantly obvious and perpetrators should not be approached. Contact local Fish & Wildlife Protection office if violation continues despite warning at number(s) listed below.

1-800-478-3377 Soldotna: (907) 262-5312 Anchorage: (907) 269-5443

WILDLIFE

The Kenai Peninsula has healthy populations of moose, bear, sheep, beaver, and various kinds of birds, all of which are present in the forest and mountains surrounding the Kenai River and its tributaries. As a matter of fact, a good portion of the river system, starting with the Kenai National Wildlife Refuge on the middle Kenai and stretching into the Chugach National Forest and the upper drainage, is a haven for wildlife. Anglers fishing the Kenai for any extent of time are quite likely to come across at least one or two large types of animals common in the region – moose and bear. Avoid close encounters, which could promote a life-threatening situation.

Moose are most abundant and at first appear as quite slow and docile creatures. Do not misjudge them as being less of a potential threat and keep a safe distance as Moose are able to cover a lot of ground in a surprisingly blaze of speed. There have been a few deadly attacks involving moose so respect is warranted as with any other wild animal.

Bears, both brown and black, are another factor to be aware of. Although usually relegated to the more remote parts of the Kenai drainage, they do surprisingly often come into more urban areas along the river, especially on the outskirts of Soldotna and Sterling, as well as in Cooper Landing. However, they are most numerous along clearwater streams in late summer and fall, scouting for salmon in the shallows. The bears forage on fish to fatten up for the long, cold winter ahead. They are for the most part very shy creatures and will avoid confrontation with humans as much as possible.

The best precautions to employ when hiking along trails away from the road are to make a lot of noise. Clap hands, sing, shout, talk loudly, wear a "bear bell," blow a horn or whistle, shake a can of rocks, or bring a boom box – whatever means at disposal to alert bears of your presence. Avoid walking on trails in darkness and through heavy brush along salmon spawning streams. If a bear is sighted in close proximity and appears unfazed by noise, leave area immediately in a calm manner. Additionally, keep all foods away from sleeping area such as a tent to prevent a potentially dangerous situation.

Report aggressive animals – both bear and moose – to the proper authorities, such as the Fish & Wildlife Service, Alaska Department of Fish & Game, the National Forest Service, or local police departments.

HIRING A GUIDE

There are probably few waters in the world that has such a profusion of specific rules and regulations catered to protecting its natural resources as the Kenai River. Seasonal, bait, and horsepower restrictions, open and closed areas, slot limits, hook size, changing bag and possession limits – all of it reflecting the myriad of rules and regulations dominating what is Alaska's most popular sport fishery. In addition, the mainstem river with its swift and cold current and multitude of game species, each with its own migrational pattern and lure or fly preference, makes for a daunting experience for many first-timers on the Kenai. Without the needed knowledge to properly fish the river and its tributaries, a novice angler may just as easily get skunked fishing here as anywhere else, or even cited for making a cast in a closed area or targeting an illegal species.

Very few people know the Kenai and its fish as the guides on the river. A guide is not just there to assist a client in catching a fish, a true professional will also offer tips and advice and explain the nuances of fishing the Kenai drainage. It is a learning experience, not just a "hit-and-run" affair, and hiring a guide is really time and money well spent, especially if only in the area for a day or two. Also, it is worth having a guide familiarize oneself with the fishery before attempting to go it alone.

Ask questions and be willing to listen, not just hear. There is a big difference. These people practically live on the river throughout the season and many of them reside on the Kenai Peninsula year-round. Local guides having spent decades in the area are a wealth of information concerning fish and their habits, water and weather conditions, and the multitude of details specific to the Kenai River and its tributaries.

It helps to know beforehand what type of experience one wants from the river, the fish, and the guide outfit. Fishing for king salmon on the lower river will provide a drastically different scenario than fly-fishing for rainbow trout on the upper river. Some guides operate with powerboats seating up to five people, others only float drift boats with maximum three in occupancy. There are outfits that also offer hike-in, fly-outs, or marine excursions in addition or conjunction to river trips. Many function as Bed & Breakfasts or operate full-service lodges with private cabins and all sorts of amenities.

There are currently more than 400 registered guides on the Kenai River. Most are reputable guides but a few fly-by-night outfits are present as well. Be certain that the business hired is licensed and insured for your own protection and that safety and following the law are top priorities.

Approximately 80% of the guides that operate on the Kenai do so by the use of powerboats, and the majority of them focus on the lower river section downstream of Soldotna. Do not expect a wilderness trip as houses line the riverbank here and there and it is common to see another hundred boats on the water at the same time, this being particularly the case during the peak of king season. Of course there is a reason why guides are here as this is where salmon concentrate in numbers as they arrive fresh off the tides and action is best. Drift boat guides mainly operate on the upper and middle river sections in much more pristine settings (and equally good fishing) but perhaps for other species.

Another big factor in hiring a guide is accessibility. If physically challenged by age or other factors impairing the ability to easily get around, fishing from a boat with a guide makes sense. A few boats are even designed to facilitate wheelchair use. The techniques employed are for the most part quite simple and the knowledge base of the guide in identifying trends, proper methods, and changes in water conditions and fish behavior play a vital role in the angler's success. In other words, relax, enjoy the experience, and leave it up to the guide to do the work.

A list of registered guides is available through the Alaska Department of Fish & Game's website (address below) by clicking "Sport Fishing Guides" or by writing to the Kenai River Center at 514 Funny River Road, Soldotna, AK 99669, (907) 260-4882.

ADF&G Home Page: *www.sf.adfg.state.ak.us/statewide/sf_home.cfm*

The following guide outfits have contributed material support to this book:

King Of The River
P. O. Box 107
Soldotna, AK 99669
1-888-478-9901
http://www.kingoftheriver.com
Specialty: Guided fishing for king
salmon and halibut.

Mystic Rivers
P. O. Box 791
Cooper Landing, AK 99572
1-907-227-0549
http://www.mysticfishing.com
Specialty: Guided fishing for salmon,
trout, and char; fly fishing.

Alaska Clearwater Sportfishing
P. O. Box 1181
Sterling, AK 99672
1-888-662-3336   1-907-262-3797
http://alaskaclearwater.com
Specialty: Guided salmon, trout,
and char fishing.

Silver Bullet Guide Service
P. O. Box 444
Sterling, AK 99672
1-888-268-0887
http://www.alaska.net/~silverb/
Specialty: Guided salmon fishing
and lodging accommodations.

Early Fishing
P. O. Box 753
Soldotna, AK 99669
1-907-262-6132
http://www.earlyfishing.com
Specialty: Guided fishing for
salmon, trout, and halibut.

Alaskan Adventure Charters
P. O. Box 4273
Soldotna, AK 99669
1-907-262-7773
http://www.alaskancharters.com
Specialty: Guided king and silver
salmon, halibut fishing.

Alaska River Adventures
P. O. Box 725
Cooper Landing, AK 99572
1-888-836-9027 1-907-595-2000
http://www.alaskariveradventures.com
Specialty: Guided fishing for salmon,
trout, and char.

Marlow's On The Kenai
P. O. Box 2465
Soldotna, AK 99669
1-800-725-3327 1-907-262-5218
http://marlowsonthekenai.com
Specialty: Guided salmon, trout, and
halibut fishing, accommodations.

KEY / LEGEND

Species Abbreviations:

KS – King Salmon   RS – Red Salmon   SS – Silver Salmon   PS – Pink Salmon   CS
– Chum Salmon   KO – Kokanee   ST – Steelhead Trout   RT – Rainbow Trout   LT
– Lake Trout   DV – Dolly Varden   AC – Arctic Char   AG – Arctic Grayling   RW
– Round Whitefish   NP – Northern Pike   BB – Burbot

Access Abbreviations:

MP – Mile Post; Measurement of distance in one-mile increments as designated by the
Department of Transportation for roads and highways. Displayed by metal posts and
reflective numerical signs.

RM – River Mile; Measurement of distance on the mainstem Kenai River in one-mile
increments, starting at the terminus at Cook Inlet to the outlet of Kenai Lake.

INDEX